Pompeii Awakened

For Maya Isabella Mahler

POMPEII
AWAKENED

A STORY *of*
REDISCOVERY

JUDITH HARRIS

I.B.TAURIS
LONDON · NEW YORK

New paperback edition published in 2015 by I.B.Tauris & Co. Ltd
6 Salem Road, London W2 4BU
175 Fifth Avenue, New York NY 10010
www.ibtauris.com

First published in hardback in 2007 by I.B.Tauris & Co. Ltd

Distributed in the United States and Canada Exclusively by Palgrave
Macmillan
175 Fifth Avenue, New York NY 10010

ISBN 978 1 78076 964 6
eISBN 978 0 85773 721 2

A full CIP record for this book is available from the British Library
A full CIP record is available from the Library of Congress

Library of Congress Catalog Card Number: available

Typeset in Palatino by JCS Publishing Services, www.jcs-publishing.co.uk
Printed and bound by Page Bros, Norwich

Contents

Illustrations

Foreword

JOHN JULIUS NORWICH

1. John Martin, *Eruption*

We were all of us brought up on Pompeii. Few natural phenomena are more exciting than a major volcanic eruption, and that of Vesuvius in AD 79 was certainly the most dramatic in history. Not only did it utterly annihilate a large and prosperous community; it passed into legend. Even now, in his letter to Tacitus, it is impossible to read the younger Pliny's description without a tremor.

> They consulted together whether it would be more prudent to trust to the houses, which now rocked from side to side with frequent and violent concussions as though shaken from their very foundations; or fly to the open fields, where the calcined stones and cinders, though light indeed, yet fell in large showers, and threatened destruction. In this choice of dangers they resolved for the fields: a resolution which, while the rest of the company were hurried into by their fears, my uncle

embraced upon cool and deliberate consideration. They went out then, having pillows tied upon their heads with napkins; and this was their whole defence against the storm of stones that fell round them. It was now day everywhere else, but a deeper darkness prevailed than in the thickest night ...

They thought proper to go further down upon the shore to see if they might safely put out to sea, but found the waves still running extremely high, and boisterous. There my uncle, laying himself down upon a sail cloth which was spread for him, called twice for some cold water, which he drank; when immediately the flames, preceded by a strong whiff of sulphur, dispersed the rest of the party and obliged him to rise. He raised himself up with the assistance of two of his servants, and instantly fell down dead; suffocated, as I conjecture, by some gross and noxious vapour ... .

As soon as it was light again. which was not till the third day after this melancholy accident, his body was found entire, and without any marks of violence upon it, in the dress in which he fell, and looking more like a man asleep than dead.[1]

Pliny's account perfectly illustrates the salient point about this particular eruption. It was not the torrents of lava that killed; it was the ash. Death came, more often than not, by instantaneous suffocation; and it is for this reason that we find, on the site itself as well as in foreign museums, entire corpses almost miraculously preserved, still frozen in the positions they had adopted in their last moments of life.

For nearly 1,700 years they, and the ruined city around them, lay undisturbed; then gradually, with the slow unfolding of the 18th century, men began to realize both the enormity of what had occurred and the astonishing riches that had been left behind. The first tentative excavations were no more than digs for buried treasure, but soon it became clear that there might be other rewards: of knowledge, of understanding, of learning for the first time how people lived and loved, worked and played, in the days of antiquity. And so archaeology was born.

All this happened in the heyday of the Grand Tour. In the 16th and most of the 17th centuries, such discoveries might have made relatively little impact; in the later 18th, the age *par excellence* of humanism and inquiry, they took civilized Western Europe by storm. The young English *milord*, travelling (with tutor and valet in tow) to admire the relics and ruins of Ancient Rome, now made a point of continuing to Naples, where he would be sure to tour the neighbouring excavations and quite possibly climb Vesuvius, only to find that Sir William Hamilton had got there first.

Although his tutor might or might not have seen the one or two examples of mildly priapic erotica that he had slipped into his pocket, he would have been sure to congratulate him on his newly acquired pieces of classical statuary, for which he had doubtless paid an infinitesimal fraction of what they would be worth today.

But the whole thrilling story is covered in the pages that follow. All that remains for me to say is that Judith Harris has chosen a wonderful subject for her book, and that she has done it full justice.

Introduction

2. François Mazois, *Empty Streets, Pompeii*

Pompeii is a city that died and was buried in one night, destroyed by a volcano which erupted with a force equivalent to many thousands of the atomic bombs that struck Hiroshima.

To historians, archaeologists and scientists, Pompeii's significance lies in its offering a total picture of the ancient world, captured at a single point in time. Other ancient cities such as Troy, Angkor Wat and Native American Pueblo habitats were burned or abandoned. The vision they offer is limited and partial.

But Pompeii was not destroyed by age or enemy. It was simply blanketed, within the space of a few hours, under a layer seventeen feet thick and more, composed of dust, rocks and, above all lightweight pumice pebbles, resembling gravel. When the pebbles were cleared away, explorers found unbroken hens' eggs still on the table, an artist's brushes by his painting, the skeleton of a woman caught in the agony of death in a gladiators' barracks, and still flaunting her best pearl earrings and snake bracelet.

When rediscovery came in the 1750s, educated Europe was enthralled. Travellers from Scotland to Russia flocked to Naples, which became an obligatory stop on the Grand Tour route. In and around Rome these visitors had seen other large and splendid ruins, visible if half-buried; now for the first time they could see inside the inner sanctum of a temple and an ancient Roman bathhouse. Until Pompeii, no one knew, aside from what could be read in books, how the ancient Romans actually *lived*.

The eruption had occurred at a particularly fascinating moment in history, the height of the wealth and power of the ancient Roman Empire, and this launched an 18th-century treasure hunt of colossal proportions. Connoisseurs and collectors were enchanted by Pompeii's fine arts, beginning with the myriad great marble statues imported from Greece. Much—not all—was repro art, copies of famous works by renowned Greek sculptors, whose originals had never been seen.

With the rise of the middle class during the Victorian era, the domestic life of Pompeii captured imaginations in Europe and, now, America. The visitors flocked to admire the ivory-inlaid beds and decorated lock boxes containing the family treasure. They saw an ancient Roman kitchen with its pots and pans on the counter. They saw, they wrote poems, they painted—and they bought.

For some, Pompeii became a model and an idyllic world. For others, Pompeii represented the ultimate in decadence and sin. In both cases, Pompeii excited passionate interest.

The dead city has never lost its uncanny power to fascinate. Indeed, it attracts over two million tourists annually, and the numbers increase every year. Ask a backpacker in jeans or a venerable scholar from any nation to describe his or her first visit to Pompeii, and you will see eyes light up like lamps.

My own introduction to Pompeii began from a distance, with a reading of an old-fashioned novel by Edward Bulwer-Lytton. Lord Lytton, as the Victorians called him, wrote many historical novels, including one that famously begins, "It was a dark and stormy night". Each year an American university holds a purple prose contest in sarcastic emulation of his florid style, made familiar by Snoopy. But Lytton's achievements are not a joke. His epic *The Last Days of Pompeii*, published in London in 1834, was the second best-selling novel in history, still selling well in the early 1900s as a novel, and still being recycled as a movie in the 2000s. Both its lasting appeal and its effect on Pompeii, discussed in these pages, are extraordinary.

Reading the novel as a schoolgirl in Ohio, I revelled in Lytton's living, breathing Pompeii of lovers, evil pagan priests and gladiators, who included cheerily rough women. Its twists of plot in tavern and temple were heart-wrenching and sentimental. It all ended with burning volcanic stones hurled down from the sky, and a blind girl sacrificing herself for—what else?—love. In the snowy evenings at the edge of the Great Plains, the dead city of Pompeii seemed more alive than my own village, so dull by comparison.

A decade later, as a student in Europe for a year, I could hardly fail to make a pilgrimage to Pompeii. It was a visit which I relate here only because so many others have had similar experiences, for better or for worse.

From a ski accident I still wore a cast as I boarded the overnight train that rattled and swayed down the bony spine of Italy to Naples. For a night and a long morning I shared the hard wooden benches of the third class with southern Italians returning home from northern factory jobs. Their belongings and my crutches were stowed overhead on a narrow shelf.

In Naples, I joined a tour bus filled with American sailors from a nearby naval base. Before reaching Pompeii a half hour south of Naples, we were shuffled by a tour guide through a workshop hustling coral jewellery. But at last we walked through the ancient gate of Pompeii. In the background rose the delightfully menacing bulk of Mount Vesuvius, wrapped in a shawl of snow.

Hard bench, fatigue, and resentment at being forced like chain gang prisoners into a coral factory slipped away. Like generations of foreign visitors before and after me, I turned ecstatic at the realization that I was stepping upon the paving stones of a street 2,000 years old. The dry street fountain of stone suddenly seemed to bubble over with water or perhaps lusty red wine from the vineyards I had glimpsed from the bus. Toga-clad men strode past on their way to some official ceremony at the basilica. By the fountain Lytton's blind heroine Nydia played her lyre.

One reason for my admittedly primitive imaginings was that I tended to be left standing, to lean against my crutches outside the buildings baking in the sun on a dead street, alone with the solitary priest in our group. In small groups, smirking sailors and a few sour-faced French male tourists would dart into a building from which women tourists were excluded. From it the men would then exit, poking each other with an elbow and casting a perhaps embarrassed glance in my direction, and no glance at all at the priest.

The romantic vision dissolved. Where was the Pompeii I had envisioned so long before, the Pompeii promised by the novel? Little could be seen beyond the polished black basalt stones of the street and endless, barren walls. Pompeii had been stripped bare. Where had all the fountain gardens, the mosaics, the fine statues and painted fresco pictures gone? Where was the life of Pompeii? What had I not been allowed to see?

Then I corrected myself, for I had the sense to understand that being excluded from the famous brothel of ancient Pompeii was the least of it. I had simply failed to understand the little available to see. The Villa of the Mysteries had remained just that, a mystery, because—the reason was simple—the past was too far away for me to grasp.

Ancient stones are supposed to speak. But if they did, I would first have to learn their language.

The truth is that for many of us the past is a far country, more remote in some ways than the moon. It is still a commonplace to praise the Greco-Roman heritage as shared by most Western countries, and all the more to be treasured in an era of regional strife. Whereas, our great-grandfathers' educations were based on classical studies, like philosophy, history, languages, ours are not; and if we contemplate the remote past at all we see it from a vast distance as vague shadows which our fancies shape into cheeses or faces or fountains.

Four decades of life in Italy have gone by since then, and for my work as a journalist in Rome I have interviewed literally hundreds of archaeologists, classicists, Pompeian scholars and cultural heritage administrators. I have visited Pompeii itself more times than I can remember. I can now report that its ancient stones may not shout, but they certainly whisper some of their secrets. They have taught me a few essentials, which are the premises for this book.

The first is that, as the birthplace of scientific archaeology some two and a half centuries ago, Pompeii has been a testing ground for every discovery, and every mistake.

The second is that ancient stones are only one component of archaeology. Today's Pompeian scholars analyse pollen, skeletal DNA, charred plant roots, and faecal matter found in ancient latrines. These very new studies sometimes build upon and sometimes contradict older verities, and some of the disputes at archaeological conferences on Pompeii, where traditional views are challenged, sound like early Christian heresy trials.

Third, the very abundance that has made Pompeii a fruitful academic industry has come at the price of acute specialization. No one,
therefore, is an expert in all that Pompeii offers, with the result that
its myriad specific elements can appear disconnected segments.

Fourth, and most important, is that the stories the ancient stones
tell are not only about the people who lived there in antiquity, but
about those who have reclaimed them for us and for future generations. The riches of Pompeii have attracted creative people from all
over the world—men and a number of fascinating women who
devoted their talents, fortunes and their lives (and in a few cases lost
their lives) in order to reclaim Pompeii for the world. Patron and
poet, architect and priest, strumpet and queen—they studied and
recreated the site in *their* imaginations, for ours, ringing changes in
the arts, society, politics, ideas, and the very look of our homes and
cities, from wallpaper to the Wedgwood ceramic candy box on the
table. Strictly speaking, therefore, this book is not about archaeology—that is the purview of the archaeologist. It is about reflections,
or Pompeii in a looking-glass.

Rediscovery began as an aristocratic treasure hunt for *objets* of
prestige to decorate stately homes and gardens all over Europe. The
rulers of Naples owned the area, just eight miles away from their
Royal Palace, and tried to keep the plunder for themselves, but
failed. Dealers and thieves snatched up and sold whole Pompeian
rooms, floors, gold diadems, silver bowls and pornographic knick-
knacks. The souvenir-hunting aristocrats making the Grand Tour
included, above all, the British, whose wealth in the 19th century
and extraordinary passion for Naples made Pompeii an undeclared
British pleasure park for decades. Later, Americans took their place.

Even as its riches attracted the treasure hunters, Pompeii's evocative emptiness provided inspiration to countless artists and poets.
As cemetery and dead city, Pompeii is romantically akin to an unfinished symphony. Its shattered walls and absence of roofs create an
aura of melancholy.

The downside of this is that Pompeii also has some of the appeal
of the macabre, and this came to be morally coupled with the bath-
house-steamy sex of Pompeii. The Catholic rulers of Naples, busily
stuffing their palaces and gardens with Pompeian statuary and
making state gifts of what they considered the lesser items, were
shocked and appalled. This did not prevent them from showing to
selected visitors the offending objects, which were kept protectively
locked away in a room in the palace.

That a link would be seen between the violent mass death and sex rampant of Pompeii was inevitable. Pompeii is also seen as Sodom and Gomorrah, and its citizens, babies, dogs and horses, got from Vesuvius only what they deserved from the angry Christian God. This view continues to this day; and in our cast of characters is a preacher who made just this connection.

One man's sermon can be another man's entertainment, of course, and little has been more entertaining than the Pompeian combination of erupting volcano, sex, death and art. Among the first entertainers was the notorious Emma, Lady Hamilton, who lived in Naples and became the lover of Admiral Nelson. At a time when other people still danced the minuet, Lady Hamilton was inspired by a Vesuvian site to create a new form of dance pageantry that lasted a century. From this elegant dawn Pompeii went on to inspire grand opera, circus acts and movie epics, beginning with early silent films.

As even the ancient Romans knew, the past is a useful commodity, and during its second life Pompeii has been a useful tool of political propaganda. All the patrons of the excavations, down to J. Paul Getty, instinctively saw the reflected halo potential of a glorious ancient heritage. This quick political fix played a role in Italian unification in the 19th century. Under Mussolini, who exploited archaeology to achieve legitimacy, the halo effect helped permit racist laws.

Not least, Pompeii is what travel professionals call a "honey pot" whose popularity requires no marketing, no private or state-sponsored advertising campaign. Money pours in effortlessly, but this easy money has become a boomerang, and today's Pompeii risks being loved to death. Patronage, poetry, propaganda, sex and death: the interplay of all these conflicting images of Pompeii is the hallmark of its second life.

This book is written to introduce the heroes, heroines and villains of the second life of ancient Pompeii. My hope is that some of those who visit Pompeii will, through their encounters in these pages, better understand the site, the sophisticated civilization it represents, and the sophistication it has brought to our own. I am also addressing the many who have already toured Pompeii and wish to recapture some of the wonder of their first visit. And some archaeologists may enjoy seeing the far-reaching and sometimes surprising results of their labours.

No less than any other fragile heritage site, Pompeii remains at risk—and not only from the predicted (and now overdue) new eruption of the volcano. One-third of the one hundred acres is yet to be explored, and decisions about future excavations will have to be made. Meantime, maintenance of the sixty-six acres of buildings already brought to light—some first excavated two centuries ago and open to the elements ever since—remains a daunting task.

The story of Pompeii begins with the volcano and with the reality that the city built in the shadow of the volcano was rich—very rich. Had this not been the case, little could have been dug from under the ashes at Pompeii. Therefore, before considering what the findings meant to the world, it will be useful to make a purely material reckoning of Pompeian wealth and the reasons for it, just as the first rumblings from the volcano sounded on a very hot day in late August in AD 79.

I have received so much help in my five years of preparing this book that I am sure to overlook many who have contributed. But let me begin by thanking the papyrologists who were so patient with my questions: the American scholar David Blank, now head of the Philodemus Project; Oxford's Alan Bowman, who showed me how computers allow the reading of otherwise lost texts on wooden tablets; the Norwegian scholar Professor Knut Kleve, who has laboured for decades to recompose minuscule crumbs of charred Herculaneum papyri; Professor Francesca Longo Auricchio of Naples University, who carries on Neapolitan commitment to the Herculaneum studies; the distinguished American scholar also working on the Herculaneum papyri, Professor Dirk Obbink; especially the late Professor Marcello Gigante of Naples, who made the Herculaneum papyri his life's work; and Professor Richard Janko, the first chairman of the Philodemus Project, currently chairman of the Classics Department at the University of Michigan. They are all unsung heroes, in an unglamorous but important and fascinating world.

The director of the National Archaeological Museum of Naples, Stefano De Caro, unwittingly inspired this book when he showed me a portrait of a Bourbon-Farnese king strutting in front of a Pompeian excavation. Clare Fleck, the remarkable curator of Lord Bulwer-Lytton's ancestral home, Knebworth, was generous with her time and illuminating in her comments.

Many archaeologists shared their experience and insights with me: the current director of Pompeii Pier Giovanni Guzzo; Anna

Maria Ciarallo of Pompeii; Teobaldo Fortunato, who introduced me to Nola; Marisa Mastroroberto, expert on Bronze Age Pompeii; the head of the British School in Rome, Andrew Wallace-Hadrill; Vincenzo Scaranno Ussani; Antonio Varrone; Akira Matsuda; Nicholas Wood and especially the former director of Pompeii Baldissare Conticello and the archaeologists from the University of Naples; Antonio De Simone, who excavated both the Villa of the Papyri and Murecine and his co-excavator at Murecine, Professor Salvatore Ciro Nappo, author of a fine guide to Pompeii published in English. Archaeologist Christopher Charles Parslow's *Rediscovering Antiquity* is essential reading for those with a serious interest in the early archaeology of the Vesuvian sites.

The librarians of the archives of Pompeii, Biblioteca Nazionale di Arte e Archeologia di Roma, Biblioteca di Storia Moderna di Roma, Biblioteca Nazionale di Napoli, British Library, Dresden Library, Getty Museum Archives of Los Angeles, London Library, New York Public Library were all helpful. The Department of Heritage Studies of East Anglia University gave me valuable insights into the politics of heritage and the effects of mass tourism on heritage sites. I would also like to thank Alex Wright of I.B.Tauris and Jessica Cuthbert-Smith.

Not least, I am grateful to the expert on early cinema, Professor John David Rhodes of York University, England, for teaching me to hear what the silent films had to say.

CHAPTER I

The Plutocrats of Pompeii

3. François Mazois, *Boat*

As today's summer sailors can vouchsafe, with a fair breeze, and using the scattered islands as stepping stones, no patch of land in the Mediterranean lies more distant than five hours' sailing time. Long before Homer sang of the Italian coast and its sirens, the sea was already a busy highway linking the coastal peoples of the Mediterranean from Egypt and Carthage to Marseilles and Beirut.

Of all those ports, none beckoned to sailors more than the Gulf of Naples. The Myceneans from Greece, who sent their ships to the gulf around 1300 BC, when Rome was barely a huddle of shepherds' huts, were not the first. For the same reason the US navy's Sixth Fleet has made a nearby port its principal Mediterranean base for the past half century.

Geology, combined with a gentle climate and fertile land, explains why this area, more than elsewhere, was favoured above all others and unique in the Mediterranean. The huge gulf and its islands, which include Capri and Ischia, are gripped between two long mountain promontories that jut seaward like the avaricious claws of a crab: Cape Misena to the north and Sorrento to the south. Their steep limestone cliffs extend far below the waterline of dappled purple and turquoise, to create the deep waters which are superbly safe for mariners.

At Cape Misena the northern claw yawns open, shaping a harbour within a harbour that the ancient Romans named "Baiae", a port so superior to all others that we remember it in our own word

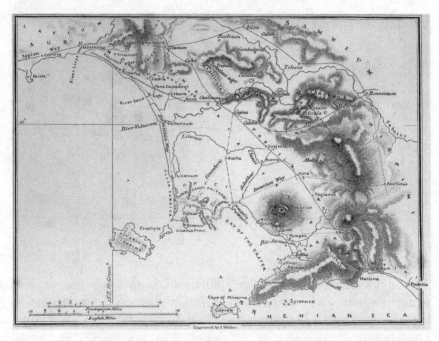

4. Architect William Gell, who represented London's Society of Dilettanti in Italy, introduced Pompeii to the English-speaking public in *Pompeiana, the Topography, Edifices and Ornaments of Pompeii*, published in 1817. Gell's map of the Gulf of Naples was astonishingly accurate even when compared with today's satellite views.

"bay". Here the hundreds of ships that composed the fleet of imperial Rome were based, for Rome's own port at Ostia was unreliable
and frustrated the emperors' admirals by silting over again and
again.

Baiae had a dual personality, however. The weather was mild, the
wine and fish abundant, the shipping time from Rome tolerable. The
coastline of steep rock cliffs and tiny coves was moreover achingly
beautiful. Just as the Hamptons became a holiday suburb of New
York, the gulf coast adjacent to the military port became a favourite
summer playground of the Roman aristocrats. There were serious
reasons to avoid the worst of the Roman heat, in any case. From
time to time the plague decimated the city while, always, the
swampy low-lying areas around the Forum bred malarial mosqui-
toes. Anyone who could leave during the danger months did so.

Julius Caesar (circa 100–44 BC) made Baiae fashionable when he
located his summer villa there, nicely distant from the eyes of
Rome's stodgy, old-school senators like Cicero, whose villa was further south, at Pompeii. In the century after Caesar, so many
luxurious summer villas were constructed atop and into the cliffs
that, as the historians of the time recorded, they made an unbroken
line down the gulf coast. Contractors vied with each other to offer
clever new conveniences, like the shower baths advertised by one
builder.

And there went the neighbourhood, or at least its reputation.
Baiae came to be known as "the golden shore of blessed Venus"—
the love coast. In point of fact it was more about sex than love, and
even gentlemen's town houses had erotic alcoves not intended for
entertaining the official wife. The later emperor Tiberius had a special "prurient and stinking room" for sex built in his mountain-top
castle on the gulf isle of Capri, as is recorded by the historian Suetonius. For the lower orders brothels were built in the very centres of
town; several have been found, one and possibly more at Pompeii
and one near Baiae at Puteoli (today's Pozzuoli).

Pompeii lay closer to the bottom of the gulf. It too had a port, but
with a crucial difference: a river. The business of Pompeii was not to
make war, nor even to make love. It was to make money. Alone in
the gulf, Pompeii was blessed with a navigable river, the Sarno,
which connected the sea and its traders to the prosperous agribusiness towns inland, like Nola and Nucera, whose populations far
outstripped that of Pompeii.

The wheelers and dealers in the Roman Forum at Pompeii did their business in an auction hall whose elaborate doorframe of imported white marble, exquisitely carved with birds and insects entwined in vines, shows the importance of the building. Its conventional name, the "Hall of the Wool Merchants", is misleading, for sold on its block, far more than wool, were wheat and slaves.

The climate and mineral-rich volcanic soil permitted twice-yearly wheat harvests, as no less an authority than the naturalist Pliny the Elder, who had a villa near Baiae, recorded. For these farmers the barges plying the Sarno were vital. Pompeii was their trading centre and gateway to the sea. Pompeii provided them with services: shipping connections, warehouses, stevedores, lawyers, bankers, money-changers, accountants, translators and factories for making the standard terracotta goods containers called amphorae.

The best customer was hungry Rome itself, whose governors subsidized wheat purchases to feed an unruly population which would ultimately reach one million. And in fact thirty per cent of the fragments of amphorae found at just one excavation site at Rome's port of Ostia bore the labels of the kilns at Pompeii.[1] The second great customer was Egypt, which bought wheat and provided slaves; the consequences showed in both religion and Pompeian houses, as we shall see.

As markings on 1,600 clay bowls found at Pompeii show, the amount of trade with the eastern Mediterranean was also notable, accounting for as much as one-quarter of Pompeii's commerce.[2] The Pompeians exported their fish-based sauce, *garum*, which came in all qualities and prices, similar to balsamic vinegar today. Trade with France was a close third, for the Pompeian aristocrats were wine snobs who preferred the better French *crus* over their own abundant but indifferent *vinum Vesuvinum*.

Slaves were the second main commodity sold. Calculating that, as scholars now believe, slaves made up about ten per cent of the general population of the Roman world, Pompeii had perhaps 2,000 slaves. The lucky worked in the households and shops. The others loaded all those heavy amphorae on the ships, or tilled the wheat fields under the southern Italian sun. A few became teachers; some, like the famous captive soldier Spartacus, leader of a slave rebellion that lasted years, were sent to the nearby town of Capua to be taught gladiatorial combat against wild animals, for the amusement of the masses assembled in Pompeii's amphitheatre.

Pompeii's flourishing economy, and the lives of its between 10,000 and 20,000 citizens, suffered a severe setback when a devastating earthquake flattened much of the city in AD 62. At least one city gate toppled, and the great temple to the trio of Roman gods (Minerva, Juno and Jove) that stood in the main forum was badly damaged. A few days after the quake Seneca (4 BC–AD 65), the great scholar who had been Nero's tutor, walked the devasted landscape. "Pompeii is almost destroyed", he wrote.

> A flock of six hundred sheep has been killed; there are some who have remained overwhelmed, they wander here and there like madmen. ...
> To what refuge, what help, can our eyes turn if it is the very earth that threatens destruction? If the earth which protects and sustains us, the earth upon which man has built his cities, cleaves and rolls, of what are made the foundations of the world?[3]

As the northern gulf cities, and especially Puteoli, picked off the business contracts, Pompeii appealed to Rome for help. The emperor Nero had just died, leaving the coffers of Rome in disarray, and so years passed before the new emperor, Vespasian, could raise sufficient taxes to be able to send money for reconstruction. Among other things, this former mule dealer—the first commoner to become an emperor—taxed the use of public latrines, a measure he defended by famously saying, "Money doesn't smell".

Smelly or otherwise, the money finally arrived, and rebuilding began. To Pompeii Vespasian also sent a contingent of slave labourers taken captive elsewhere in the empire. As if overnight, Pompeii was again a boom town and giant construction site, further reviving the economy. Marble masons and brick makers worked overtime to rebuild government buildings. The old Greek temple honouring Apollo was repaired and new temples and chapels built, including one facing onto the forum which, not surprisingly, honoured Vespasian. New temples reflecting the trade routes were erected and dedicated to imported deities like the Egyptian Isis (in earlier centuries her worship had been outlawed) and the Persian god Mithras. Wealthy private citizens renovated and expanded their walled garden compounds.

The presence of the Roman fleet at Baiae, where Pliny himself had just been named its admiral, further contributed to the return of prosperity. No less than the other towns, Pompeii was fattened by the military contracts issued by the imperial navy to replace the galleys lost to storms or battle.[4]

What the hundred or so Pompeian families who lived in town houses did with their new wealth was first of all to show it off. Pompeii had been settled in the 8th century BC by Greeks, and Greek culture was still prized. On their walls were painted copies of Greek masterpieces. For atrium or back peristyle garden—the Greek-style garden, that is—the Pompeian plutocrats imported directly from Greece newly minted copies of sculptures by famous Athenian artists. Those without the money for imports purchased a copy of a copy, sometimes made by a Greek émigré craftsman.

To keep out bad weather and cat burglars, most town houses had no windows open to the streets outside. Even the wealthy rented their street frontage for shops. This left the main entrance door of the house as the place where the show of status began. When the great bronze-studded wooden doors were swung open, anyone looking in was expected to be bowled over. The view began at the vestibule, where realistic portrait masks of family members might be hung like a boastful family tree. This display was so important that a law was passed forbidding hanging someone else's illustrious ancestor in your display. Strictly speaking, not all of the plutocrats owning these grand town houses could be classified as gentlemen; one of the richest Pompeian entrepreneurs held the cart delivery concession, a monopoly for town deliveries of goods.

Although the foremost Greek god of Pompeii, Apollo, was still honoured in his already ancient shrine temple, the Romans who had conquered Pompeii in the mid-4th century BC had centred the new forum around a larger, higher temple to their own gods of the Capitoline hill, the trio of Juno, Minerva and Jove. But this was a merchant town, and the Pompeians showed specific gratitude for their prosperity by erecting a host of smaller shrines to the business gods, beginning with Mercury, god of commerce. Similarly they honoured, in paint and sculpture, the spirit of the Sarno River, portrayed again and again as a reclining river god holding a cornucopia spilling over with delights. Harking back to the town's Greek roots was the goddess Persephone, whom the Romans insisted upon calling Proserpina; wreathed in flowers, in another sign of abundance she is usually shown holding a pomegranate (which may explain why a church near Pompeii has, to this day, a statue of Mary holding a pomegranate).

Perhaps the most important inheritance from the Greeks who founded Pompeii was the mystery cult of Dionysus, as is seen in a sequence of ambiguous paintings in the Villa of the Mysteries. One household shrine painting, now in the Naples museum, shows his Roman variation, Bacchus, the god of the mystery rites and everlasting life, standing draped in grapes and vines against a painted Vesuvius. The mountain, significantly, had one hump.

By August of AD 79 the fix-up, paint-up phase was ending at Pompeii. In the kitchen of the traders' hospitality inn by the river, renovation was almost complete, and the brand new, numbered marble paving slabs for the baths had arrived from northern Italy. The jewellers were back in business, manufacturing fine gold bracelets that weighed a pound, and the ornate table silverware—spoons, plates, platters, cups, engraved with amusing allusions to the theatre productions—in use even on the richer farm estates. The prostitutes were plying their trade in the brothel and in their private rooms with street entrances.

Elsewhere on the gulf, life was also amusing, at least for the elite. In his villa near Baiae, which had suffered no damage from the earthquake, the already famous Pliny, a martinet who disliked wasting time, had an educated servant read improving literature out loud while his guests dined.

The resort town of Herculaneum, midway down the gulf coast, had suffered little from the earthquake. Its denizens were, like the Pompeians, wealthy. But they were otherwise different, for they were the powerful and politically well-connected. Many were from Rome, but spent their summers far from that malaria-infested city, in spacious villas with fine sea views and private boat landings.

By day they took the sun, swam, read and talked. Evenings were spent in the theatre or dining on fish, flatbread, ewes' milk cheese, vegetables, figs and grapes. Setting the tone, some dressed up in Greek-style clothing for the lively lectures and discussions of speculative Greek philosophy, and especially Epicurean thought, for this was a centre of Epicureanism, established by émigré scholars from Alexandria. The summertime intellectuals listened to works by Epicurus and his followers like Philodemus, and by their own beloved Roman poets, like Virgil and Lucretius.

The talk would continue into the night with music on the belvedere terraces under the stars. In certain upper-class circles the fellowship was easy enough that, shockingly, a slave or two and occasionally even an aristocratic woman might be included. Only the stodgiest were offended when the host withdrew to a love alcove for a moment of bliss with a woman or a male partner, part of the whole "Greek" way of life still maintained at Herculaneum and another neighbouring town whose name betrayed its Greek origin, Neapolis (Naples).

This was the wealthy, intelligent, convivial and ostentatious Gulf of Naples on the eve of the eruption. Not one of its citizens, not even an erudite scholar of natural sciences like Pliny, reading his book after lunch on 24 August, had the least inkling that their mountain was a volcano, and dangerous. Yet there had been premonitions. Like a few of the crooked old lanes left within the city walls by the inland tribes called the Oscans, traces of the old-fashioned religions celebrating the spirits and sprites of field, spring and mountain had survived both Greek and Roman conquests. As is known only today, before AD 79, Vesuvius had erupted six times on the same scale. Some of the very oldest religious themes hinted tantalizingly at fire, as if drawn from a collective memory.

One Vesuvian myth in particular spoke of fire and violence. Cyclops was the one-eyed giant who forged lightning bolts for Zeus (and lightning bolts regularly figure in Vesuvian eruptions, including in Pliny's description). Cyclops, it was firmly believed, lived in a cave on Vesuvius's high peak. In another myth, Vulcan, god of fire, worked his smithy's forge and bellows on Vesuvius. These earlier eruptions, like that of 1800 BC, seem to have survived in language as well; the very name Vesuvius may derive from the Sanskrit word for fire, *ves*.

None of these gods was heeding prayers when disaster came.

24 August AD 79 was recorded at Pompeii as hotter than most summer mornings. At around midday a thunderclap rocked the mountain, cleaving its single hump into two. A column of volcanic debris burst from the heart of the cleft peak. Soaring miles into the sky, it formed a flat-topped cloud shaped like an umbrella pine tree, the *pinus maritima*.

Speeding toward the sea in a south-westerly direction, the low cloud began to dump ton after ton of poisonous, volcanic matter onto countryside and towns. Pompeii was the first. As day turned to night, the sky disgorged torrents of golf ball-sized black basalt rocks, dust and lapillae.

Braving the darkness, some of the inhabitants of Pompeii raced outdoors, covering their heads with pillows as protection from the falling rocks, described by an eyewitness as appearing "charred and split as if by fire". Some made it to safety. Most did not. A slave was found chained to a post like a dog; so was a dog. A guard by the Herculaneum Gate (another of our heroes in these pages) remained at his post out of duty.

Other Pompeians hid in their houses. Theirs was a fatal choice, for as ash and pumice pebbles piled up, the weight eventually collapsed the roofs. Attempting to see, they also lit torches and oil lamps. As the roofs caved in, the lamps overturned, setting fires in houses where fallen roof timbers had blocked exits.

Herculaneum lay on the coast due north of Pompeii and was spared that initial onslaught. But when the wind shifted, so did the cloud. Gathering speed now with the afternoon breezes, the ashy, gaseous grey-black mass in the sky rushed forward, toward Herculaneum, at an implacable forty miles per hour.

Watching from a safe distance at the northernmost outpost of the Gulf of Naples at Baiae were two observers standing upon a rocky beach. Admiral Pliny, fifty-six years old and stout, had been sunbathing and swimming with his nephew, a youth of eighteen. He had adopted the boy as his son, who would go down in history as Pliny the Younger. After a late breakfast both were reading when the elder Pliny's sister called them to look at the strange dark cloud.

For Pliny, the appointment as admiral was a sinecure. Soldier, historian and naturalist, he was famous for having compiled a thirty-seven-volume encyclopedia called *Historia Naturalis* (*Natural History*). Its subject, as Pliny explained boldly in its preface, was "the nature of things, that is, life". The bibliography for Volume One alone listed 2,000 works by 473 different authors, only half of them Roman sources. Most were works by Greek authors. Now lost, many exist only in Pliny's references to them.

Its entries cut a wide swathe: art, astronomy, botany, crop rotation, diet, geography, horticulture, Latin translations of the Greek names for plants, magic, medicine, metallurgy, mineralogy, poisons and their antidotes, statues (including one now in the Vatican, the *Laocoön*), and the wisdom of large-scale farming, the lack of which is "the ruination of the Romans", in his opinion. In an agricultural section he describes an ox-drawn grain harvester, which he said he saw while soldiering in Gaul. Scholars assumed this was imaginary until 1958, when one fitting his description turned up in bas relief on a Roman-era stone panel found at an archaeological site in southern Belgium. Students were still studying from Pliny's encyclopedia long after Columbus discovered America.

Pliny himself had studied in Rome, then travelled widely. At twenty-three he entered the military and rose to command a cavalry unit in Germany. Returning home he seems to have studied law before Nero sent him off to Spain as an administrator (*procurator*) for the Roman legion there. Pliny had the busy man's dislike of wasted time. He reproached his nephew (from whose letters these accounts are taken) for strolling on foot around Rome rather than riding in a sedan chair borne by running men. In a sedan taxi, his nephew could study. Walking wasted time.

It was wasted time not to take notes of one's reading, and he habitually penned notes into the margins of his own papyrus scroll volumes. For what was the point of reading, he declared to his nephew, if one fails to note down what is read? Even at dinner Pliny kept his secretary by his side, seated at a low scribe's desk so as to take down the great man's thoughts on whatever book was being read aloud.

One evening the reader mispronounced a word. A dinner guest intervened to correct the speaker's pronunciation. Pliny turned severe,

"Did you understand the word?"

"Well, yes", the guest acknowledged.

"Yet you made us miss ten lines", Pliny snapped.

This was the man who stood watching the spectacle of the bizarre cloud over the sea. It intrigued him, for, as he remarked to his nephew, he had never before witnessed such a sight. In his *Historia Naturalis* he had listed all ten active volcanoes known to exist, but had not included Vesuvius. Here was a chance to remedy the lack as well as to test his theories on vulcanology.

"Prior to an eruption", he told his nephew, "several things happen". The first was an earthquake; then the air would turn calm, and the sea lapse into quiet. The reason was that, he believed, winds caused a volcano by plunging into the earth and then re-emerging, in the form of a volcanic eruption. For without the winds entering the volcano, how can they exit?

Here was a fine chance to observe all this in action. His nephew later described the scene in a now-famous letter to the historian Tacitus, a dear family friend:

> Calling for his sandals, he climbed up to a place that would give him the best view of the phenomenon. It was not clear at that distance from which mountain the cloud was rising. Afterward it was known to be Vesuvius. Its general appearance can best be expressed as being like an umbrella pine.[5]

This cloud hovered high in the sky for hours, then suddenly appeared to tumble straight down. Pliny could not know that beneath that chute an entire city was already being buried. Indeed, until recent years and more precise knowledge of the effects of volcanoes, no one credited the description of the sudden dropping of the cloud. Worse still, until only a few centuries ago, scientists still believed that a volcano was caused by winds entering it and pushing out the plug as they exited.

Pliny was still standing watching the cloud and making observations to his sister and nephew, when a man in a boat was spotted rowing frantically toward them. The exhausted boatman carried a note from Pliny's well-born Roman friend, a widow named Rectina, in her villa at Herculaneum among the holidaymakers. Rectina begged the admiral-cum-professor to send a ship to save her and her neighbours from the catastrophe.

Four oared boats from the Roman fleet were immediately readied. Within an hour Pliny and his nephew set sail. The older man took personal command at the helm of his ship to brave the rising sea. From Baiae the ships had to cross the gulf on a diagonal to reach Herculaneum. "He was entirely fearless, describing each new movement and phase of the portent so that it could be noted down exactly as he observed it", his nephew later wrote.

There was much to describe. "Broad sheets of fire" rose from the volcano interior like slow-motion lightning. On land terrifying fires were burning; to reassure his sailors Pliny explained that those fires had been set by farmers burning the hayfield stubble. Then, when the ships neared Herculaneum, a shower of ash, pumice pebbles and stones began to rain down as the vapour-filled clouds shifted toward Herculaneum.

Approaching the shoreline, the ships were blocked by a rising sea. The terrified men at the oars began to lose control of their ships. Wind and wave forced a heart-sick Pliny to give up; he could not save Rectina and her friends.

Next they risked losing their own lives. The high seas would not allow them to return to Baiae. They were forced to continue southward, past Herculaneum, past Pompeii. Regaining control of the ship, the sailors finally brought it to anchor on the beach at Stabiae. A friend had a villa there, and here the exhausted party sought refuge. It was afternoon, but the sky had turned black. Exhausted, Pliny washed to remove the sea salt from his skin, then sank onto a bed in the villa. He fell into a deep sleep, "breathing loudly and heavily".

The bedroom where Pliny lay opened onto a courtyard. Suddenly the same ashes mixed with pumice stones that had afflicted the ships began falling into the courtyard. Pelting the tiled roof, they made such a racket that Pliny woke. He joined the others as the houses, "now shaking with violent shocks, seemed to sway to and fro as if torn from their foundations".

To remain indoors had become dangerous. Servants helped the admiral make his tortured way toward the seashore once more, gasping at the stifling stench of sulphur. The aim was to try to escape by boat, but the turbulent sea cut off that route. Servants tied pillows onto their heads and began to flee on foot. They begged Pliny to follow them, but by then he was too exhausted. "He struggled to his feet, leaning on two slaves. Then he collapsed." He never rose again.

"What he had begun in a spirit of inquiry, he completed as a hero," his mourning nephew wrote to Tacitus, who quoted the letter in full in his *History*, making it the most famous eyewitness account in history of a volcanic eruption and Pliny the Younger (AD 62–114) the world's first vulcanologist.

With his mother, the frightened youth sought what shelter could be found as the explosions continued until dawn. The two were still alive, the terrified survivors of "the darkest of the darkest nights ever seen".

The scattered inhabitants who had also survived the cataclysm found the landscape of the gulf transformed beyond recognition. From dromedary, Mount Vesuvius had become a camel, with two humps. Then rains came, slowly snuffing out ash and ember until all that remained was a black, rolling sea of death. In the rewritten geology of Vesuvius, the survivors could find no trace of where their towns had been. Pompeii, Herculaneum and Stabiae had vanished into nothing. So they would remain, lost for over sixteen centuries.

As has been recognized only recently, the two Plinys described the eruption with remarkable scientific accuracy. They described the vertical column, topped by an umbrella pine-shaped cloud in which lightning blazed. They gave a careful scientific account of the hailstorm of ash, dust and pumice which filled lungs. They described the total darkness, the accompanying earthquakes, the flows of hot ash and horizontal blasts, and the tidal waves that accompanied the quakes.

It is interesting to compare Pliny's account with a recent study of the eruption by a multidisciplinary group of scientists, including forensic anthropologists, from the University of Naples.[6] Their reconstruction is that six successive surges took place. The first, at around 1 pm, shot a column of gas and pyroclastic materials some fifteen kilometres into the air. This was immediately followed by a cloud of cinders that began to blanket the area close to Pompeii on the south-west slope of Vesuvius.

With the passing of the hours the heavy cloud soared twice the initial height, to about thirty kilometres high. Around midnight it shifted direction. When the column partly collapsed at 1 am on 25 August, it shed about one-third of its content. The swift collapse triggered a new surge of wind-driven gases mixed with fine cinders whose heat is estimated at between 400 and 500°C. This mixture of materials was almost certainly what had killed the many hiding in cellars at Herculaneum or who had, like Rectina, stood in anguished wait on the beaches for boats which would not arrive.

The progressive surge waves at Herculaneum gradually piled up the pyroclastic matter, including waves of lavic mud, to a thickness that varied from twenty-seven to sixty-three feet. Torrential rains then packed the lava foam, mud flow and cinders into what would, over the centuries, coalesce into layers of generally hard stone.

Although a few earlier attempts had been made, most of Herculaneum remained unexcavated until 1934. Few skeletons were found in that time, and it was assumed that most inhabitants had safely escaped by boat. But more recently scores of skeletons have been found in cellars and by the original shoreline. Their DNA bone content shows that the women and children had lodged in one place, the men in another; presumably the men had gallantly tried to arrange help for the waiting women and children.

At Pompeii, the few who had made it through the night fell victim to the fifth and particularly devastating surge at 7 am, when the majority of those who had failed to flee the town died. And many did escape: remains of fewer than 2,000 individuals have been found so far at Pompeii. The final and worst surge, ending the eruption, came about an hour later. During its violence Vesuvius had spat into the atmosphere some ten billion tons of magma, plus hundreds of millions of tons of water vapour and other gases, expelled at a veloc-ity of some 9,000 feet per second.

In coming centuries other severe eruptions added more lava lay-ers, further burying the ghost cities of Vesuvius: in 305 and again for three years in a row after 471, when clouds of powdery ash fell upon points as distant as Constantinople and Tripoli. In 512 a new layer of lava blanketed Herculaneum, bringing such destruction that the ruler, Theodoric, refunded the taxes paid to him from the area around Naples, the Campania. Worse came in 1631, when an erup-tion killed some 3,000 people and 6,000 farm animals.

In the long meantime the mineral-rich earth had brought flourish-ing crops. The bleak, rolling sea of post-eruption grey had long since disappeared beneath fields of grass, farms and vineyards. Only an occasional trace of ancient Pompeii rose from the fields. Summering along the gulf, Rome's boy emperor Severus Alexander (209–35) had noted handsomely fluted columns standing in the fields. He had his slaves cart them away for his palace. More humbly, a few stone walls or a building dome from Pompeii would be tall and strong enough for reuse as a stall.[7]

However, even if they did not know how it came to be there, farmers knew well that valuable plunder lay underground. Count-less narrow tunnels were dug into the darkness in a search for buried treasure. Small boys were sent to crawl down these amateur tunnels, to shout descriptions to their elders, who could then decide whether it was worth proceeding on a larger scale. Their small skel-etons, recovered by today's archaeologists inside the walls of Pompeii, testify to ancient greed and ancient cave-ins.

Otherwise for many hundreds of years no ray of light penetrated the darkness of the lost Vesuvian towns. Even scientific interest in Vesuvius and in volcanoes in general waned in the Middle Ages as the Christian view crept in, linking volcanoes to sin and to hell itself. That view, however, revived interest in volcanic behaviour, so that some monks began to keep diaries of volcanic activity.

After Columbus discovered the New World, his enriched Spanish sponsors wrested control from the French over the south of Italy. For the two centuries before the rediscovery of Pompeii the Italian south was a Spanish province. Its capital, Naples, with 300,000 people liv-ing within its walls, became the third largest city of Europe after London and Paris. By far it was the poorest of the three.

The Spanish rulers of Naples, eight miles from Pompeii, were mil-itary leaders whose tasks were clear and simple: collect taxes to send back to Spain and defend the territory from others. On the eve of rediscovery, therefore, Spanish construction of ports, defensive walls, towers, and docks for warships testified to the Spanish vice-roys' military priorities. The problems of the countryside had gone ignored, even when famine drove hordes of young men from their farm homes and into the impoverished capital city.

The viceroys had little interest in higher education, and the imported Spanish Inquisition, which stifled freedom of thought, was at its height. Although Naples was home to one of the most important universities, under Spanish dominion the south, includ-ing its capital city of Naples, was cut off from the rest of Europe, including Central Italy, as if by a high wall.[8]

A glimmer of light arrived in the 1590s, when the celebrated Roman architect Domenico Fontana was summoned to Naples to build a suitably grand palace for the viceroy of Spain. Fontana was famous for having built the dome of St Peter's Cathedral from the designs of the late Michelangelo. But the architect had fallen upon hard times and took what he could get.

What he got was a ditch. The Neapolitan landowners were bat-tling to wrest control of the lucrative milling of wheat. Needing water to turn his mill, a local duke hired Fontana in 1592 to excavate a long ditch for the pipes of a new aqueduct. A portion was to pass underground through open fields eight miles south of Naples. Fon-tana set to work—and sliced directly into ancient Pompeii, which he immediately recognized as such.

Fontana's diary entry is the first description after Pliny's of the effects of the volcano upon the buried cities:

> Beyond any doubt what we see before us is the celebrated city once called in its country Pompeii, irrigated by the currents of the chill Sarno River. … A strange and certainly horrendous way to die … We approached close to the city, which she herself shows us through her towers, houses, the theatres and temples which one can discern, almost whole.[9]

Fontana asked his employer's permission to explore the buried city, but the duke's interest was in milling that same wheat which had built the fine towers and houses of Pompeii so long before. A dis-heartened Fontana was ordered to rebury the ruined houses and walls of Pompeii. In doing so, Fontana wrote, he took care to do as little damage as possible so as not to compromise future excavations; and one of the touching moments of a visit to Pompeii is to walk over the hump made in the road a hundred yards or so from the amphitheatre by Fontana's large water pipes.

Fontana's ploughing through Pompeii left no more impression on
his era than did the water coursing through the aqueduct he took
eight years to build. And by the dawn of the 18th century the handsome palace built by Fontana to house the Spanish rulers of Naples
had fallen half into ruin. Spain's two hundred years of dominion
over the Kingdom of Naples and the Two Sicilies were drawing to a
dismal end. The last viceroy's rule was so feeble that a mere handful
of Austrian soldiers seized Naples and kept it as a trophy of Vienna
for fifteen years.

In 1734 a new monarchy would arrive. Fontana's Royal Palace
would be restored to its original splendour and enlarged. Naples
would be rebuilt into a European showplace celebrated as a cultural
capital. Rediscovery of lost Pompeii would be the star in its crown.

CHAPTER II

Tunnels

5. Mosaic panel, House of the Faun

The town of Portici lies on the sea five miles south of Naples, on a coastal road called the Golden Mile for its gracious, sun-drenched villas and fountain gardens. Most of these houses were built by the Spanish viceroys who had ruled Naples for two centuries. Beneath them lay others, the ghosts of the shorefront villas of the ancient Romans. These too had made an uninterrupted file along the coast; they survive in the town's name, taken from the Latin word *porticus*, for their elongated shaded porches and walkways overlooking the sea.

   In the year 1709 few other traces of ancient glory survived on the Golden Mile. When a Neapolitan publisher, catering to the reviving tourist trade, issued the first guidebook to the area that year, the author apologized for being unable to give indications for the great cities of Herculaneum and Pompeii. Both were still lost to "the vomit of Vesuvius", he admitted, and no one knew where they lay: "On the basis of some vestiges of rediscovered ancient buildings, the latest opinion in the field is that Herculaneum sat atop the summit of Mount Vesuvius, where the crater opens".[1] The latest opinion in the field was wrong. Within a few months Herculaneum was rediscovered, beneath a town called Resina less than a mile from Portici.

With Naples, Portici had just become an Austrian province. After their two centuries of brutal, indifferent rule the Spanish had finally been swept out of the Kingdom of Naples and the Two Sicilies by Austrian troops. An Austrian governor now occupied the Royal Palace.

The Austrian cavalry corps was under the command of an enterprising young French prince named Emanuel d'Elboeuf. Within a year of his arrival d'Elboeuf had married the daughter of a Neapolitan duke—"a native princess" as a woman tourist described her snidely in a letter home to England. Overcrowded Naples was endemically unhealthy in hot weather, and so the next obvious step was for the couple to acquire one of the coveted summer villas on the famous Golden Mile safely far from town.

D'Elboeuf found and purchased a rundown church property overlooking the sea at Portici, which he set out to remodel on the grand scale with the addition of a great horseshoe staircase.[2] Learning that d'Elboeuf was in the market for fine marble panels to decorate the house, a mason from Portici stepped forward with an offer of coloured marble panels recovered nearby, from the bottom of a dried-up well in a field where a farmer grew flowers. While the well was being deepened in the search for water, the drill, turned by an ox plodding in a circle, had spun to the surface fragments of colored marble. They proved so precious, the mason claimed, that he had already sold some for the construction of church altars in Naples.[3] D'Elboeuf happily agreed to the purchase. Then he had second thoughts. Why pay peasants for marble which he could dig up himself?

From Naples, d'Elboeuf cannily obtained a permit to expropriate the well and all its contents on behalf of the Austrian government. A winch was placed atop the well. Then a mason was strapped into a sling and dropped down into the utter blackness of the well.

Thirty feet or so below, the shaft unexpectedly widened. Still unable to see, the mason found he could stretch out his arms. A few minutes more, and his feet had touched ground. A torch was lowered, permitting him to see that he stood inside a vast, round cavern. Broken statues lay on the floor; others stood in niches.

Now the excited d'Elboeuf himself descended in the sling. Venturing further in the underground space, d'Elboeuf saw by torchlight a curving wall faced with marble panels, set in a vari-coloured, geometric pattern.[4] Returning above ground, he reported that he had found either an ancient Roman temple or amphitheatre. In coming days, the well shaft was enlarged. The traffic grew brisk as the winch was worked up and down by prison labourers, helpfully dispatched to Portici by the Austrian government in Naples.

Three of the statues still standing in their niches were larger-than-life marble sculptures of women. The pleating of their long tunics of marble was so deftly carved that the garments appeared to be made of fine linen, fluttering in a breeze. Incredibly, the three large statues were intact and in perfect condition. It was an extraordinary find, and d'Elboeuf knew it. He also knew that to haul the buried treasure to the surface up through the well would be impossible. The problem was resolved by having the labourers dig slanting tunnels, as if for a mine.

Finally seen above ground, the three female statues in their seemingly diaphanous draperies of marble were hailed as masterpieces, so skilfully carved that they fairly flaunted that they were the works of sculptors from ancient Greece. Next a huge male nude statue was found and identified as Hercules, legendary founder of Herculaneum. The Austrian governors of Naples gleefully trumpeted that they had found one of the famous lost cities destroyed by the eruption of Vesuvius in AD 79. The news was rushed back to Vienna and, from Vienna, circulated throughout northern Europe. The stunningly high quality of the marble statues and objects removed roused a furore of curiosity about the new property of the Habsburg emperor in Austria deemed to be Herculaneum.

The excitement reached fever pitch when the circular hall at the bottom of the well shaft was identified as a theatre. Measuring fifty-four metres across, with an orchestra diameter of just under nineteen metres, it fitted precisely the harmonious proportions prescribed by the Roman architect Vitruvius.[5] It was, moreover, a Greek-style theatre, the first ever found.

Two more tunnels were built, and within nine months d'Elboeuf had stripped the decorations of the entire high proscenium arch — the only one ever found intact — to the last marble pebble.[6] A dismaying list of what had been found was published in 1711 in *Giornale de' letterati d'Italia*:

> ... a statue of Cleopatra, seven female statues belonging to a series of twelve in the niches between 24 columns found in a circle between columns on the exterior of the building, fragments of columns of African [marble], of *giallo antico*, of *cipollazzo*, and of flowered alabaster, some

Greek-style statues, but broken, and various cornices of excellently
carved Pario marble of the Corinthian order.[7]

In the space of nine months the theatre had been stripped to the
last marble shard. The rewards had, like the well above it, gone dry.
To explore further would have required the digging of expensive
new tunnels, deep underground. In 1714 the three that had been
excavated were sealed. D'Elboeuf—now Duke d'Elboeuf—and his
native princess were posted abroad. A wealthy local duke purchased their well-stuffed villa at Portici. The bill of sale in 1716
shows that, from the theatre, d'Elboeuf had managed to acquire a
rich trove of plunder: 177 statues and objects, or enough to outfit a
small museum.

Missing from that impressive list were the original three elegantly
draped female statues (now known to be 4th-century BC copies of
originals) which had been found intact standing in the niches of the
Greek Theatre.[8] D'Elboeuf had apparently planned to sell them, but
the Austrian consul in Naples abruptly declared them crown property and had them shipped to Vienna. The Habsburg Prince Eugene
installed them in the garden of his magnificent royal Belvedere Palace, to suffer the stings of the Viennese winter.

At Portici meantime the tunnels in the fields by Resina, which
d'Elboeuf's prison labourers had built for extracting the plunder,
were being used as rubbish dumps. When the farm houses above
began to show cracks in their foundations, the farm families protested. The tunnels were entirely refilled with rubble as a safety
precaution.

That was the end. Once more Herculaneum was obliterated, left
to subside into darkness and silence.

The dawn of the 18th century had found Italy, and particularly
Rome, in a physical, financial and intellectual shambles. It was still
Europe's foremost centre for the arts, but 200 years of religious warfare had taken their toll. *Nouveau riche* Catholic Spain, France and
Austria on the one hand, and Protestant northern Europe on the
other, had filled the breach. The Italian economy was in tatters, with
skilled textile workers leaving to find work in the north of Europe.
Aggravating matters in Rome was the Inquisition, which stifled
intellectual development; Galileo Galilei's heresy still echoed in the
ears of the prelates who ruled Rome. This acted as a brake on the
economy as well.

The coming of a general peace revived secular tourism to Italy. Once again people travelled for the sake of travel, rather than as part of a religious pilgrimage; between 1700 and 1710 the number of foreign visitors to Florence and Rome quadrupled. The ancient world had been these foreigners' schoolroom, and long before they saw Rome they knew its classical literature, philosophy and languages. They liked to call at the places they had studied in their books. Because Virgil had died near Naples, that now-Austrian city was part of their secular pilgrimage.

"There surely does not exist a place in the world where a man can travel with more pleasure and profit than Italy", reported an enthusiastic Joseph Addison, visiting Italy in 1705 as one of the new generation of travellers.[9] A recent graduate of Oxford and future contributor to *The Spectator*, young Addison was even planning to write a guidebook to Rome.

The institution of the Grand Tour was a peculiarly British custom filling the gap between school days and marriage. During the period the British university system showed a sharp decline in enrolments, and this was a factor encouraging a long period abroad. Two years were normally spent away from home, more when marriage had to be postponed until a convenient death in the family allowed the handing over of an estate. In the meantime the heir was shipped out of the way and told to study other countries and their languages, polish his manners, meet his foreign peers, and improve himself by looking at art and statues. From Britain the custom of the Grand Tour spread to the gilded youth of other countries—Germany, France, Holland, Sweden, Poland and Russia.

The Tour usually began in France, where a carriage would be hired and language study begin. After a month or so the gentleman and his retinue of servants and preceptor (his "bear", as he was called) would venture down through Switzerland and cross the mountain passes to their primary destination, Italy—meaning, in order, Venice, Florence, and Rome. The winter stop of choice was Naples, where the palm trees, flowers and midwinter sunshine made it "the garden of Europe", a place to escape from coughs and foul weather.

Life on the road was harsh and the bedbugs many, as letters home reported. Bandits infested every mountain range of Europe (though shortly these too would be celebrated in art and literature as part of the tourist experience). The Italian peninsula was divided into a dozen or so statelets and duchies, and each required a certificate allowing passage and a health certificate. One English Grand Tourist was advised to carry two health certificates: one to guarantee good health so he could cross borders, the other to certify illness so that he could lay claim to the best food.

As with package tours today, the Grand Tour spun rituals. Certain Renaissance art works had to be seen and admired, certain contemporary artists sought out. A portrait painted in Rome by Pompeo Batoni was nearly obligatory (he churned out some 500 for these foreigners, always with a chunk of broken column or urn in the background as witness to the Roman setting).

Other young foreigners, less well heeled, flocked to Rome to study art and architecture. The atmosphere they found was a beguiling blend of the clubby and international. A large contingent was French. The Villa Medici, where the French Academie scholarship students lived for an obligatory two years, at the top of the Spanish Steps, was already a venerable institution. The others, Italian as well as foreign student artists, were less organized, but many were provided studios at the Accademia di San Luca, a short walk from the Piazza di Spagna at the foot of the Spanish Steps.

All congregated there, even as young tourists do today, or indoors at the Caffè degli Inglesi (the English Café). This strategically situated café occupied a corner by the low, boat-shaped fountain at Piazza di Spagna. The café walls had been fancifully decorated by Giovanni Battista Piranesi, in a capricious blend of Egyptian antiquities that the young artist had seen in the Vatican Museum. The French students also frequented the Caffè Greco, a few steps further on.

For the local dealers of art and antiquities plying their trade in Rome, the influx of Grand Tourists came as manna from heaven. The wealthiest of the "milordi" ("the My Lords", as the Italians called the British aristocrats) were particularly keen on buying original statues from ancient Rome. Imperial Rome had been a forest of perhaps 6,000 statues, and Italian noble families would find them in their vineyards and fields by the hundred. But for the foreign Grand Tour shoppers sources were limited. The princely Roman families always had a cousin who was a cardinal, if not pope, and managed to keep the best for themselves.

Despite this, when formal archaeological excavations were opened at Hadrian's Villa in 1724, the market for genuine antiquities in Rome became suddenly lively. Some of the gleanings finally went to the foreign buyers. Subsequently a few Grand Tourists, beginning

6. Late 18th-century art students met at Rome's English Café, where they were befriended by G.B. Piranesi, author of the café's Egyptian-motif wall mural (above). Through the friendships kindled there, news of the discoveries at Herculaneum, and of the destructive excavating methods, travelled abroad.

with the British, managed to wangle a permit to conduct their own, personal excavations.

Statuary was the primary choice, but paintings from antiquity were also a popular purchase. These too were rare and tended to disappear even before they came onto the market. In his diary written in the late 18th century, Welsh artist Thomas Jones, who worked in both Rome and Naples, described seeing a painting being hacked from the wall of an ancient Roman villa near Tivoli and carted away.

Most visitors therefore made do with lesser souvenirs of the picturesque Roman ruins. The Roman workshops were all too delighted to oblige with repro antiquities created by clever Italian and some foreign immigrant sculptors and artists. Moving further downmarket, the less well-heeled souvenir hunters could buy engravings and drawings of the visible antiquities. To take home to the ladies, on offer were excruciatingly miniaturized, micro-mosaic parlour bibelots and jewellery—necklaces, earrings, brooches—depicting the ancient monuments of Rome.

One of the many catering to the flourishing Grand Tourist market was a gifted young Roman artist named Camillo Paderni, who worked as the equivalent of a sous-chef in the busy *bottega* of a prominent painter of large-scale historical scenes, Francesco Imperiali. A particular favourite of the Grand Tourists were copies of an authentic ancient mosaic of birds. This charming bird scene was so popular that it was sold in half a dozen versions worked in diverse materials, from mosaic to engravings and drawings. On commission for an English milord, "I drew some of these mosaic birds myself", Paderni acknowledged cheerfully.[10]

Paderni's other specialty were landscape paintings "in the manner of Poussin". Poussin was a French artist who had worked in Rome the previous century and had set the fashion for fantasy Arcadian scenes showing a Greek temple in the background and, in the foreground, nymphs and satyrs with wineskins, cavorting beneath a pink-gold sky. For Paderni, repro Arcadia was a living.

The Roman world of the junior artists was small. One day young Paderni met two students from Edinburgh, who were living in rented rooms above the Caffè degli Inglesi at the Piazza di Spagna. One was Allan Ramsay, the future portrait painter. Paderni invited them to a Sunday art outing organized by Paderni's maestro, Imperiali. Another participant was portrait painter Pompeo Batoni. In a far cry from the religious tourism of the previous century, the little group moved from church to church while Imperiali lectured on the works of art. The friendship continued: Paderni, in turn, visited London, where he became a member of the Royal Society.[11]

In 1738 Paderni learned that antiquarian artists were being hired in Naples to copy ancient paintings and objects just then being found in a new excavation there, twenty-nine years after d'Elboeuf's wholesale plundering of the Greek Theatre of Herculaneum. From Rome, Paderni travelled to Naples to apply. In the back of his mind was the possibility that he might find objects to sell through his new friends from Edinburgh. He was hired.

Paderni found a new Naples, no longer Austrian, and just beginning a great boom. Four years previously, an ambitious new royal dynasty, unconnected to any nation but the Kingdom of the Two Sicilies, had been installed in the capital city of Naples. Finding the capital shabby, the new rulers raised money for reconstruction by the simple expedient of lifting tax exemptions from the myriad Neapolitan churches and monasteries. With these funds the new ruling family had launched a vast building programme that was already changing the face of Naples. Everywhere great new buildings were under construction: three new palaces, a fine opera house, factories, a prison, hospices, a cemetery. Even the shabby royal palace was being lavishly rebuilt.

Though officially Spanish, this royal family was the usual inter-related and mongrel breed of European aristocracy. It had no blood connection whatsoever to the Spain over which it ruled. Elizabeth Farnese, the mother of the eighteen-year-old sent to Naples as king, was descended from the Medici dukes of Florence and the Farnese dukes of Lombardy. The father, Philip V, was French; a cousin of the French king Louis XIV, he had grown up at Versailles. Through clever manipulation, these non-Spanish monarchs of Spain had successfully claimed the south of Italy as a personal kingdom. To keep them from claiming more important territories, the other great European powers had agreed, and the Kingdom of Naples and the Two Sicilies had been handed over to the Bourbon king of Spain and his Tuscan wife in 1734.

Grandeur had been bred into both parents, and their points of reference and ambitions for their teenaged son, who reigned as Charles III, were palatial. Versailles was their model along with the vast Palazzo Pitti of Florence, where the boy Charles had whiled away his adolescent summers with his Medici cousins, shooting arrows at the hares woven into the tapestries on the walls.

Naples was to be no less. Charles's father suffered from what would today be diagnosed as severe depression (for two years he never spoke), and so Charles's tough-minded mother, Elisabetta Farnese, commanded. Her goal, as she wrote to her son in a letter, was to make Naples, the family kingdom, into "the Florence of the South". To this end she gradually removed the aristocratic but inept Spanish staff sent to Naples with her son and replaced them with men from her own north Italy, beginning with a brilliant Tuscan prime minister for Naples, Bernardo Tanucci.

Prestige for the new dynasty was the goal. Elisabetta Farnese was due to inherit an immense treasure of fine ancient Roman sculptures and old master paintings, which belonged to her uncle, the

7. Strong-willed Elisabetta Farnese sent her young son Charles to Naples as king in 1734. This Tuscan queen of Spain remained the power behind the throne, and her tastes indelibly marked Naples, its arts, architecture, and museums at the dawn of scientific archaeology. Anon., Royal Palace, Caserta.

Farnese duke. Museums were prestigious; in Rome the Capitoline Museum had just been opened to the public. For Naples, Elisabetta planned that one of the new palaces would be a showcase for her inherited treasures, which she expected to send to her son for a great museum. New additions would reflect more glory upon the brand new dynasty. To this end the old tunnels excavated by d'Elboeuf at Herculaneum in 1709, and abandoned less than a year afterward, were reopened and being extended with new tunnels underground.

Little was known about them in Rome, however, and as Paderni prepared to leave for Naples, he had little idea what he would find there. Nevertheless he eagerly packed up his paints and brushes. Bidding farewell to his maestro and his friends at the Caffè degli Inglesi, he set out by carriage from Rome, to rattle his way down the old Appian Way to the coaching station at Resina.

Carlo Paderni had barely arrived when a sculptor, Giuseppe Canart, rushed forward to greet him. Canart was hired shortly after the reopening of the Herculaneum excavation in 1736. Many of the statuettes, lamps and other ancient objects of bronze being hauled to the surface were broken. Canart's job was to repair and restore them.

Canart also showed Paderni thirty paintings that had just been hacked from walls somewhere deep underground. The slave labourers and hired farm workers had hauled the pictures to the surface in wheelbarrows. Paderni was expected to make copies of them and, where necessary, retouch them. Even when he compared the paintings before him with the fine ancient paintings from the excavations at Rome, Paderni found those from Herculaneum "exceedingly beautiful ... coloured to perfection, and as fresh as if painted a month ago", he wrote in a letter to a friend in London, "worthy of a Raphael".[12]

Eager to see the excavation for himself, Paderni crawled down through one of the shallow, slanting and airless tunnels. It was not a pleasant experience: "This Place is a Pit, it's like a Well", Paderni wrote. "The lava is hard as a Flint. ... They dig their way (after the manner of our Catacombs) under the Bituminous Matter, thrown out of the Mountain the Time of Great Eruptions".[13] There is no doubt that the difficulties facing the excavators in the tunnels were immense. The buried city lay too deep for an open excavation and could be reached only by sinking tunnels like mine shafts. Yet to do so the available equipment—pick, shovel, barrow—was no more advanced than when the Etruscans mined the isle of Elba for iron ore. Poorly clad and ill-fed forced labourers and hired workmen, their skin tanned mahogany from the sunshine above ground, found freezing conditions deep below as they worked in airless tunnels less than five feet in height. Assailed by poisonous fumes, they hacked away at endless walls of rock in the uncertain light of torches which consumed what little oxygen reached them from far above. No one had time to pay heed to the position of statue, chair, lamp, bed, table, lump of bread, frying pan, tool, or even painting; and so they did not.

A further difficulty, as Paderni noted angrily, was that the rubble from digging underground remained underground, shifted now here, now there, as excavators entered a new area. For this he blamed the Spanish artillery engineer in charge of the excavation, Captain Rocque Joachim Alcubierre. For his part, the Spanish engineer took nothing but pride in his tunnels, for it was he who had promoted reopening the abandoned Herculaneum excavation.

Alcubierre had been summoned to Naples from a military post in Tuscany in order to oversee construction of an elaborate new royal hunting palace at Portici, near d'Elboeuf's old property, to be called La Reggia, set within an immense estate stretching from the sea to the mountains. On learning that an Austrian prince had found a treasure trove of antiquities in caverns deep below the neighbouring town of Resina, Alcubierre ordered the removal of the rubble from d'Elboeuf's old tunnels. The following year a formal excavation began with a team of twenty workmen. Alcubierre directed the excavations, and hence Paderni's work.

As the excavations proceeded beyond the small area that had been explored nearly three decades previously by d'Elboeuf, a gratifying jumble of antiquities was hoisted above ground: painted pots, bronze buckets and urns, ornate oil lamps and marble panels useful for paving floors, all for the benefit of the royal sponsors, and for the career of Alcubierre himself. The stunning amount involved was described by one of the earliest outside visitors permitted into subterranean Herculaneum. What the visiting French magistrate Charles de Brosses saw were:

> Pieces of furniture from rooms and kitchens, some of terracotta, most in bronze, … vast numbers of lamps, vases, instruments for sacrifices, for war or for baths, urns, etc.
>
> I don't want to neglect some singular objects, such as a marble table, having not the feet of a goat, but of a lion, and all around it an inscription in Oscan or Etruscan, whose characters I would have liked to

copy. There was a mirror of an off-white metal, a hunk of bread, and walnuts and olives that have kept their appearance even though carbonized.[14]

Scientific archaeology was yet to come, and so the finding of bread and walnuts at that time was a mere folkloric curiosity. Marble mania prevailed, and what mattered were large statues. It was a personal triumph for Alcubierre to have discovered the Hercules and the other important statues, which he had installed in an annex buildings to La Reggia.[15]

The Hercules marble had special importance because it was seen as definitive proof that the town underground was indeed Herculaneum. It was another triumph for Alcubierre when an inscription showing the word "theatre" was found, and a date placed it in the age of Augustus. Finally another inscription identified the city for the first time as the celebrated lost Herculaneum.

D'Elboeuf had left only a rudimentary map, but Alcubierre took care to make careful maps of the new excavations, showing his own and the original tunnels. From the Greek Theatre his workmen had advanced to its entrance on the main street, the Decumanus Maximus, where they came upon two life-sized, splendidly carved white marble equestrian statues of ancient Herculaneum's most eminent citizens, the Roman senator Balbus and his son. They were a sensational discovery.

Paderni meantime went on grumbling because he had other objections as well. Because the strata of hard volcanic rock varied, when workmen were confronted with an especially tough patch, they simply abandoned a half-explored room to move on toward another, easier. In addition, rather than tunnel along a wall in a time-consuming search for door or window, they smashed straight through walls, damaging them. This was serious because all wall surfaces were painted, some crudely, but others with elegant decorations. Unable to see what might be on the other side, this brought needless destruction.

Alcubierre also permitted the workmen to hack paintings from the walls for viewing while still deep underground. When he decided they were too similar to those already above ground, he had the supposedly repetitious pictures smashed to smithereens because they were not worth the bother of hoisting to the surface. The sole wall paintings left untouched were those judged to be inferior. As a result, in the 1950s, when a central part of Herculaneum was excavated from above, rather than by tunnel, a small number of paintings were therefore fortunately found in their original positions. This was important, even though they may not have been the best in Alcubierre's eyes.

This was collection-driven archaeology at its most brutal and a year after his arrival Paderni sat down to write just this to one of his new friends in Britain. In what was not precisely the sort of regime propaganda the Neapolitan monarchs desired, Paderni meticulously described the sorry manner in which Alcubierre's excavations were conducted.

> When they meet with anything that seems valuable, they pick it out, and leave the rest. But I am afraid, that after they have searched, they throw the Earth in again; by which means many Curiosities may be lost, not being understood by these labourers ... They pry out the pictures without making a drawing of the position where they had been found, such as the niches. ... Before being copied, elegant figures and animals were destroyed. The same fate will befall the rest. [16]

Paderni deplored the fact that no records were being kept of provenance, no sketches were made. Entire decorated walls and mosaic picture floors were detached and hacked into sections small enough, he reported, to be squeezed into a wheelbarrow through the tunnels for raising to the surface. The letter could not have been more damning.

Thanks to his old student friends from the Caffè degli Inglesi, his letter was read aloud to the Royal Society in London and published in its review. This was the very first serious informed account of the Herculaneum excavations to appear in any scholarly forum outside Naples itself. Paderni's report was therefore keenly anticipated, but when it came, the reaction was shock and dismay. The excavations were expected to bring the Neapolitan crown glory, not scandal.

Nevertheless Paderni continued to work with amazing industry. In this pre-photography era his hundreds of detailed drawings of the wall paintings, sculptures, and household objects of buried Herculaneum became a treasure trove in their own right. The paintings he was reproducing were in the style of pure realism the Romans preferred. For the artists and art theoreticians of the ancient Roman world, the point of art was to make an exact copy of reality, used to decorate the walls of houses and porticoed gardens. Water seemed to run from painted fountains, and painted bowls of glass were exquisitely transparent. Cherries and grapes glistened beneath what

looked like thin netting to keep away the birds, which were painted
meticulously down to the last feather.

In addition, in their homes the cultivated, wealthier families surrounded themselves with pictures on the walls with themes familiar
from Greek paintings; indeed, some were reproductions of famous
Greek paintings. Scenes from Greek mythology, as familiar to everyone as Jack and the Beanstalk nowadays, appeared again and again:
Theseus, Narcissus, Hercules, Venus and Mercury.

Most were painted *al fresco* in a complex process that required up
to seven layers of preparation, but some paintings were on wooden
boards. These pictures were set inside painted fake frames, faux
marble panels, architectural fantasies or garden fences. Miniature
landscapes and seaside views (in them the viewer can see the elongated porches) alternated with summery garden scenes; their
purpose was often to give a tiny, dark room a look of the outdoors.
And there were everyday scenes of men working, gambling, or selling food to customers.

In copying these works, in recording their literal representations
of Roman reality from daily bread to deities, Paderni became the
first modern man in history to see life in the ancient world unfold.
As if by magic lantern he saw and, copying them, painted daily life
in Roman villa, temple, harbour, farm and town. And then the pictures took him beyond the gulf of Naples, beyond Rome and the
sea, to the flooded Nile and villages in Africa where pygmies
cavorted.

The gleanings from underground did not stop. Like one of the
cornucopias in the arms of a river god or temple statue, Herculaneum went on gushing forth marbles and bronzes, statues and
statuettes, twisted columns and decorative mosaics, bronze lamps,
buckets, tripod tables, utensils. As the exploration crept forward,
one improvement arrived: a broad staircase that descended into the
Greek Theatre. Another addition was the appointment of a Neapolitan scholar named Marcello Venuti to serve as official royal
antiquarian at Herculaneum. Venuti's first task would be to guide
honoured guests, including fellow antiquarians, on a tour of the
Greek Theatre, already famous but seen by only a handful of
outsiders.

For the first time important visitors descended into the cavern-
like, open area of the theatre, rather than were dangled down into
the old well or bent double in the low tunnels. Antiquarians from
Rome, Florence and as far away as Britain arrived, some curious, but

many hoping to snatch up the leavings from the already rich crown collection. Their acquisitions and the tales they told back home further whetted interest in Herculaneum.

Their reports were not always flattering, however. A shocked scholar from Verona in northern Italy, Scipio Maffei, toured the site in 1746. "The workmen go forward blindly", he reported. "Who knows how many precious and desirable objects have been lost in the rooms and cabinets?"[17]

A few of the visitors went so far as to suggest that buried Herculaneum in its entirety should be declared a museum. But instead, it became a business. A particularly decorative central panel was always set protectively aside for the rapidly expanding royal collection. However, the framing panels that surrounded it tended to be snubbed as merely decorative; many, therefore, were sold. No record was kept of the entire scene, which may have covered the walls of a whole room (to see what this means, today's visitors can visit the more recently excavated Villa of Oplontis, where wall scenes are intact).

If Paderni objected to the methods, what infuriated Alcubierre were the curiosity-seeking trouble-makers, who wheedled permission to see the sights, only to write unflattering accounts later. Alcubierre put the blame for the bad publicity squarely on Venuti, the scholar who had been made chief tour guide, with the result that Venuti was fired. This was patently unfair; the earliest historian of the Herculaneum excavations, Michele Ruggiero, blamed Alcubierre himself, who had been sent to Herculaneum "to ruin it", as Ruggiero wrote bitterly in 1885.[18]

The problems continued. Above ground at Resina, terrified villagers saw cracks appear in the foundations of their cottages. Underground, too, there was terror, for good reason. The new staircase led only into the Greek Theatre. The houses and streets of the buried city proper could be reached only through a rabbit warren of narrow tunnels, into which poisonous gases continued to seep. Alcubierre himself fell sick repeatedly—his eyes were affected—and for long periods refused to descend underground with his work crew, whose own illnesses obviously went unnoticed.

Presumably Alcubierre did not read English, for the man who replaced Venuti as director (*custode*) of the Herculaneum antiquities was none other than the first to criticize Alcubierre's methods, the artist Camillo Paderni. Theft was an obvious risk, and Paderni was concerned to keep track of all findings from Herculaneum and to keep all paintings and objects safely locked away. The future museum under construction for King Charles high atop the Capodimonte hill in Naples was not yet finished. But d'Elboeuf's old seafront mansion at Portici was available. Incorporated into the estate flanking the hunting lodge, it became the first Herculaneum Museum.

Having been the first to tell tales, Paderni was now obliged to enforce the secrecy ruling. The excavations were financed by the crown, and information about them was counted upon to lend lustre to the kingdom. The Neapolitan Establishment therefore demanded total control over the news from Herculaneum.

The foreign interest persisted, however. In France in 1750 magistrate Charles de Brosses's collected *Lettres sur Herculaneum* were published. Many in his own circle had read or heard of his letters when they were first written fifteen years before, but now they were circulated in Britain, Germany and other countries as well. They show that de Brosses had instantly grasped the importance of the frescoed paintings he had seen at Herculaneum: "Almost nothing else of the kind has survived from antiquity. ... The very paucity of the pictures by ancient painters which have come down to us renders those we have most precious."[19]

Six years later a philologist-monk named Jean-Jacques Barthelemy began secretly preparing a report on Herculaneum for the Academie Française after visiting the excavation in 1756. Hovering guards had forbidden him to take notes. To dodge them he was forced to become an archaeological spy; as he later wrote, he had to pretend a need to urinate in order to steal away to a quiet corner and jot down all he could remember.

Court self-promotion was not the sole reason for the Neapolitans' cult of secrecy. The sale of engravings was an important source of income. Each connoisseur-collector kept his items private for his stable of artists to copy for sale. Their model was Giovanni Battista Piranesi, and, like him, their style was to embellish ancient buildings, objects and sculptures into fantasy compositions drenched with emotion. This was a vogue which some serious antiquarians considered unscientific. One of the critics of the fantasy interpretation of the ruins was a young but already successful Prussian art historian named J.J. Winckelmann, just then in the employ of the Vatican in Rome.

Despite the pressure, official publication came belatedly in a traumatic process. In 1755, nearly two decades after the Bourbon-

Farnese excavations began at Herculaneum, the Neapolitan estab-
lishment finally produced its first scholarly tome describing the site,
Le antichità di Ercolano (*The Antiquities of Herculaneum*), edited by a
famously dull court-appointed antiquarian named Camillo Bayardi.
So dense and verbose was Bayardi's prose that Prime Minister
Tanucci called it "Thick as a mattress".[20]

However, the copies of the Herculaneum pictures and treasures
which had been drawn by Camillo Paderni and other artists who
had flanked him over the course of twenty years excited quite
another reaction. Copies of the Bayardi book with Paderni and company's pictures were rare as hens' teeth. Normally they were
bestowed as gifts from the Neapolitan king to his peers, and so they
were seen by very few scholars. Nevertheless, the sensation they
created was extraordinary. The cultivated Europe of the early
Enlightenment was already besotted with Greek antiquity. Because
Greek and Greek-influenced colonists, including the Etruscans and
the Samnites, had settled in the Neapolitan gulf coast and ruled over
it for five centuries, the wonders found at Herculaneum were considered—and, much of it, correctly—Greek art.

The appetite to know more was enormous, and somehow foreign
publishers made plates and issued their own editions. In addition,
as a gift for the king of Naples, Charles III, Paderni fashioned a
special sixty-page report on the excavations. This hand-written
book, containing forty-eight of Paderni's own illustrations,
disappeared until the 1890s, when a descendant of Napoleon
donated what is one of the treasures of the Vesuvian sites to the
French School in Rome, which published a facsimile copy in the year
2000.[21]

Scholars had long surmised that Paderni had kept a personal
diary covering the earliest, least known and formative years of the
Herculaneum excavation. For two centuries the diary was completely lost, until it surfaced in the Naples archives in 1979. The
delays in finding Paderni's report to the king and his diary meant
the loss of a critical portion of the early history of the excavations.
Until recently his contribution was therefore considered insignifi-
cant. Even the year of his death was commonly given incorrectly, by
a decade.

Today, on the wall of my living room, hangs one of Paderni's
engravings, taken from a German edition. The beautifully executed
picture shows a pensive seated muse holding quill and scroll as she
pauses to reflect—whether upon love letter or poem, we do not

know, any more than we know in what parlour of what salon the original painting may be hanging today, or who cruelly tore the page from the German edition to sell.

What we do know is that, in the reckoning of what was lost at Herculaneum, Paderni's contribution has helped to restore Herculaneum to life.

CHAPTER III

Papyrus

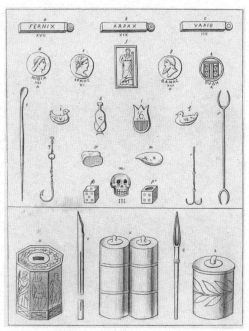

8. Ink boxes and theatre tickets, engraving

For his good deeds Colonel Alcubierre won a promotion, after which he tended to disappear from the stinking tunnels. He was indeed ill from the gases released underground, but he was also ambitious, striking out and testing for more and better sources of ancient treasure throughout the coastal area.

This was the best of luck for Herculaneum, for in his ever more frequent absences, a thirty-eight-year-old army engineer named Karl Weber was appointed to supervise the excavation at Herculaneum on 25 April 1750. Under the methodical Weber the excavations began to be conducted in an orderly fashion for the first time. Weber was born in 1712 in the Swiss mountains and educated by Jesuits in Lucerne. Moving to Pavia in north Italy, he attended high school there, then in short order married an Italian woman, joined the Spanish army and took a degree in engineering.

His first job in Naples was to make a topographical map of the Vesuvian area. A week later a handful of coloured ancient marble fragments were dredged up a mere hundred yards from the entry to one of Alcubierre's tunnels. The court in Naples was eager for new excavation sites, and Weber was reassigned to hunt the source of the ancient marble pieces. Within a month he had opened an air shaft, and work could recommence. As he probed forward into the mystery of the past, Weber had no sense of what, if anything, lay one pyroclastic wheelbarrow load before him.

But suddenly he came upon a patch of finely worked mosaic floor, unlike any yet found at Herculaneum. As the men wielding picks widened the floor area, the entire mosaic design became visible. It was a giant marble pinwheel which, in geometric circles, widened out from the centre, creating patterns within patterns, all in subtle harmonies of colour. The rosetta pavement was an almost magical display of the ancient stone mason's craft.

Similar mosaic floors were often found paving shallow pools or the floor of a dining room (*triclinium*). Puzzlingly, however, no trace of wall was found—only an exterior ring of holes at the border. Weber decided that this was a circle of post holes, for beams which held up a circular roof above the pinwheel, trompe l'oeil floor. The building would have had no walls and must have resembled a child's merry-go-round. Its extraordinary beauty spoke for the unknown rest. The quest continued. As Weber worked he made a carefully precise map—the first ever made of the site.

From the pinwheel floor, Weber's men found themselves tracing a long, narrow pavement. This siren walkway lured the excavators forward into the blackness to the crash of pick against stone. Post-holes lining either side showed that the walk was a long portico, Weber wrote in his report to the crown, and the circular pavilion a covered, round lookout post called a *belvedere*, accessible by the porticoed walk. This was a stunningly evocative notion, for it suggested long-ago summer strolls toward the belvedere, and summer strollers gazing seaward, meditating or speaking earnestly in Aristotelian fashion.

Chief engineer Alcubierre, Weber's superior officer, had little interest in the general layout of the belvedere or its social uses. His goals never changed: work the men hard, spend little, bring home treasure. Inevitably the two clashed. Nevertheless, Weber burrowed forward along the walkway pavement. After some 300 feet it led him straight into one of the great finds in the history of archaeology: the magnificent villa now known as the Villa of the Papyri (Villa dei Papiri, sometimes also called the Villa Pisone).

This particularly large villa revealed itself in thrilling fits and starts. As became clear only gradually, it had once sprawled hundreds of yards on a bluff overlooking the sea, just outside the city walls of Herculaneum. In order to trace its interior, Weber opened two parallel tunnels, which he then connected by a network of cross-tunnels. From these tunnels, the doors to villa rooms and to its various open courtyards and a peristyle garden were slowly located and explored. His map now resembled a honeycomb as, adding more tunnels, he could extrapolate the spaces into their larger whole.

It was a breakthrough when Weber found himself in a recognizable space, an exceptionally long porticoed garden. Dubbed the Great Peristyle, as it appears on Weber's maps, it stretched 900 feet in length and was 111 feet wide. On the map Weber also marked all columns and their placement (twenty-four on each long side of the Great Peristyle, and ten on the short, he recorded). Down its centre, amid garden and statues, ran a long, narrow pool.

Scattered in the peristyle garden were life-sized ancient Greek marble and bronze sculptures (many still on view in the National Archaeological Museum at Naples). They included a white marble group of two figures, roughly three feet tall. They were locked in an embrace. Otherwise, in the smoky darkness, Weber saw little and did not or could not immediately realize what, if anything, they represented.

The exciting new finds at Herculaneum were being followed by the court of Charles III with the utmost excitement, in part because most of his courtiers had little else to occupy their time. The court happened to be on hand, attending a hunt in the woodlands of the grounds of the new royal hunting palace called the Reggia at Portici, when word came that the mystery troupe of workmen underground had made magnificent new discoveries of ancient statues. Servants rushed ahead to prepare a picnic and raise an improvised canopy tent alongside the entry to Weber's tunnel. Then the entire court converged to see what was being hoisted to the surface. A court artist stood by, to capture the first impressions for the painting he would complete in his studio.

Amidst a flotilla of courtiers in silks and befurred velvet finery, Charles and his Prussian wife Queen Maria Amalia arrived in a rustling, stately procession and took their seats on folding chairs. From the bowels of the earth the carved white marble group of two embracing figures, which Weber had found in the Great Peristyle, appeared at the mouth of the tunnel, borne upon a litter carried by prison labourers. A shiver of excitement rippled through the court. Already the dainty turn of that horn revealed the prized Greek look. When the whole sculpture group hoved into view two heads could be seen and two bodies. One seemed to be a man of sorts, though at closer look he wore two small horns on his head. He gazed fondly into the female's languid marble eyes. For locked in his embrace was a female goat, surely the prettiest in the flock, whom he was in the act of penetrating.

The educated among the observers would have recognized in this garden sculpture from antiquity nothing more than an amusing allegory. The lover was Pan, forest god and the Arcadian protector of flocks and shepherds. Pan, a denizen of woodlands, notoriously startled people walking in a wood (his surprising them gave us the

9. The Bourbon King Charles III was only eighteen when he assumed the throne of Naples in 1734. During his remarkable quarter-century reign Naples flowered, Herculaneum was explored, Pompeii discovered, and the first museum of Vesuvian antiquities created. Anton Raphael Mengs, Lazaro Galdiano Museum, Madrid.

word "panic"). To such later and more sophisticated Greeks as Soc-
rates, Pan represented the search for beauty of soul. This statue was
a playful representation of a myth relating how nature (Pan) gave
poetry to mankind (the she-goat). The statue had stood, a garden
party background prank, along the flank of the elongated pool in
the Great Peristyle.

In the sculpture group Charles saw no amusement, nor redeem-
ing metaphor. It mattered little to him that it was superbly well
crafted. When his new opera house, the San Carlo, was opened he
had been scandalized by the ballerinas' bare legs and had ordered
them to wear ankle-length black pantaloons ever after. This priggish
side now made him order a halt to the entire excavation at Herculaneum. Outraged, Charles led Maria Amalia and the entire court
away in pious haste.

Not long afterward a French visitor, Gabriel Seigneux de Correvon,
toured underground Herculaneum. Returning home, he penned a
gushing paean of praise in which he lauded the patrons of the excavations for their having given "new life" to antiquity, history,
architecture, and all the arts: "The discovery crowns the glory of a
magnanimous King whose sensible authority directs and leads this
great undertaking".[1] "Immortal praise"—no patron of archaeology
could have asked for more. King Charles's prohibition on excavating
was soon forgotten. The she-goat and her lover were locked into a
cupboard, whose sole key was tightly guarded by the secretary of
the new Herculaneum Academy, the Accademia Ercolanese.[2]

Weber returned to work at Herculaneum. From the Great Peristyle he and his force of workmen plodded slowly into another area
of the villa. This was a classical entry hall (*atrium*) open to the skies,
with, in its centre, a small square pond called an *impluvium*. From
there his excavators penetrated into what appeared a private household area of rooms, bedrooms and a bathroom.

At that time very few ancient Roman villas had been seen in modern history even though, strictly speaking, it was not so much
"seen" as extrapolated by Weber on the basis of his patchwork view
deep inside the stinking labyrinth of underground chamber and
tunnel. Yet from his careful soundings Weber imagined the whole:
the villa, its rooms and their purposes, its belvedere and gardens,
seaside position and relation to the town of Herculaneum. His being
able to envisage, in exceedingly tight spaces, the entire, large villa
required an extraordinary flight of the imagination.

Having discovered the pinwheel mosaic and the Great Peristyle with its statues, another discovery of immense importance was made, though not immediately recognized. A workman shovelling rubble from the private household area noticed a heap of charred lumps lying in a tumble on the floor. Each was from eight to ten inches long. Resembling fisherman's floats, the blackened lumps were considered of no importance.[3] Some, picked up, disintegrated into dust on the spot. The workman chucked others into the rubble, where they were lost forever.

Because it was so cold below ground and the lumps resembled charcoal, still others were tossed into wheelbarrows and hauled above ground as fuel for the fires that warmed the workers after their long hours of toil in the chill bowels of the earth. Countless "charcoal" was burned before one, caught in the brilliance of daylight, revealed odd markings, rather like writing. Indeed it was writing, but more time passed, and more were lost, before recognition that this was ancient Greek script, and that each charcoal lump being consumed by the workmen's fire was in reality a book of history, poetry or philosophy from antiquity.

The secretary of the Royal Society of Agriculture at Tours, a Monsieur Verrier, happened to be touring underground Herculaneum in 1754 and creeping through the tunnels when a second cache of papyri was discovered in the same villa. Once above ground he wrote to his friends in France that charred scrolls were being culled from the cinders of Vesuvius. They looked, he said, exactly like "a pastry rolled upon itself" — a swiss roll, but one made of puff pastry since the fragile outer layer tended to crumble the moment it was touched, as he wrote.

"I saw a good many scrolls being extracted from the ashes", Verrier wrote in an article published in France in 1763. "Some of the writing could be deciphered by raising the external surface, but the effort to save one fragment often caused the loss of another ten. My heart bled at the spectacle."[4]

Underground, in the room where the charred hoard of scrolls had been found, Weber's men now discovered a wooden table and cupboards which appeared to be for books. A visiting Spanish bishop witnessed this discovery, which he dramatically recounted in a letter to his brother in Madrid. All the precious furnishings were lost:

> Against the walls stood two cupboards, barely taller than a man, while in the centre of the room was another cupboard with space for books on either side. These cupboards immediately fell into bits. ... On the floor

below the cupboards lay a big pile of scrolls, so fragile that with the touch of a finger they dissolved into powder.[5]

But there were also joys, and a euphoric Paderni wrote to a friend in England that the room—the first recognizable library from antiquity ever found—had a "not inelegant mosaic" floor and corniced cupboards inlaid with different kinds of wood, "as in our own day".[6] Atop the cupboards stood small bronze busts of Greek philosophers, among them Demosthenes and Epicurus; together with the original of Weber's map showing its location, these busts are among the finest treasures of the Naples National Archeological Museum.

The findings—scrolls, bookshelves, busts of philosophers—confirmed that at the heart of the villa was a library. That such libraries existed throughout the Mediterranean by the late 2nd century BC is well established. Libraries came to Rome itself somewhat belatedly. In the 1st century BC, when the Herculaneum villa was constructed, Rome was a city of landowners, military men and lawyers, but nevertheless lacked the institutions of higher learning. Serious students went to Greece and Alexandria for higher learning; Julius Caesar studied at Rhodes, and Cicero attended lectures at three different schools in Athens, where libraries were a standard part of school life.

After a late start, the Romans became prolific writers, and, the papyrologist's one-liner goes, "A publisher wants to issue a one-volume edition of Cicero". The faint humour comes from knowing that Cicero's collected works fill several bookshelves. It was not only the upper-class gentlemen like Cicero and the Plinys, Elder and Younger, who wrote. Ordinary people, including some slaves, were literate, as Pompeii has demonstrated in the large number of scribbled graffiti in various languages and in the election campaign slogans written in Latin on walls.

The physical work of writing was done by highly skilled scribes. In Egypt they sat cross-legged at a low table; at Pompeii and Rome they sat on a stool by a low desk to write in neat columns in black and sometimes red ink, occasionally with illustration. A chief scribe hovered over them, as text corrections in a careful, second hand show. All this amounted to an industry of book agents and dealers and publishing; Cicero himself once became involved in setting up a scribe school as an investment.

The scribe would take notes on a slate, then write a fair copy in ink on the papyrus scroll. Because scrolls were important discoveries at Herculaneum, we must take a moment to explain what they are.

Some papyrus was of high quality, some cut-rate and even recycled; the very best was made by cutting a foot-long section of the inner stalk of the reed into extremely thin strands, laid out side by side. Atop this a second layer of strips was placed crossways and the double layer pounded with a mallet until the two layers naturally adhered into a sheet that was dried in the sun, polished and, for a perfect writing surface, finely glazed to create a brilliant surface. The sheets were then bonded by more pounding into a long strip that was wound around a wooden peg, to make a book or *volumen*. Each scribe developed a characteristic hand, which might vary from the plain to an almost Gothic-looking, ornate script; today these variations are studied in the Herculaneum papyri as an aid to dating texts.

In any library, philosophy was the main topic, but to the Romans, like the Greeks, "philosophy" was a catch-all word embracing physics, geography, music and theories of governing. Along with literary works expressing the aspirations of man and his thoughts about the gods, there were also pragmatic treatises on medical treatment, how to grow crops, what a nursing mother should eat, architecture and, perhaps obviously, how to cook a fine meal. There was even a convenient Roman *Who's Who*, with tiny illustrations of the personalities described. Scholarship was a tool of power, and so ancient libraries contained treatises on the design of a war ship and data about a conquered province—its gods, laws, class structure, economy, farms and, not least, how to speak the language. New citizens had to know their future tax and military obligations.

Ancient cities possessing great literary libraries therefore guarded them with pride and jealousy. Rome was still a bellicose backwater when Alexandria in Egypt fell heir to the wisdom of Greece. The Ptolomies built the greatest library of its time at Alexandria, a cultural centre with sculpture gallery, performance hall and library of nearly half a million scrolls; a nearby temple library housed another 36,000. Among its works was a multilingual dictionary of words for fish. Translating, like lecturing, was an important profession; famously, the Alexandrians seized from foreign ships anchored in port copies of any book they lacked, and had translators at work full time.

Alexandria's primacy in books and scholarship, which lasted the two centuries before the birth of Christ, depended upon royal patronage, but also on its cornering the market in papyrus. Papyrus was power, and the reed *genus cyperaceae* flourished on the Nile River banks, and nowhere else. When the Egyptians wanted to cut down to size their rival on the north shore of the Mediterranean, Pergamum, they halted papyrus shipments there (Pergamum fought back by inventing parchment, made from stretched lambskin).

With the collapse of the Roman Empire, the libraries became the victims of war and politics, fire and flood. To hide collections of books from barbarians the Romans buried them underground, where they rotted from the humidity. By the 4th century AD those of Rome were all lost, "all sealed, for evermore, like tombs", wrote an historian from that time, Ammianus.[7] The final blow was the annihilation of the greatest of all, the Alexandrian Library, with the Arab conquest of Egypt in the 7th century AD.

The single exception is the library discovered by Karl Weber in the villa at Herculaneum. More than the sculptures or the Greek Theatre, more than its great mosaic masterpiece of the belvedere, the buried library at the Villa of the Papyri is the greatest single treasure of Herculaneum and one of the greatest finds of all archaeological research. The quantity alone was astounding: despite the losses, during the twenty-two months between October 1752 and August 1754 Weber recovered some 1,100 scrolls and broken or otherwise partial chunks of scrolls, or one-fifth of all Greco-Roman papyrus scrolls extant today (and this figure includes all recent findings).

Other troves of writings from antiquity have survived in tombs and rubbish dumps, but they are small. With the exception of the Dead Sea Scrolls, most deal with commercial or property questions—wills, tax lists, commercial orders, marriage contracts, homesick letters from soldiers. Herculaneum's collection differs from these because the trove was, beyond discussion, a library, thoughtfully planned as a storehouse of knowledge, rather than a random finding of documents. On the basis of references in existing ancient books, scholars have deduced that only one-tenth has come down to us, of the entire classical heritage of literature, history and scholarship. There was also a question of the authenticity of medieval copies of the works of antiquity. Mid-18th-century European scholars longed for more ancient literature, more authentic voices speaking directly without the mediation of generations of copiers. In their laborious copying and recopying works again and again, medieval monks incorporated mistakes, including in mathematics. Some were wilful additions, others incorrect corrections, general misreadings, and pious omissions.

The finding of the Herculaneum papyri therefore raised high hopes among the best minds of Europe. Before the first scroll was read, scholarly interest was at fever pitch. The reason for the excitement was spelled out by the same Gabriel Seigneux de Correvon who had gushed thanks to King Charles at Naples and to his father-in-law Augustus in Dresden for their patronage of the excavations. From Herculaneum, he wrote, "We long to recover the library collection of a Roman intellectual. There surely were some, considering the fact that Cicero, Lucullus and other illustrious Romans owned magnificent country villas at Pompeii, Herculaneum, Pozzuoli, and elsewhere nearby."[8] Echoing his words, French visitor de Lalande hoped the papyrus scrolls would yield unknown texts and hence expand all knowledge of the classical world:

> What a memorable date in the history of the human spirit it would be if they prove to contain the complete works of Diodorus Siculus, of Polibius, of Sallust, of Tito Livy, of Tacitus or of the six last works of Ovid's Fasti or the 20 books of the German war, which Pliny began in the years in which he served in that country.[9]

Following the finding of the first trove in the library proper in October 1752, papyri were discovered in four other locations in the villa. A number were found tucked inside the bucket-shaped travelling case for papyri called a *capsa*, discovered in a separate, small room near the library, perhaps a private study or storage room. Mysteriously, in the Great Peristyle a batch of scrolls were found packed inside wooden crates—whether crated for carrying to safety or sale, or whether newly arrived and not yet unpacked remains an intriguing and hotly debated mystery. The last tantalizing finding was in August 1754.[10]

No title page showed the contents of any scroll. A *volumen* begins on the column closest to the wooden winding peg, a pencil-like stick, and is rewound as it is read. The title appears inside, by the peg. It is also written on a string-tied tag called a *sillybos*, which dangles from the top of the peg, but in the case of Herculaneum, this fragile tag, shown in ancient pictures, was instantly burned. Other factors made unrolling and deciphering the brittle, flaky scrolls difficult: the age and condition of the scroll at the time of the eruption, the handwriting style of the scribe, the number of times the scroll had been copied in antiquity (even then each copier-scribe introduced errors).

Among the first to make an attempt to unroll scrolls was a personal friend of the king, the Duke of Sansevero. This handsome and arrogant youth dabbled in alchemy and Masonry, as those who visit his fascinatingly eccentric chapel in the heart of old Naples will see

10. Working underground by torchlight at deeply buried Herculaneum, Roman artist Camillo Paderni was the first to copy ancient wall paintings, like this of the history muse Clio with a scroll container (*capsa*). Beginning in 1755 the drawings were published in the eight-volume *Le Antichità di Ercolano*.

in the Masonic symbols of its labyrinth-design marble floor. Attempting an alchemical opening of the scrolls, the duke soaked several in a pot of mercury. The scrolls dissolved.[11]

Next a Neapolitan philologist stepped in, offering his help. Black ink on a black scroll being hard to read, he reasoned, sunlight would make the ink fade, and the writing would stand out as pale against the background. He tucked a scroll inside a glass bell jar in brilliant sunshine and waited. The writing vanished altogether.

A third improvised expert advised dunking the charred scrolls in oil or alternatively in boiling water, then leaving them to unroll by themselves in a damp basement. This too was attempted. But because papyri are subject to mildew, a reason why they were little used in damp northern Europe, they rotted. Needless to say, the scrolls chosen for the hapless "experiments" were those where the writing appeared the clearest and easiest to read.

No one had yet read any of the charred scrolls. Tucked away under Paderni's watchful eye in the new Herculaneum Museum, the secret treasures they contained remained a mystery. In desperation, an expert calligrapher priest named Padre Antonio Piaggio was called from the Vatican in Rome to try to transcribe them so that the scholars of Naples could begin to study them. Born in Genoa in 1713, Padre Piaggio had been working as Latin scribe in the Vatican Library when the first charred cylinders had been found.

In Naples Piaggio was given a tiny room in a corner of the Herculaneum Museum in d'Elboeuf's old house. There he encountered a new and unexpected battle: to protect the papyrus rolls from damage. Already, countless had been destroyed by benighted attempts to open the scrolls with a knife.

This was the solution devised by none other than the artist Camillo Paderni, now Piaggio's superior as director of the royal museum at Portici. Deaf to Piaggio's pleas, Paderni would slit the charred, brittle cylinders down the middle lengthwise as if they were cucumbers. Then he placed the two elongated halves adjacent to each other and tugged out the inner leaves, one by one alternately, convinced he had recomposed the scroll.

Paderni also had another system, according to Mario Capasso, one of today's foremost experts on the Herculaneum papyri.

Paderni wanted to show the scrolls to the king. So instead of just slicing one vertically, he might cut it in three cylinder chunks. The centre

chunk, being the least damaged, would give him a fairly good, uninterrupted section. He would therefore clean the scroll, as it were, almost
always to deleterious effect. Almost always, the title would be lost.[12]

Once bisected vertically along the central pole, the layer was basi-
cally destroyed. Scribes who spoke no Greek would make a
transcription, more or less accurately, of the folio before it was
removed usually destroying it in the process so as to see the layer
below. For many scrolls therefore only this haphazard transcription,
called by scholars a *disegno*, has survived in archives in Naples and
Oxford.

When other scrolls were sliced lengthwise, some leaves came
away as a single slip, but where heat had bonded pages together a
clump of several, appearing to be one page but in fact several,
would result. When the slashed and clumped pages were reat-
tached, nothing matched. The supposedly recomposed page made
no sense.

Even this was difficult to understand because most were written
in ancient Greek, and only a few in Latin or ancient Oscan. None
were languages Camillo Paderni or, for that matter, Padre Piaggio
knew. (Today's papyrologists are still struggling to re-separate these
erroneous compositions and reassemble them correctly into a logical
whole. In one of the most dire cases, some papyri were assembled
entirely backwards by 19th-century scholars—and read and interpreted, an error corrected only recently by two papyrologists
working independently, the American Dirk Obbink and the French
Daniel Delattre.) When Padre Piaggio objected, Camillo Paderni
turned on the little scrivener priest—and went on slashing papyri
vertically and horizontally. In this way Paderni lost or destroyed at
least fifty.[13]

Piaggio's own hopes were pinned on a wooden contraption of his
devising—his "*macchina*", he called it. Resembling a small loom,
Piaggio's *macchina* worked by unrolling the central cylinder chunk,
though this tended to eliminate the more fragile charred exterior.
First the outer shell of blackened papyrus was softened with a cocktail of unguents devised by Piaggio. The outer edge was bound
with soft leather, from which dozens of silk threads were slowly
tightened by screws at the top of the *macchina* onto bobbins. This
tugged the scroll open at the painfully slow rate of a half or three-
quarter inch during Piaggio's customary solitary workday of five
hours.

Four years after he had begun, Piaggio's *macchina* successfully opened the first scroll, perfectly intact for logical reading of its thirty-nine sequential columns. His was a lonely life, far from home, in a hostile world. But soon he would have an unlikely new friend.

By the mid-18th century the excitement of the discoveries being made at subterranean Herculaneum had swept all Europe. The passion for the classical was being called "the religion of antiquity", and this made the treasure from Herculaneum fine fodder for the ambitious dynastic crown of Naples.

In the trickle of distinguished foreign visitors permitted to descend into the celebrated Greek Theatre one crucial figure was completely barred: Johann Joachim Winckelmann. Born in Prussia in 1717, Winckelmann had achieved overnight fame throughout Europe for his treatise on the meaning of ancient Greek art published when he was thirty-nine. Confident he would be welcomed in Naples and Herculaneum, Winckelmann was stunned when his visa application of 1756 was flatly rejected. Winckelmann had come to Rome from Dresden the previous year to accompany a Prussian aristocrat, Heinrich von Bruehl, on a Grand Tour. On his departure, the Prussian royal family had offered Winckelmann a stipend in exchange for keeping the court abreast of all the fresh discoveries of antiquities in Italy, including Naples.[14] This made of Winckelmann a sort of spy.

Von Bruehl returned home alone. A new convert to Catholicism, Winckelmann was enchanted by Rome. He found a position working for a well-placed cardinal, and then inside the Vatican itself as an all-round arts advisor. This intimate Vatican connection, combined with Winckelmann's fame as an art critic (and perhaps a report that he was in the pay of the king at Dresden), terrified the Neapolitan administration. No foreigner was to undercut Naples itself. Winckelmann was all too well known and even feared; Charles's wife, the queen of Naples, moreover, was the daughter of the king at Dresden.

Winckelmann had written about the Greeks but had never seen a "Greek" city. How dare the Neapolitans deny him the opportunity to see Herculaneum for himself? He chafed against this bitter rejection.

That Winckelmann's father was a shoemaker suggests that he emerged from poverty. In reality, his grandfather was manager of a

textile factory, and young Johann was well educated. He had studied classics in Berlin, theology at Halle, and mathematics and
medicine at another university at Jena. Moving near Dresden, he
was hired by a local aristocrat to tend his library and catalogue a
picture collection.

The Dresden in which Winckelmann came of age was a magical
city, "the Athens of modern times", in the words of English musicol-
ogist and organist Charles Burney.[15] Endowed with abundant halls
for concerts, with museums, Baroque churches, imposing squares,
and bridges arching over the Elbe River, the Prussian capital was an
established station on the Grand Tour itinerary. For its flourishing
arts Casanova called it, in his *History of My Life*, "the most brilliant
court in Europe".

Sovereign of this "brilliant" court was connoisseur and collector
Augustus III—that very King Augustus whose adolescent daughter,
Maria Amalia, had been dispatched to Naples in 1738 to marry King
Charles. The royal antiquities housed in Dresden's Antikensammlung Museum included a number purchased from the Chigi
banking family in Rome and several from Herculaneum (now
housed in Berlin), which had been acquired by a royal princess, Wil-
helmine von Bayreuth.

Of all the antiquities at Dresden the most sublime treasures had,
surprisingly, come from Herculaneum—the trio of marble statues
which cavalry general d'Elboeuf had raised from the Greek Theatre
at the bottom of the well at Portici during its first exploration. Seized
as crown property, the three had been shipped to Vienna. Three decades later, heirs to the Austrian throne put the Herculaneum trio on
the art market. An enterprising Italian sculptor crafted a small clay
model of one, which he shipped to the famous connoisseur-king at
Dresden. A delighted Augustus purchased all three statues. The
entire citizenry of Dresden lined the quay of the Elbe river port to
watch the unloading of the huge, heavy crates and their careful
removal to the Antikensammlung Museum.

Shortly afterward, young Winckelmann saw them in the museum.
The vision sent him into a state of near delirium. The sight of their
marble draperies, fluttering like fine linen in the grip of invisible
breezes, showed him instantly that these were among the finest
ancient statues the world had ever seen. "Divine pieces", he
declared them, for "the grandiosity of the draperies, the straw yellow marble, their nobility and elegance ..., meditative air, and the
hair done in carefully executed melon wedges".[16]

Even such lavish descriptive praise was not enough for Winckel-mann. For months he pondered the question *why*: what made the three Herculaneum statues so divine, what explained the genius of the Greek artists who had conceived of them and carved them so long before? Previous writers on art had merely passed judgment — this is good art, that is bad. Even Giorgio Vasari in *The Lives of the Artists* (1568) and Christina of Sweden's librarian Giovanni Bellori in *Lives of the Modern Painters, Sculptors and Architects* (1672), had pro-vided biographies of artists without analysing the work itself.

Winckelmann analysed the reasons in a seminal essay of 1755 that brought him overnight fame. Within a decade it would be published in translation throughout Europe.[17] He argued that sculpture was the finest of all the arts because it embodies "more of the ideal" than architecture or even painting, and that, of all sculpture, ancient Greek was superior because its authors sought the *essential*. The con-sequent refined simplicity went beyond adornment, and the search for the essential that informed Greek works made them elegant, and in so doing ennobled life itself.

But there was a corollary: that ideal beauty was not detached from life, but a product which reflected a specific culture — in this case, the culture of ancient Greece.[18] It followed that: "The only way for us to become great, or even inimitable, if possible, is to imitate the Greeks", he wrote in an oft-quoted phrase. And as models for imita-tion he offered the three "divine pieces" from Herculaneum, the buried city he had never seen.

Winckelmann had been given an office in the Vatican archives and an apartment in the Cancelleria building, where he was already working on a new book, *History of Ancient Art*, which would be pub-lished in 1764 in Dresden. In this, his masterpiece, he reiterated the superiority of ancient Greek art — and this was the heart of his thought — which existed because nourished within a democratic state which had a "constitution and government, and the habits of thinking which originated therefrom".[19]

Britain alone had a Magna Carta: this was pure political heresy. Kings did not need constitutions, for they ruled by divine right. Yet Winckelmann was a child of his times, and radical political change, associated with ancient Greece, was already fluttering in the winds like the marble linen of the Herculaneum statues. Montesquieu had glorified the democracy of ancient Greece and denounced tyrannical kings in his *Considerations on the Grandeur of the Romans and on their*

Decadence (1734). Similarly, Voltaire was teaching that knowledge derives from observation, as it had for the ancient Greeks, and not therefore from divine inspiration (not uncoincidentally, Winckelmann had called the Herculaneum statues "divine"). Winckelmann's linking Greek art to democracy was therefore a manifesto. However inadvertently, the father of art history used art to validate democracy.

This reasoning placed Winckelmann squarely within the radical intellectual ferment of the European Enlightenment at mid-century and the ideas of philosophers like Denis Diderot in France, Immanuel Kant in Germany, and David Hume in Scotland. For decades to come the use of reason—logic, maths, art, sciences, pure thought—remained identified with ancient Greece, which explains why the passion for the ancient world was being called "the religion of antiquity". The ideas lived on, as the later Hegel (1770–1831) spelled out explicitly: "Europeans have their religion from a further source, from the East ... but what is here, what is present,—science and art, all that makes life satisfying, and elevates and adorns it— we derive, directly or indirectly, from Greece".[20]

At mid-century the kings of Europe, like Charles and Augustus, could hardly foresee where their antiquarian pursuits were leading them. To them art was still just "art"—beautiful in itself and conveniently decorative propaganda. Yet the century ushered in by the finding of coloured marble chips in a Neapolitan well would be ushered out by the guillotine. The royals of France would lose their heads, those of Britain would lose their American colony. In their echo Naples itself would stage an important revolution.

After his visa request was rejected in 1756, Winckelmann contrived to obtain a letter of introduction to the queen of Naples, signed by her brother, Frederick. This procedure took two years, but finally the visa arrived. In Naples at last, the optimistic Winckelmann now expected to be received with due courtesy as art historian and a member of the Society of Antiquarians in London and of the Accademia Etrusca of Cortona. And indeed he was invited to dine at the Royal Palace. But to his consternation, Charles openly snubbed him.

Then it transpired that the room in the convent where Winckelmann was to sleep, in any case inconveniently far from Naples, had somehow become unavailable. The celebrated art historian had nowhere to sleep, and so Piaggio gave him hospitality in his own rooms at Portici. In the long evenings there with Piaggio, Winckelmann listened—listened, and took notes. Later, writing to a friend in Germany, Winckelmann had unstinting praise for Padre Piaggio.

It was another story for Camillo Paderni, whom Winckelmann called "a most astute and ignorant man", a weaver of nasty little plots who grovelled before the queen. It was a sad sentence for a man who had done so much to preserve for all time the paintings when they were first found at Herculaneum. For his part, Winckelmann found at Piaggio's lodgings at Portici unexpected hospitality and even a kind of bliss. The two gossiped and dined together on delicious cauliflower grown on the slopes of Mount Vesuvius, their meal all the finer for the Lachryma Cristi wine.[21]

In Piaggio's modest home, as Winckelmann has written, he fell asleep soothed by the waves lapping against the shore.

CHAPTER IV

Dynasty, Neapolitan Style

11. Glass bowl with fruit

Charles found an occasion to broadcast the glory of his Hercula-neum excavation in 1749. He was thirty-three years old and had reigned for fifteen years. In a tradition dating back to the Middle Ages, the Catholic monarchs of Naples travelled to Rome every year to kneel down before the pope in a ceremony of fealty called the "Chinea", from cavalcade. Customarily the homage included donat-ing to the pope a splendid white horse and a bag of gold coins.

For the Chinea, architect Michelangelo Specchi created a horse-drawn parade float, a *macchina da festa*. Specchi worked from imaginative drawings made by Ennemond-Alexandre Petitot. An uplifting religious theme might have seemed appropriate to the occasion, but Specchi made instead a giant model of the Greek Thea-tre of Herculaneum. This pagan boast in papier mâché about the kingdom's great new archaeological treasure trove was intended to bowl over the princes of the Church and all Rome.[1] The importance of this Chinea reflected the consolidation of the still fragile dynasty which Charles represented, and whose patronage was financing the renewed excavations.

This dynasty was barely fifteen years old. Charles's mother, Elisa-betta Farnese, was queen of Spain and lived at the court in Madrid.

Born and bred in the north Italian town of Parma, she possessed "a Medici brain and Lombard heart".[2] Tall, lanky, with a big nose and pockmarked face, she had grown up in the gloomy, minor Duchy of Parma, in the flat Lombard plain between Florence and Milan. At twenty-one, she was definitely an old maid by the standards of the day. But when the wife of the king of Spain died, leaving him two young sons, Parma's ambassador in Madrid proposed Elisabetta as an appropriate new wife. She was Catholic, she was available, she spoke four languages, and—the clincher—she was a direct descendant and probable heir to the fortune and fabulous sculpture collection left by her ancestor Alessandro Farnese of Parma, Paul III—that pope for whom Michelangelo built Palazzo Farnese in Rome.

Her proposed husband, the Spanish king, Philip V, was not in fact Spanish, but French, a grandson of Louis XIV and raised at the court at Versailles. Philip's hopes for the French throne had been dashed when he was passed over for a cousin and given the now-diminished Spanish crown as a consolation prize. Ever afterward, Philip felt defrauded.

Elisabetta's dowry came from Alessandro Farnese, the first pope to buy antiquities for himself rather than for the Vatican. His finest single piece was a sculptural group called the "Toro Farnese", or "Farnese Bull", found in the ruins of the Baths of Caracalla in Rome in 1545.[3] To display this and his other classical sculptures, the pope had Michelangelo design a special sculpture gallery in the Palazzo Farnese in Rome. As later Farnese princes opened personal excavations, the collection expanded.

With the honeyed lies permitted of matchmakers, Parma's ambassador to Spain promoted Elisabetta ruthlessly as, on the one hand, an heiress and, on the other, something of a simpleton:

> She was raised in the shadow of her own home, a timid lass to be done with as one wishes, uninterested in anything but her weaving; and, what counts for more, she is sole heiress not only of the duchy of Milan but of other lands situated in the Kingdom and of Tuscany, where the Medici are fading out.[4]

Philip accepted, and the two were wed by proxy in the Cathedral of Parma in 1714. Elisabetta travelled toward Madrid at snail's pace, and for three months Philip had to make do with the unpromising portraits of his unseen bride sent from Parma. As Elisabetta finally approached Madrid, the king's bossy official mistress rode forward to greet her in a show of power. She was the widow of an Italian prince but, like Philip himself and most of his courtiers, French. Forewarned about her French rival, Elisabetta tossed one haughty glance at the mistress, summoned the guards, and on a pretext had the mistress arrested, hauled ignobly to the border and deported, permanently.

When Elisabetta arrived in Madrid, a choir sang a joyous *Te Deum* in the cathedral. Immediately afterward Philip took Elisabetta (the Spanish called her "Isabella") to his bed, apparently for days on end, to the scandalized amusement of the Spaniards, the rage of the French, and the delight of historians. The court at Madrid was staffed by French aides who, having seen Elisabetta's treatment of the mistress, were distressed. Their dismay increased when Philip made the matchmaking ambassador from Parma, Giulio Alberoni, foreign minister of Spain; shortly afterward the pope made Alberoni a cardinal. From French sideshow, Spain seemed on the verge of becoming an *Italian* sideshow, even as fears mounted that Elisabetta would encourage Philip to make a bid for that French throne he coveted.

The new cardinal, Alberoni, cosseted his protégée. He had Italian foods imported to Madrid for Elisabetta, and when she was pregnant he personally whipped up a genuine north Italian *ragù*. But even he was startled by her ability, as he confided in a letter to Parma. "I don't know where she learned all that she is saying and doing, when I think she is only twenty-two years old and was raised within four walls without seeing people", he said. "She's as sharp as a gypsy".[5]

In quick order she bore Philip five girls and, crucial for the royal succession, two sons. Charles was the elder, but not seen as a candidate for the Spanish throne because of Philip's two sons by his first marriage. However, Elisabetta began to sit in on court audiences. Scandalized French diplomats at the court sent Paris secret dispatches calling her "cruel and petty … the worst yoke a king can bear. This disaster is beyond repair."[6] A report of 1714 called her "a despot who controls the king". She had a violent streak, her servants feared her, she gorged on oysters and sausages, she stank of garlic, and (worst of all in French eyes) she did not know how to dress.

Within two years of their marriage Philip began to suffer bouts of what the royal doctors described as melancholy, some lasting months.[7] He would lie prostrate, unable to govern or even to speak. He forgot to wash. He suffered from amnesia, headaches, hallucinations, fainting spells, hypochondria, insomnia and paranoia; he believed the French were trying to poison him. At other times he thought he was dying of illness; yet again he seemed suicidal. The occasional call to arms would buoy Philip up only briefly before his depression returned. "I've seen the king go one year without going to bed, one year without getting *out* of bed, and one long year when he never spoke", the usual French spy wrote Paris.[8]

In January 1724, when Elisabetta was thirty-two, a despondent Philip renounced the throne in favour of his sixteen-year-old elder son by his first wife. The youth died within a year; his brother was too young to reign. A reluctant Philip picked up his crown again— and collapsed from stress.

During Philip's numerous absences, Elisabetta Farnese took over. The cardinal whispering advice at her side, she sat on the state council as a minister, which endeared her still less to the French. She ordered all communications to Philip to be sent directly to her, bypassing the resentful state counsellors. Philip had already abdicated once, and since Elisabetta wanted no new letter of abdication, she ensured he had no access to pen and ink.[9]

In truth Elisabetta's only power was her wit, for she owned nothing whatsoever, not even money. When the French clique in Madrid campaigned against her mentor Cardinal Alberoni, she reluctantly sent him home to Parma. That hard decision left her truly alone, with the knowledge that, if her husband died, *sicarios* of either Spain or France might do away with her children.[10]

In the nick of time the Duke of Parma died in 1731, giving Elisabetta a duchy, however tiny. There she sent her first-born son, Charles, age fifteen, as the new duke. A stunning diplomatic windfall followed that very year. After two centuries of ceaseless war, the great powers of Europe negotiated a general peace by which the Habsburgs of Austria, who had seized the south of Italy in 1707 from Spain, agreed to return the Kingdom of Naples to Spain. Because the other great powers at the conference still feared Spain with its dread Armada, in a bizarre compromise the accord stipulated that the Kingdom of the Two Sicilies *had never actually belonged to Spain*. It would therefore logically become a personal holding of the Farnese-Bourbon family just then ruling in Spain. To Spain this was no loss; the French-dominated court wanted Charles and his meddling mother well out of the way.

This meant that, at age eighteen, Charles would enter Naples as king, while his younger brother replaced him in Parma. For the first

66 POMPEII AWAKENED

time in centuries, southern Italy would not belong to a foreign country. Two sons, two kingdoms—Elisabetta must have pranced and danced around the Prado.

At the moment, Naples did not appear a great bargain. The city that was to serve as capital for Charles was an intellectual shut-in, "kept by its Spanish rulers a recluse behind a wall for two centuries", to quote modern Neapolitan historian Antonio Ghirelli.[11]

The wall was literal, for the Spanish had forbidden construction of new housing outside the city walls for 200 years, and in its brief rule Austria had not rescinded the law. Famine had drawn thousands of desperate farm workers into the city and made the population density appalling. Naples was Europe's third largest city after Paris and London and in absolute the poorest of the three, with a populace that lived in hunger, pestilence, superstition, poverty and unrequited prayers.

The feudal aristocracy brought no relief. Nobles abounded: "50 princes, 65 dukes, 106 marquises, and 60 earls", by the count of one visitor. They lived lavishly, but on rents paid by desperately poor tenant farmers. "All travellers notice the luxury and licence that obtains in Naples", wrote a contemporary historian.[12]

Nor was the Church helpful. Southern Italy's largest single landholder, its monasteries were wealthy from farm rents and other privileges, such as the Jesuit monopoly on sales of wine. The greatest privilege of all was a status of tax exemption on all Church properties. But nothing daunted Elisabetta. In a proud letter to her son she described the Neapolitan throne as "the finest in Italy". Then she and her advisors set to work to make it so.

Having finally turned eighteen, Charles III rode into his new capital in his carriage on 10 May 1734. In his hand he carried a diamond-studded sword given to him by his uncle, Louis XV of France. At the cathedral he placed a fine diamond and ruby necklace upon the statue of San Gennaro, the most beloved saint in Naples.

Prisoners released from jail joined the festivities as gold and silver coins were tossed to the *scugnizzi* jamming the streets for a look at the new king. A *cucagna* basket was dangled from a high pole, but in the general hilarity too many boys shimmied up it to grab for prizes. The *cucagna* collapsed, killing several.

Charles's Spanish tutor, who functioned as Elisabetta's prime minister, accompanied him to Naples, with orders to send daily reports

back to Spain. Elisabetta eased out the tutor and all the other Spaniards, whom she replaced with north Italian professional ministers
and advisors. As prime minister she chose Bernardo Tanucci, a talented Tuscan law professor, who would oversee the family interests
for the next thirty years.

In consideration of Tuscany's ancient tradition of Guelf anti-
clericalism, it is not surprising that, to finance reconstruction, this
supposedly Spanish-flavoured crown declared fiscal war on the biggest landowner in the kingdom: the Roman Catholic Church. For
the first time the Church was taxed on the vast holdings of its many
religious orders in Naples and the surrounding Campania. Tax revenues trebled, paying for the rebuilding of Naples, including the
excavation of Herculaneum which would shortly begin.

The Church prerogatives were undermined in other ways. For a
century local scientists had pleaded for a chair of astronomy at the
University of Naples, but hard-line Catholics still resented Galileo
for his heresy and refused. Young Charles, which is to say his
mother and her Tuscan advisors, authorized the teaching of astronomy, and a promising young astronomer was given a royal
scholarship to study in Paris.

With stunning rapidity new royal palaces—still the pride of
Naples—were designed by architects like Ferdinando Fuga and
Luigi Vanvitelli. Elisabetta continued to hold the reins of control;
when Charles was to marry, the decorators of the bridal suite had to
send the drawings to Madrid for her approval, which arrived only
after three months.[13]

Philip had hoped to put Charles on track for a claim to the French
crown and had therefore favoured a French bride. But Elisabetta
prevailed, choosing the fourteen-year-old daughter of the Prussian
King Augustus III. The girl was "very young, with an air of malice,
... a nose like a ball, a face like a crayfish, and the voice of a mag-
pie", as French magistrate de Brosses wrote.[14]

The adolescent Princess Maria Amalia had grown up in a palace
in cultivated Dresden filled with splendid antiquities. Ironically,
these included the very trio of statues excavated by d'Elboeuf.
When the couple married in 1738, Elisabetta sent them her famous
inheritance of Farnese antiquities and old master paintings,
beginning with a portion stripped from Palazzo Farnese in Parma: a
hundred Renaissance paintings, twenty-six ancient sculptures from

Rome, and additional antiquities from the family excavations in the
north.

Coincidentally the popes, kings and dukes elsewhere in Italy
were throwing open the doors of their private museums to the
Grand Tour gentlemen. In 1734 Rome's Capitoline Museum with its
vast halls of antiquities was opened, "for the curiosity of strangers,
for dilettantes, and for the comfort of scholars", to quote its mani-
fest. The Uffizi Galleries in Florence were opened to tourists that
same year (mornings only). And in 1738 the Vatican opened to the
public its Braccio Nuovo, crammed with splendid sculptures from
ancient Greece and Rome—those statues that Michelangelo had
sketched.

In keeping with this spirit, Elisabetta ordered that as soon as
Charles arrived in Naples construction begin on a vast new royal
museum, the Museo Farnesiano, to show off the Farnese collection.
Designed to impress, the building would sprawl across the Capodimonte hilltop overlooking the Gulf of Naples. Its vast halls had
ample room for future acquisitions.

The museum was not ready when the first crates of Farnese treasures arrived from Parma by ship and so they had to be stored
temporarily at Naples University (today's National Archaeological
Museum). Time passed. That curiosity-driven Frenchman, de Brosses, was exploring the university basement, when he saw the
crates. "For three years the paintings have been left at the bottom of
a stairwell, where everybody goes to piss", he thundered. *"Oui,
Monsieur, pour pisser sur Guido et Correggio"*.[15]

The rest of the collection, including the "Farnese Bull" sculpture
group, took longer to arrive, for the papal will stipulated that his
collection must remain in perpetuity in Rome. Elisabetta claimed it
anyway, and litigation began; again she won, and the entire Roman
portion at last was sent to Naples. Other buildings were under con-
sruction: a royal factory for the manufacture of prized china, a silk
textile factory, another for weaving tapestries and a new opera theatre—the San Carlo, or Saint Charles—was built in just nine months
and inaugurated in 1736, when Charles was twenty. Construction
also began on a multi-storeyed hospice, the Albergo dei Poveri
(Hotel of the Poor), whose elephantine dimensions were meant to
demonstrate that the king took care of all his people. A new, star-
shaped prison was built on an island in the gulf. The care extended
to the grave, and so a new cemetery with 356 plots for the poor was

built. Each mass grave was covered by a big, flat stone marker showing only a gigantic number, the day of the year; when the plot was full, the bones disappeared, and the plot was re-used. The building boom which generated work and put food on the table for countless Neapolitan craftsmen and their families also made Charles exceptionally popular. One of the three new royal palaces under construction for Charles happened to stand above the buried city of Herculaneum; this was the hunting lodge called "La Reggia", located on a broad swathe of land between Vesuvius and the sea at Portici, five miles south of Naples.

In 1744, when he was twenty-eight, war entered Charles's life. To some degree Elisabetta's acquisition of the Kingdom of Naples and the Two Sicilies had destabilized the balance of power in Europe, and Austria suddenly marched on Rome. Charles charged off to fight the Austrians and defend the sovereignty of the papal state. On his white horse at the head of his troops, Charles met and held off the Austrians in a pitched battle in the pope's backyard at Velletri, on Rome's outskirts.

Pope Benedict XIV was obliged to thank him. In a white wig Charles met the pope in a pavilion at the Quirinal Palace in Rome. Considering that Charles's gigantic building programme had been paid by taxing Church properties, the meeting had to be cause for some tension. But for Charles it was a gloating celebration, recorded in paint by Roman artist Giovanni Pannini.[16]

As a commemorative gift for the pope, Charles carried to Rome an etching of an imaginary festival taking place inside the Greek Theatre of Herculaneum. The picture was blatant propaganda showing the importance the Neapolitan court attached to the new excavations. Encircling the phantom merry-makers in the theatre was a halo of cartouche portraits showing Charles himself. The delight which his excavator-engineer, Alcubierre, must have felt on seeing his portrait included can only be imagined.

Two years later Charles's relations with the Church soured again. In Naples, Charles encountered an agitated mob gathered around the Church of the Carmine. On hearing that the Bishop of Naples had just installed an Inquisition court in that very church, Charles stalked into it. At the altar, he knelt and drew his sword, which he raised toward the sacrament while proclaiming loudly that no Inquisition court would ever be convened in his kingdom. The outraged bishop resigned and in short order withdrew huffily to the papal state and Rome.

Back in Spain, Elisabetta was still the power behind the throne. Indeed, much of the time she was in front of it, and no less querulous in her dotage than in her youth. When a French prince rejected one of Charles's daughters as a bride, Elisabetta sat down and wrote to the queen of France (!) a letter of insult calling her son "beastly". Elisabetta had every right to be arrogant, for in two decades she had achieved much. Her younger son was duke of Parma. Her elder, Charles, had a fine kingdom. The children of Maria-Amalia of Prussia, the wife Elisabetta had chosen for Charles, included two sons who would carry on the Bourbon-Farnese dynasty.

The San Carlo Opera Theatre was now home to musicians like Cimarosa and famous ballet performers. The Royal Palace with its fabled grand staircase by the Neapolitan port had been restored and new royal palaces built. From the depths of Herculaneum new treasures were being added daily to the Farnese collection of antiquities. Naples itself was now celebrated as "the most beautiful part of the finest country in the world, on the loveliest bay in the world", as Cambridge student Thomas Gray burbled in a letter of June 1740 to his milliner mother back in England.[17]

Then the disaster that Elisabetta had always feared occurred. Philip died in 1746. The surviving son from his first marriage—who, not surprisingly, despised Elisabetta—became king. Elisabetta had to leave the court.

Eight years later she was back from her rustic exile as regent after her stepson the new king of Spain died in 1754. Elisabetta's son Charles was his half-brother and next in the line of succession. For the coming five years Charles sorrowfully contemplated his obligation to leave Naples—contemplated it and postponed it.

The erotic statue forgotten, Charles had rediscovered his passionate and personal interest in the progress of the excavation at Herculaneum. In emulation the entire court now succumbed to the passion of finding buried treasure. In the gold rush all had become collectors. Everywhere Neapolitan farmers looked hopefully down their wells and churned up fields in hopes of profiting from the treasure hunt.

As the archaeological pace had grown feverish, Alcubierre opened possible sites further afield. Two hundred prison convicts and slaves from Tunisia and elsewhere in North Africa, watched at gunpoint by soldiers, were dragged to the sites to dig new tunnels, their clanking chains a rude counterpoint to the refined gossip of the Neapolitan courtiers.

One of Alcubierre's tentative trenches was dug in an empty field called "Cività" on the elongated seafront plateau just south of Vesuvius. In April 1748, farmers digging the usual well in a field found bits of obviously antique coloured marble mixed in with the pebbles and soft lavic stone. Alcubierre sent a few men. The terrain was soft, and so a test trench was dug. The men worked at a gratifying speed, particularly in comparison with the harsh toil of Herculaneum.

At a mere ten feet or so below the surface the shovels struck roofing tiles. A shard of painted surface appeared— an obvious patch of wall. No one knew it then, but Alcubierre's excavators had dug directly into the outside wall of one of the largest and most handsome town mansions of Pompeii, the House of the Faun.

Just then a more exciting rumour recalled Alcubierre elsewhere. Returning to Cività several weeks later, he once again put fifty men, mostly slaves, to work digging with shovels.[18] They soon struck the

12. The Neapolitan authorities reluctantly allowed the already famous Johann J. Winckelmann to visit a newly discovered site they thought was "Stabiae". It was, in fact, ancient Pompeii, and the Prussian art historian was the first to catalogue and to disseminate news of its treasures. Angelica Kauffman, Kunsthaus, Zurich.

tiles of collapsed roofs beneath a scanty few feet of ash and lapillae, quite unlike the seventy feet of rocky husk covering Herculaneum. As work proceeded, streets could be made out.

Plainly this had been a town—Stabiae, Alcubierre guessed. The houses were buried shallowly enough for exploration from above, open to the skies. The immediate and visible results galvanized the interest of the entire court. King Charles stood by watching the new exploration, and at one point plunged into the digging himself. To his immense delight, among the volcanic pebbles he came upon a gold ring set with a finely carved cameo. He popped the ancient ring upon a royal finger and wore it as long as he remained in Naples.

But time had run out. Amid tears and fanfare all Naples stood at the shore to watch Charles and his weeping queen take their sorrowing leave by sea in October 1759.[19] Charles asked to be kept abreast of all the developments at the excavations and to receive regular reports, maps and plaster casts of the findings.

Leaving, Charles bequeathed the greater part of the crown antiquities, including his mother's heritage of Farnese sculptures, to the kingdom of Naples. In a tearful moment he removed the ring from Pompeii from his royal finger and handed it to the prime minister, for Naples and its people.

Charles's departure for Spain in late 1759 posed serious problems. His first-born son was severely mentally handicapped, to the point that he ran around sexually assaulting servant girls. The succession thus fell to the boy's younger brother, eight-year-old Ferdinand. A watercolour depicts the optimistic leave-taking: Ferdinand stands, a slip of a boy, between Charles and the man who would rule until Ferdinand would come of age at sixteen, the grave Tuscan premier Bernardo Tanucci—that same Tanucci who had been hand-picked by Elisabetta Farnese and her family advisors in Parma a quarter of a century previously.

Handed his father's diamond-spangled parade sword, a gift from the king of France twenty-five years before, little Ferdinand pranced about the palace, brandishing the sword like a toy and shouting, "Now I am king, now I am king".[20] King he was, monarch of a butterfly realm which had emerged almost amazingly over the past quarter century from its misshapen chrysalis.

As a minor, Ferdinand could govern only at age sixteen. For eight years Tanucci would be regent, premier and, incidentally, director of the Herculaneum Academy. Such power came at a cost; in contemporary portraits his face, careworn and deeply furrowed, betrays fatigue and age. Charles wrote daily letters of counsel. But he was hopelessly distant and absorbed in running a vast realm which stretched to the New World.

Young Ferdinand never wrote at all. He hated writing even the obligatory letters to his father. He despised studying. Dressed like a street urchin, he roamed the miserable alleys of downtown Naples, where, in the Neapolitan equivalent of Cockney dialect, he hurled insults for fun. The louts retorted, and then he laughed as they were arrested by his bodyguards for insulting the crown.

Tanucci and the state councillors, all elevated to ministerial rank, did not bother to consult a churlish boy in short pants. To add Ferdinand's signature to court documents, Tanucci had a stamp made. Other problems required more than a stamp. Under Tanucci's regency Neapolitan life became "more confused than that of a [papal] conclave", as court architect Vanvitelli wrote to his brother shortly after 1759.[21] Political turbulence increased, with the result that for most of the next hundred years, north Europe, and especially Britain, would draw greater benefit from the discoveries at Herculaneum and Pompeii than did the Kingdom of the Two Sicilies.

When Tanucci proposed a much-needed land reform, the landowners screamed, and Tanucci dropped the proposal. Sensing the power vacuum, local potentates built their own power bases, cemented into place by corruption. The treasury fell seriously short of the funds required to maintain the court's opulent status quo. To repair the damage, Tanucci again struck at the Church. All Jesuit properties were seized, and in 1762 Tanucci cancelled the monasteries' tax exemption on sales of their manufactured silk fabrics and then abolished the 700-year-old tradition of the "Chinea", the kingdom's annual cash tribute to the pope in Rome.

Already under Charles, the Bourbon-Farnese show-off architectural finery, designed by Vanvitelli and other outstanding architects, had been financed by removing the tax-free status of Church properties, at a time when the Church owned some two-thirds of the landed property in the kingdom.[22] In another assault on Church wealth, in 1750 Charles's advisors had dropped the Church's right to act as his tax collector.

In 1763, when Ferdinand was thirteen, the kingdom's finances suffered when drought destroyed the wheat crop and a famine year began. For lack of wheat the bakeries locked their doors. The poor died in the streets from hunger. Bread riots broke out. Tanucci's solution was harsh repression of the riots, which lasted until the famine ended because foreign businessmen began importing wheat. Meantime, the famine had drawn tens of thousands of desperados to the city. They slept in caves and doorways and ate, when they ate at all, in the streets. Lacking other solace, the poor of Naples gave themselves over to religious cults like those of the Virgin Mary and San Gennaro, and gaudy folk festivals with fireworks.

The Italian south was a feudal state economically, and rare was the entrepreneur interested in creating new wealth, at a time when north Europe was industrializing under a new, energetic and profit-minded class. The social gap widened, and a wall developed between the classes, which had notably less contact with each other than even in the medieval past.[23]

Centralization remained the rule in the Italian south, and civic and religious institutions were all headquartered in Naples, where the aristocrats resided in order to be close to the court, but were otherwise largely inactive. Naples also was home to the small southern Italian middle class of lawyers, teachers, scholars, architects and doctors, whose chief function was in effect to defend the aristocrats' traditional privileges. Even the university was slow to propose innovations; it was 1740 before the first lecture at the University of Naples was in a language other than Latin.

The centralization dated from the days of the Spanish military viceroys, who had made all decisions regarding the entire kingdom, from the price of bread to the university curricula—decisions made mostly on the basis of politics rather than on practical reality, fairness or efficiency.[24] This tradition endured under Tanucci until Ferdinand finally came of age in 1767. Overnight, in this centralized state, he held untrammelled power, which he exercised wilfully, ignoring his elderly and exhausted ministers. A new element was added to the dismal equation in the shape of a foreign bride. At seventeen Ferdinand was forced into a politically useful marriage to a daughter of the widowed Habsburg empress Maria Theresa of Austria, who was busy settling her children on half the thrones of Europe. Her eldest son would succeed her in Vienna, while other sons would rule Tuscany and Lombardy, and her younger daughter would become known as Marie Antoinette of France. The Neapolitan wedding was arranged, down to the sewing of a hundred gowns, when the girl died of smallpox. Ferdinand was delighted, but only briefly, because back in Madrid, Charles needed to ally the south of Italy to Austria as a counter to British sea power and trade.

To this end, he arranged for the empress to send a substitute, sixteen-year-old Maria Carolina, who was the fifth daughter down the line.

Told she would marry Ferdinand, Maria Carolina rebelled, famously retorting, "You might as well cast me into the sea". Many times Ferdinand must have wished someone had cast Maria Carolina into the sea. Dragged kicking and screaming to Naples, the adolescent bride endured some eighteen pregnancies and eight live births. Nevertheless, she possessed in spades the intelligence, political instincts and willpower her husband lacked. By 1765 she sat on the state council, the equal of her ministers, just as had Elisabetta Farnese in her time in Spain. One of Maria Carolina's coups was to manoeuvre Tanucci out of power, which helped to sever the last links of the south of Italy to Spain, in favour of new alliances with her own Austria and with that England which her father-in-law in Spain, Charles, feared.

Naples did not particularly like Ferdinand and showed it by dubbing him "Re Nasone" (King Big-Nose). He was at least foolish. When his dying younger brother begged the adult Ferdinand to journey from Sicily to his bedside in Naples, Ferdinand declined on the grounds that he was going hunting. He wrote to his brother that, if he died, it didn't matter, and if he didn't, a gift of wild game would be welcome. The hunt lasted three days—longer than his brother, who died.

Hoping to provide Ferdinand with a more erudite kingly model, Maria Carolina trotted her foolish husband up to Florence in 1785 to meet her brother, now Grand Duke Leopold. Ferdinand was untouched. "Really", he sniffed to his brother-in-law, "I can't see what use all that science is to you. You and your people read constantly. But your towns, your city, your court—they're all dismal and gloomy. I know nothing at all, and yet my people is the liveliest there be."[25]

His relations with his wife fell to such a low point that Ferdinand overcame his dislike of letter writing and wrote whining and futile letters to his father in Madrid, claiming that his Austrian wife mistreated him. "And when you reply do not let on that I've written you secretly", Ferdinand begged his father. "She reads all my mail". Speaking of Maria Carolina much later, Napoleon's verdict was "She is the only man in Naples". Nevertheless, Ferdinand was king. For better or for worse he would rule for sixty-six years, long after Maria Carolina's death.

In Spain in the meantime, where Charles had put his shoulder to the wheel, his mother, Elisabetta Farnese, the first patron of Herculaneum, died and was buried in Parma in 1766.

During the intervening years since Charles's departure for Spain in 1759, the court's interest in its Vesuvian sites had waned. The Herculaneum Academy began to fall into a torpor the very year he left. Even funds for excavating had dwindled. The lack of money particularly affected costly Herculaneum, seventy feet underground.

Work continued at various sites open to the skies, however, including the presumed "Stabiae" (Pompeii), under the supervision of Karl Weber. In late 1763 Alcubierre intervened and ordered him to return once more to Herculaneum. Weber, by then fifty-two years old, was ill, suffering from a lung disease he believed was caused by the poisonous gases underground. Frightened at the prospect of returning to subterranean Herculaneum, he wrote to Elisabetta's hand-picked premier Tanucci that to excavate there would present a "clear danger to my life".[26]

Questioned by Tanucci, Alcubierre scoffed. If Weber had a health problem, it was due to his being overly fond of the bottle. Weber was obliged to return underground. Three months later he was dead; friends in Naples whispered that his death had been hastened by Alcubierre's harassments.[27]

Lack of money, Weber's death and the light-weight lapillae of Pompeii, which made that city easier to excavate, sealed the fate of the Herculaneum excavations for over a century and a half. European historians and papyrologists were disconsolate. If papyri from the library had been found in five places in the villa, which was still only half explored, was it not logical that more could be found in other rooms, left there by students or perhaps blown down flights of stairs from the hot air surges of the volcano?

They were ignored. The site was shut down, the entrances to the costly, painfully constructed and death-dealing tunnels filled with rubble. For all intents and purposes Herculaneum was at an end.

There was one survivor of Herculaneum: the patient priest Padre Piaggio who, through the chill winters and hot summers, had remained doggedly bent over the Greek manuscripts which he could decipher but not read, while his *macchina* tugged away at the manuscript treasures of the Herculaneum scrolls, a precious half-inch each day.

CHAPTER V

The Moon and Crabs

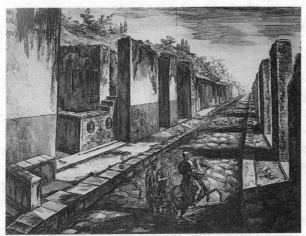

13. G.B. Piranesi, *Pompeii street*

In Rome, Winckelmann watched from afar. He had become curator of the collections of the wealthy and suave Cardinal Alessandro Albani, Rome's foremost antiquarian and a nephew of Pope Clement XI, who served the Vatican by meeting discreetly with envoys of the English royal family and other important Protestants with whom the Vatican otherwise had no diplomatic relations. In Albani's famous library at Palazzo del Drago by the Piazza Quattro Fontane, the well-connected, well-heeled Grand Tourists took tea and surreptitiously negotiated export permits for antiquities.

Cardinal Albani first set Winckelmann to work on a catalogue of carved ancient gemstones from a collection begun in Florence by a late Prussian antiquarian, Philip von Stosch. Before his death von Stosch had, curiously, worked as a spy for the British. It was a connection which alarmed outsiders, including in Naples.[1]

Portraits painted by Winckelmann's affectionate artist friends at that time show a slight and slender man with chestnut hair, lively

brown eyes and an oval face. There is also intelligence and sensitiv-
ity, with no hint of duplicity—even though, living cheek by jowl
with princes and popes, and to judge by a few whiplash comments
in his letters, the Prussian art historian was fully capable of self-
protective parrying.

In 1762, Winckelmann made his third visit to Naples. Again he
was Piaggio's guest. The kindly, hard-working calligrapher priest
who had been summoned to Naples as copyist of the Herculaneum
papyri again found a listener who was both keenly interested and
intelligent. At their vinous meals they discussed the papyri, the tunnels, the eruptive nature of Vesuvius (one of Piaggio's particular
passions), and the artists and the engineers of the Neapolitan court.
Piaggio recounted poor Karl Weber's heroic underground struggles
against the forces of evil in the form of the Spanish military engineer
Alcubierre and the dull antiquarian Camillo Bayardi.

Winckelman was in Naples because Alcubierre had uncovered the
new site erroneously called "Stabiae," and for the first time Winckelmann was given access to follow the work there for a full month. The
site was, in fact, Pompeii, excavated on and off for nearly a decade
before the city was identified correctly in 1768, with the greatest of
fanfares. This was a stunning coup for the Prussian scholar, who
immediately produced the first catalogue ever made of the treasures
being found at Pompeii. *Unpublished Ancient Monuments*, about Pompeii, was his first book to be published in Italian and the first attempt
for a scientific study of a Vesuvian site. The discoveries of new works
in marble there also provided Winckelmann with countless examples demonstrating the distinctions between Greek and Roman art.

Aside from making an inventory of the findings at newly discovered Pompeii, Winckelmann had become interested in the figure of
Priapus, the ithyphallic god (the word refers to the huge fake phallus carried during processions at festivals to Bacchus). He also asked
to see the notorious fine Greek marble statue of Pan, the god of
flocks who gave man poetry, making love to a she-goat, found in the
Villa of the Papyri at Herculaneum. Permission was denied.

Returning to Rome, Winckelmann launched an energetic attack
on the Neapolitan establishment. *Open Letter on the Discoveries of
Herculaneum* was officially addressed to his old friend at Dresden,
Christian Heinrich von Bruehl. The "letter", written in the calm
magnificence of Cardinal Albani's new hilltop villa at Castel Gan-
dolfo outside Rome, was the most informed report yet to appear on
the excavations. Winckelmann's authority was such that his opin-

ions were immediately trumpeted to every court and scholarly academy in Europe.

For Naples it was a public relations disaster. Only the Swiss engineer Karl Weber came in for praise:

> He [Weber] drew up an exact plan of the underground passages and the buildings above-ground, in all sorts of scale … clear and intelligible through the use of other drawings showing the building elevation as would have been visible if the earth covering them were removed, and this were an aerial view. … The first thing he did was to make an exact map of the underground galleries and the buildings they led to. This map he rendered more intelligible by providing a minute historical account of the whole discovery. In it the ancient city can be seen as if free of all the rubbish which presently encumbers it.[2]

Winckelmann assailed Camillo Paderni for slashing the precious papyri. He attacked the Neapolitan scholar-scrivener Bayardi for incorrect identifications. Above all he savaged Alcubierre in an insult which has gone down in the history of archaeology:

> The direction of the work was given to a Spanish engineer named Roch Joachim Alcubierre, who had followed His Majesty to Naples and is now a colonel and head of the corps of engineers at Naples. To borrow the Italian proverb, this man knows as much of antiquities as the moon knows of crabs. His incapacity caused the loss of many antiquities.

Showing what a small world the antiquarians of Europe inhabited, von Bruehl forwarded Winckelmann's letter to an aristocratic connoisseur in Paris, Count Anne-Claude-Philippe de Caylus, whose theories on the arts of the classical world had originally helped to inspire Winckelmann. De Caylus had the letter translated into French and published in Paris.

A storm of criticism rained down upon the Florence of the south, and for the precise reasons—its antiquities—which its rulers had hoped would bring it amazing recognition and status. Nevertheless, in a back-handed compliment even Prime Minister Tanucci admitted that Europe had learned more about the glories of the Bourbon-Farnese excavations from Winckelmann's writings than from any of the publications of the Neapolitan Accademia.

King Ferdinand's indifference to the excavations, just when excavations had begun at Pompeii, meant that, for literally decades to come, the fruits of the Bourbon-Farnese dynasty's efforts to achieve grandeur would continue to be harvested by others. The plodding Accademia Ercolanesi nevertheless moved slowly, and it was 1792 before all seven volumes of *Le Antichità di Ercolano* had appeared, with contributions from outstanding artists like Carlo Nolli and Nicolò Vanni.

Foreign interest had remained relentless, in particular by the British. As a sign of the times, the first guidebook to Naples was published in English by Carlo Barbieri, in 1774. It offered twenty-five illustrated itineraries which showed the archaeological sites (Pompeii, Stabiae, Virgil's tomb), plus "all Roads ... the Posts, the prices of Horses, and the Principal Inns".[3] This was a windfall for the musicians, artists, hotel keepers, and dealers of antiquities of Naples, enriched by the foreign travellers and foreign collectors, primarily British, given that nation's power at sea, its merchant wealth and new riches accruing from the first industrial revolution. British interest in the classical world, which in turn promoted travel for purposes of education and that spin-off, collecting, was further stimulated by the publication in 1776 of the first volume of Edward Gibbon's hugely successful *Decline and Fall of the Roman Empire*.

But Naples had fallen behind in knowledge of its own archaeological treasures. First, the writers and scholars of Naples had long been locked within narrow intellectual confines. Although Charles had established a print shop and financed publication of the gift books about Herculaneum, the kingdom had antiquated printing presses and small print runs, of under 500 copies. Distribution was inefficient, the paper and ink inferior. Of necessity most books in circulation were therefore imported, but with a customs duty of fifty-five per cent.

Secondly, censorship rules originally imposed during the long twilight of Spanish rule were still observed. Even the catalogues offering imported books were rigidly controlled by the censors.

Realizing something of this, and because national pride was at stake, in 1767 the elderly premier Tanucci had urged his ambassador to Paris, Ferdinando Galiani, to arrange for the publication of the Herculaneum Academy's books on the excavations in French, in France. A popular Neapolitan man-about-town, Galiani retorted sarcastically that few wealthy antique dealers in France were literate enough to read anything published by the Neapolitan Academy—a polite way to say how dull the Neapolitan production was.

On the other hand, Galiani continued, only half mockingly, new pictures of objects from the excavations would be welcome, for the few in circulation had become unbearably trite because Herculaneum was already such a vogue in France:

The goldsmiths, costume-jewellery makers, painters of carriages and of ornamental wall panels—all need such a book. Is Your Excellency aware that everything these days is made *à la grecque*, which is the same as saying à l'Herculaneum? ... Bronzes, engravings and paintings from Herculaneum are all being copied. I have seen that painting of a woman selling cherubs as chickens at least ten times. So Your Excellency can see the importance of a (complete) reprint of Herculaneum as, without the whole book, the poor artists have to cope with just bits and pieces.[4]

In fact, it was already too late. Ignoring the Neapolitan censors, ignoring the prohibition on notes and sketches, a French publisher had long been selling copper-plate engravings of pictures of the Herculaneum treasures drawn by the Count de Caylus—that same count who had translated Winckelmann's critical letter about Herculaneum into French.

De Caylus was a serious scholar. For a pioneering art school in Paris, the Académie des Inscriptions et Belles Lettres, he had created the world's first academic course in the arts of the classical world. In 1752 a book of his engravings of the Herculaneum antiquities, *Recueil d'antiquités égyptiènnes, étrusques, grêcques, romaines et gaulôises*, began appearing in Paris, preceding the Neapolitans' own publications on Herculaneum by three years. Unlike theirs, this was addressed to a broad audience, and indeed had been studied in Dresden by Winckelmann.

The first volume of *Le Antichità di Ercolano*, that ponderous work by Bayardi, appeared in Italy only in 1755, but it was an edition distributed solely for royal gifts. The first edition in Italian aimed at the educated public arrived only in 1789, whereas outside Italy, cut-rate versions of the same book were already being read in Britain in 1767 and in Germany in 1780; Leizeilt of Augsburg's elaborate, nine-volume German-language edition was published in 1777. To read about Herculaneum in their own language, therefore, the Italians had to wait twenty-two years after the British and a decade after the rest of northern Europe, or acquire costly imports in foreign languages.

In 1766, Jérôme Richard, the Abbé de Saint-Non, visited the little Herculaneum Museum over which Paderni ruled at Portici. It was, said Richard, the most beautiful collection from antiquity ever assembled. The visit inspired Saint-Non to organize publication of an illustrated, multi-volume work that would describe and illustrate the art, architecture and archeological treasures of the Italian south, to be first published in the 1760s as *Voyage pittorèsque a Naples et en Sicile*.

Other illustrated books had already popularized the lesser items found at Herculaneum, such as household furniture, introduced first in the Count de Caylus's 1759 *Recueil d'antiquités égyptiennes, étrusques et romaine* and then in *Voyage pittorèsque* by Saint-Non. One of the drawings showed an exceptionally finely wrought three-legged bronze charcoal brazier table from Herculaneum. Tripod tables were common at Herculaneum (both the real and those painted on walls), and all had captured French interest. This one in particular caught the eye, for its legs were shaped like ithyphallic satyrs.[5]

In Naples, Saint-Non met a young chargé at the French embassy, Dominique-Vivant Denon, who had been trained in Paris as an engraver. Saint-Non enlisted him to take charge of a team of young French artists, trained at the French Academy in Rome, who would make a daring tour of the whole south of Italy in order to paint and record its finest views, paintings, sculptures and monuments.[6]

At the dawn of the 18th century, French student architects, artists and classicists had been awarded Prix de Rome scholarships to study in Rome for a period of up to three years. Some were trained at an arts preparatory high school in Paris created specifically for that purpose, the Ecole des Elèves Protégés.[7] Whereas young artists and architects arriving from England and Scotland had to make do with happenstance student lodgings and a few introductions, the more privileged French students in Rome were fed and lodged at the French Academy.

Later in the century they spent a period in Naples. On site at Herculaneum the scholarship students sketched what they could of the Greek Theatre and the Portici Museum collection of marble statues, bronzes and other artefacts. Their sketches later were shown in Paris exhibitions and drawing rooms.

Nothing on the scale Saint-Non proposed had ever been attempted. The young artists drafted for Saint-Non's project included the brilliant Jean-Honoré Fragonard and the prolific landscape artist Hubert Robert, both friends of G.B. Piranesi in Rome.[8] Twenty years after Saint-Non's *Voyage pittorèsque* first appeared, with its hundreds of drawings, an expanded edition was published, showing more of the furnishings of Herculaneum and Pompeii: tables, pitchers, ritual buckets, lamps, chairs.

The reaction was ecstatic, and *Voyage pittorèsque* is still considered the finest travel book of its century. However, its wealth of illustrations confounded some French scholars, for these depictions of antiquity were unlike any other, because more accurate; the training the French scholarship student architects and artists had received in Rome made them more highly skilled than any other group in representing the literal reality of the ruins and the buried cities. A few waspish Parisian intellectuals considered this a defect. In their eyes, the literal-minded Prix de Rome fellows lacked the creativity of Piranesi, whose engravings were already a fashion in France; in 1763 Louis XV had pictures from Piranesi's *Prisons* hung in his private study.

Other *savants* were distressed by the art itself. Before seeing the Saint-Non pictures, they had imagined the classical world as immensely, overwhelmingly majestic. The literal French, like the late 17th-century illustrator of Roman ruins, Antoine Desgodetz, had always measured monuments and presented them as they were, but Piranesi's pictures in particular had presented ruins as immense, their grandeur heightened by shrinking the human figure to ant size: he saw no need for mathematical truth in ancient monuments. As Piranesi wrote to a French friend on the abbé's team, the young artist Hubert Robert, "My drawing isn't on my sheet of paper, but entirely in my head—you'll see it on my drawing board".[9]

The French had been captivated by Piranesi's enlarged, romanticized views of the buildings of classical antiquity, and not least the Greek Theatre of Herculaneum. Before their eyes too was the reality of gigantic architecture exemplified by the palace at Versailles. When the first accurately scaled drawings made by meticulous French architects came into circulation, the French were startled and disappointed to discover that the real temples of Vesuvian antiquity were small by comparison.

Further, the new vision of antiquity called into question previous concepts of Greece itself, otherwise based mostly on literary and intellectual conjecture. The Greek statues, furniture and other objects found at Pompeii, and then sketched and painted meticulously by the French artists and architecture students, tended to conflict with the era's conventionally accepted canons of beauty. Statues believed to be pristine white were in fact painted, for instance. The very concept of what was meant by "classical" art and architecture had to be reformulated.[10]

In the meantime, Piranesi's own engravings of Herculaneum were circulating. Piranesi was already well known in every art academy and had important clients in France, Germany and England, where his work contributed to the development of neo-Classical architecture.[11] Born near Mestre, inspired by the Venetian painters like

Tiepolo and Canaletto, Giovanni Battista Piranesi reached Rome around 1745 to study under Sicilian engraver Giuseppe Vasi. He lodged near the French Academy and became friends with its student artists, showing them the Roman ruins and the latest archeological discoveries.[12] Together with the French student artists he produced a series of drawings of monuments for a small guidebook to Rome.[13]

Piranesi's depictions of antiquities often held an almost grotesque quality, and some of his ancient buildings seemed like visions or nightmares, as in his book, *Prisons*, which showed demonic variations on the theme of Hadrian's Tomb. The Piranesi quality of mysterious unreality was such that Sigmund Freud himself admitted being at a loss to define it.[14] During the 1770s Piranesi and his son Francesco made several visits to the Vesuvian sites, and Piranesi painted at least fifteen views of Pompeii, which Francesco later turned into copper-plate engravings.

What most captivated the public were Piranesi's ten engravings of the imaginatively reconstructed submerged theatre of Herculaneum, published in 1783 by Francesco after his father's death. Karl Weber, the Swiss engineer who had excavated Herculaneum by tunnel, had himself made drawings of the theatre exterior, but these had somehow been irretrievably lost.[15] Weber's gas-filled tunnels too had long since been refilled with rubble, and only a portion of the theatre interior could be entered.

In his version Piranesi seems to have added elements from other ancient ruins, such as Hadrian's Villa, the foremost Roman excavation of the day. Still, the sensation was enormous, for his work—a full half-century after its exploration began—was the first to show the Greek Theatre of Herculaneum as an intelligently conceived architectural whole.

Piranesi's gloomily theatrical but entrancing engravings of the Herculaneum theatre circulated throughout Europe for the rest of the century, augmenting the popularity of all the Vesuvian sites. No less a figure than Johann Wolfgang von Goethe, author of the quintessentially sad Romantic novel, *Young Werther*, related that in his childhood a Piranesi print hung on his bedroom wall. This memory, he said, inspired him to visit Italy in 1787.

At the Piranesi establishment in Rome, it was not all art for art's sake. Piranesi *père* owned a vast private collection of antiquities, which he hustled to the well-heeled foreigners. To encourage a prospective buyer, he would engrave a picture of it and then dedicate it to a specific wealthy tourist. One engraving of an ancient marble cinerary urn, carved with damsels pouring libations, was dedicated to Edward Knight, "English cavalier". Shamelessly, the inscription advised that the piece "*si vede nel Museo dell'Autore*" (can be seen in the Museum of the Author), the "museum" in question being Piranesi's studio.

On commission for the Count of Exeter at Burghley, Piranesi designed and had a mason build a patchwork "Pompeian" fireplace in which he incorporated three original bas reliefs of carved pink Egyptian marble which he had acquired from an unspecified ancient site. Above it, in a whirlwind of Piranesian arabesques, was his marble reproduction of a painting just then discovered on the wall of a garden at Pompeii, showing a reclining nude Venus on the half shell.[16]

Among Piranesi's acolytes was the wealthy young British architect Robert Adam, who came to Rome in 1755–6 to study ancient temples. To Adam, who would go home to become the most important British architect of his day, Piranesi dedicated his great map of ancient Rome, published in 1762, *Il Campo Marzio dell'antica Roma* (*The Campus Martius in Ancient Rome*). Its frontispiece shows the two artists' heads together in a medallion like Roman consuls.[17]

Like Piranesi, Adam toured Herculaneum:

> We traversed an amphitheatre with the light of torches and pursued the tracks of palaces, their porticoes and different doors, division walls and mosaic pavements. ... Upon the whole this subterranean town, once filled with temples, columns, palaces and other ornaments of good taste is now exactly like a coal-mine worked by galley-slaves who fill up the waste rooms they leave behind them according as they are obliged to go a-dipping or strikeways ...
>
> With great pleasure and much astonishment we viewed the many curious things that have been dug out of it, consisting of statues, busts, fresco paintings, books, bread, fruits, all sorts of instruments from a mattock [pickaxe] to the most curious Chirurgical probe. We saw earthen vases and marble pavements just discovered while we were on the spot and were shown some feet of tables in marble which were dug out the day before we were there.[18]

Returning home, Adam, fascinated by the colours of the ancient walls he had seen at Rome and Herculaneum, utilized them in the interiors of buildings adapted from halls of the buildings of antiquity. The Adam style was then imitated in the design and décor of fine libraries and drawing rooms throughout Britain and elsewhere in Europe.

Herculaneum moved into east Europe thanks to a Roman artist
named Ludovico Mirri, whose book of hand-coloured copper-plate
engravings appeared in 1784. Mirri was well known for his paintings of the wall decorations in Nero's Domus Aurea. As assistants at
Herculaneum, he hired two artists who had worked in Poland and
Russia, Francesco Smuglewicz and Vincenzo Brenna. Their contacts
at home promoted the Mirri book in those countries, and knowledge
of Herculaneum further east in Europe than Dresden for the first
time.[19]

The Grand Tourists also brought the sunlit Neapolitan landscape
into its own as a subject. Like the engravings of the ruins, its portrayal gradually evolved away from the static toward the more
emotional and evocative.

During the 1600s a literal-minded Dutch painter, Gaspare Van
Wittel, had been the foremost landscape artist of Naples (his son,
known as Vanvitelli, was the architect of Charles's outsized royal
palace at Caserta). Van Wittel specialized in delightfully meticulous
topographical illustrations of Naples, its coastline and buildings.
But in the 1740s a French artist working in Naples, Joseph Vernet,
invented a new way to portray the Neapolitan countryside. Shun-
ning the topographically accurate, Vernet added a quality of
imaginative mystery which art historians call the "aesthetic of the
picturesque". A whole flowering of the Neapolitan magical landscape painting occurred as, inspired by Vernet, French artists and
painters from England, Denmark, Germany, Russia and Northern
Italy also arrived to emulate Vernet's dreamy views of the serene sky
and shimmering waters of the gulf.[20]

Side by side with the Vernet-style renderings of the magical,
shimmery *paesaggio*, came tiptoeing in another style that became
known as "the emotionally picturesque" Neapolitan landscape.
Here the sky was storm-racked, as waves crashed against the jagged
coastline of the gulf of Naples. Gradually the choice of subject matter broadened to include vividly coloured and sometimes almost
abstract views of the narrow alleys and humble hamlets of the poor,
as painted by foreigners like the Welsh artist Thomas Jones and the
English John Robert Cozens.[21] Jones, the subject of a National Gallery, London, exhibition in 2003–4, was a precursor of modernism.
He arrived in Rome in 1776 and then moved to Naples, where he
produced small and almost abstract oil paintings of the Neapolitan
skyline during the early 1780s.

Mount Vesuvius, that favourite goal for the excursions of the Grand Tourists, became a painterly subject in its own right. In the late 16th century it had piqued the scientific curiosity of the German Jesuit bibliophile and ethnologist Athanasius Kircher (1602–80), who lived in Rome. When Vesuvius erupted, Kircher travelled to Naples and had himself lowered into the crater to study it. He constructed a shadowbox model of the volcano in papier mâché. To show that the red-hot lava lay deep in a pocket inside the volcano he had it lighted from behind by a candle glowing through crumpled red waxed paper.[22]

To the increasingly moody painters of the last decades of an increasingly difficult century, such scientific views and rational explanations of Vesuvius were beside the point. Vesuvius was their nightmare vision of life itself. Vivid fireworks and violent streaks of red paint would tear across a black background while lava gushed in horrific, marvellous torrents down the slopes. The volcano was a spectacle, all light, form and colour—an emotional and aesthetic thrill, "the most beautiful thing one can see in nature", in the words of Joseph Wright (Wright of Derby), an English painter active in Naples in 1774 and 1775.[23] When twenty-seven of his oil paintings of Vesuvius erupting were put on view in England, they helped to launch a minor vogue for nocturnal paintings of volcanoes in eruption even though, ironically, his visit to Naples ended before Vesuvius actually erupted; his was an incredible work of the imagination (see Chapter X on Turner's version of the Vesuvius eruption which, like Wright, he had never seen).

Particularly influential among the late 18th-century painters was a German, Philipp Hackert, who first visited Naples in 1770 and returned in 1785. For four years he worked for the court. The independent-minded Queen Maria Carolina commissioned him to paint frescoes on the walls of various royal properties and also hired him to teach the royal princesses to draw. Of an evening Hackert, cribbing from a one-volume, instant-learning German encyclopedia, lectured on art to the entire royal family. As he wrote to his friend Goethe, the encyclopedia had indifferent scholarship, but was "quite good enough for society people".

In 1787 the queen sent Hackert to Rome to negotiate the final shipment to Naples of the remaining classical sculptures that had belonged to the Farnese family and included the famous Farnese "Hercules" and the "Farnese Bull" sculpture group, which Charles had been claiming since 1734. Hackert's mission succeeded and he had the Hercules installed in the public garden of the Villa Reale in Naples. In Rome it had been found without legs, and Michelangelo had carved replacements. The original legs being found, Hackert had the ones carved by Michelangelo lopped off and replaced. The spare limbs were placed beside it so that the ancient and Renaissance sculptors' abilities could be compared.[24]

The publicity from all this, the books of engravings of Herculaneum and Pompeii, the magical and mysterious paintings of the gulf and countryside, the nocturnal views of Vesuvius erupting, all contributed to the appeal of Naples for the Grand Tourists, but more than tourism was involved. Britain's new wealth and growing power was stimulating an early interest in public buildings that would be seen as appropriate to the new political and economic leadership, who looked to the classical world for inspiration.

In the wake of Robert Adam, the English architect John Soane arrived in Italy in 1777 on a travel grant offered by King George II, to spend three formative years in Rome, Naples and Sicily. He was from a poor family, but a benefactor, George Dance, had paid for him to study at the Royal Academy. Returning from Italy, Soane joined Adam in promoting the classical style for public buildings.[25] He became personal architect to William Pitt, the prime minister, and worked on such great projects as the Bank of England and the Parliament building.

CHAPTER VI

Vulcanology

14. Leda and the swan

In 1764, when excavations had been underway at Pompeii for nine years, an exceptional find was made: the Temple of Isis. Dating from the 2nd century BC, this was the first Egyptian temple ever found in Europe, complete with its dowry of religious artefacts and wall decorations illustrating the cult. The excavation director was the competent Italian archaeologist Francesco La Vega, one of the first to keep careful records. The news launched a wave of Egyptomania as countless drawings circulated throughout Europe showing the temple slowly emerging from its grave.

Following the death of Alexander the Great, Pompeian trade with Ptolemaic Egypt had revived, as is shown by an Egyptian coin of 230 BC found at Pompeii's neighbouring agribusiness town, Nola.

The rediscovered temple, like the Egyptianized decorations of various Pompeian houses—elongated garden pools that supposedly recall the Nile, Nilotic scenes in mosaics, like those in the House of the Faun—echoed the business interests: wheat from the Campania in exchange for commodities, such as marble and slaves from North Africa.

The temple also illustrated the ancient Romans' eclectic attitude toward religion. To the Pompeians, Isis was in many ways a familiar figure. In the elegant statue in the National Archaeological Museum, Isis is depicted as if a sister to Venus. For the Pompeians, in any case, the cult based around Isis's brother-cum-husband Osiris was akin to that of the already worshipped Dionysus, in its representation of fertility, death and rebirth. Isis, who had kept Osiris's body from rotting, was to the Roman world a prototype of the good wife and mother, and hence patroness of all mothers. Important in a seaport, she was also protector of sailors in their fragile crafts. And she was a goddess of magic, who presided over the transformation of things

15. The discovery of the temple to the Egyptian goddess Isis at Pompeii in 1764 caused a sensation throughout Europe. Mozart utilized it for the setting of Act I of *The Magic Flute*, first performed in 1791. In an 1815 production German architect Schinkel painted Mount Vesuvius behind the temple.

and of living creatures. Further heightening interest in the discovery was the ancient Egyptian priests' fame as medical doctors and pharmacists. Their ministrations were seen as magical, and they were known for their magical potions, which may have been the same opium-based "tea" (boiled seeds of opium poppies) that young European hippies stewed up in the 1960s.

The same year, 1764, when excavations of the temple began, the future vulcanologist Sir William Hamilton and his wife Catherine set sail from England for Naples, where he was to serve as His Majesty's ambassador to King Ferdinand. On board Hamilton entertained himself by reading from a friend's farewell gift: Winckelmann's *History of Ancient Art*. Hamilton was the quintessential gifted English connoisseur and amateur scientist. Born at Henley in the Thames valley in 1730, the son of the governor of Jamaica Lord Archibald Hamilton, William had a lively mind, charm, and a remarkable feeling for both the arts and sciences. Taking a job at the Foreign Office, he wed an heiress from Wales who, like him, loved music. In their early thirties the couple were still childless. Then Catherine developed lung problems. Hoping that a mild climate would improve her health, Hamilton asked to be posted to Naples.

The Hamiltons took up residence in a portion of a former monastery overlooking Naples, the Villa Sessa. Naples already had a large foreign colony of artists, aristocrats, shipping agents, and tourists, and the Hamiltons' colourful diary entries and letters record lively social evenings, William at his violin, Catherine at her harpsichord.

In the Garden of Europe Catherine's health improved sufficiently that she could arrange a piano concert for the Scottish community living in Naples. Herr Mozart and his adolescent son performed, as artist Pietro Fabris has recorded. In reality, the artist was English, and his real name was Peter Fabris, who had come to work in Naples in 1773; he had just completed a painting of the Temple of Isis being dug from the cinders of Vesuvius.

The concert took place in the drawing room of Lord Fortrose, and Fabris showed the young Mozart by the piano; in the background, a sign of the times and showing their ready availability from the Vesuvian sites being plundered by dealers (and by William Hamilton), is a long shelf lined with ancient Greek painted vases.[1] Young Mozart wears the same elegant light-blue suit given to him by the Empress of Austria, a cast-off from her own children. Amadeus and his father, Leopold Mozart, remained at least five weeks in Naples that year, and it is more than likely that at the Hamiltons' the genius child of eight would have heard of the discovery of the strange Egyptian temple. Whether or not he did, the setting for Act I of Mozart's final opera, *The Magic Flute (Die Zauberflöte)*, first performed in Vienna in 1791, was a Temple to Isis. Mozart, a Freemason who had already written specific funeral music for Masonic funerals, was a member of the Crowned Hope Lodge, and the score of the opera is filled with Masonic references. The opera's specific association with Isis and Pompeii was underscored in an 1815 production. In this production, the Temple of Isis of the opera set stands against a painted backdrop of a smoking Mount Vesuvius, the work of another of the brilliant foreigners who had spent time in Naples, the German architect Karl Friederich Schinkel.

Having settled themselves into the roomy monastery overlooking the Gulf of Naples, the Hamiltons then acquired two more residences: a cottage on a picturesque bay at Posillipo, directly below the Villa Sessa, and a more remote and rustic farm house at the foot of Mount Vesuvius. Little about the slipshod and downmarket court of King Ferdinand, its political diplomacy and congeries, engaged the mind of Hamilton, true son of the Enlightenment. Hamilton had time, energy and a scientific cast of mind. When Vesuvius entered a dramatic eruptive phase shortly after their arrival, Hamilton, leaving Catherine at home, would move into the farmhouse.

There Hamilton fell in love with the volcano. He had always been fond of collecting. Now he gathered thousands of samples of volcanic rocks and sulphur samples as he wandered the countryside and climbed the volcano, the first of his sixty excursions to the crater. In 1767, after three years of life in Naples, the thirty-seven-year-old Hamilton observed that the volcano was coming alive for the second time, and that its cone was changing shape. For four months he made careful sketches and paintings of the changing volcano and its gradual expansion. That October, Vesuvius erupted.

The eruption had summoned other recognized scientists to Naples, whom he would befriend: the eminent French geologist, Nicolas Desmarat, who had written an eye-witness description of the 1754 eruption of Vesuvius for Diderot's illustrated *Encylopédie*; the noted Scottish geologist, James Hall, and the famous Professor Déodat de Gratet de Dolomieu of the School of Mines in Paris. Fortified by their instruction and his own astute observations, Hamilton became one of Europe's foremost vulcanologists, a pioneer of the rational approach to understanding the formation of the earth.

The volcano is one of nature's trickier puzzles. Because the fertility of volcanic soil attracts farmers, despite the well-known risks, for more than 2,000 years the best minds of their times had studied volcanoes. Their goal, in antiquity no less than today, was to try to find a way to control an eruption, or at the very least to predict its coming in time for inhabitants to flee.

Attempts to understand the *causes* of a volcano were frustrating, however. Until recently scientists had no tool but to study and analyse its *effects*, since no human being could penetrate its interior. Observation and deduction were the only methods available, with the result that in the sulphuric air theories were advanced whose wildness shows, first, the difficulties in understanding a volcano and, secondly, the genuine contribution Hamilton made.

Because, as was observed, hot and liquid lava gushed from a volcano and then invariably hardened into rock, lava was evidently molten rock. Ergo, somewhere underground a giant fire burned, for otherwise the rock would not have melted. To tame the volcano required therefore putting out the fire—but no one knew where or how deeply beneath the earth's surface the presumed fire burned.

In addition, as observation showed, a fire had to be ignited. Because lightning often accompanied eruptions, it was assumed that these flashes of lightning ignited underground gases. Alternatively, because the smell of sulphur hung over volcanoes, it was thought that the rays of the sun, penetrating deep into the bowels of the earth, toasted underground sulphur, which then burst into flames. Fuel too was needed to feed the flames that melted the rock that became the lava; this could be a layer of buried fat left from the bodies of millions of decayed animals. Again, to burn, fires need air, so air vents had to be located somewhere on the surface of the earth. Find the vents and block them—that would smother the fire.

Christian theology discouraged sharper thought because the idea that the earth was still in some process of formation and transformation rebutted the accepted Biblical version which allotted one day for creation of the earth. To claim otherwise was heresy, and even Descartes, in a study of the earth's formation, tried to sidestep conflict with religious authorities by claiming that he was writing fiction.

In Pliny's era, philosopher-scientists from Greece and Rome had speculated upon the why of natural forces, and tossed about theories about the atom and the notion that the earth was round. With the fall of the Roman Empire that sort of naturalistic speculation

came to a halt. Western man in the Middle Ages became less interested in the search for rational explanations of events like
earthquakes and volcanic eruptions than in the spiritual life. As science historians say, it was as if a rational explanation was not
considered terribly useful. Thus the Christian emperor of Constantinople saw the clouds arriving there from an eruption of Vesuvius in
473 and read in them a warning of the wrath of God. He took notice
and set out on an urgent pilgrimage of repentance.

In the time of St Gregory the Great (590–604), Vesuvius had
become explicitly the abode of the devil and indeed was hell itself;
and one horrific stretch of the volcano peak was named just that, the
Valley of Hell. Scholarly monks became volcano watchers as a
result. Today's scholars cherish their accounts, like that of the anony-
mous 6th-century Benedictine monk who saw and described a
violent eruption in Iceland. In it, he added, Judas Iscariot was
roasting.[2]

By the 11th century the explosions of Vesuvius were not considered the results of natural forces at all, but "pranks of supernatural
beings, whose sole power over humanity was the infliction of hell".[3]
Pietro Damiani of Castigliano specified in 1062 that Vesuvius was
the receptacle of some of the souls not yet consigned to hell. And a
priest at Beneventum heard his dead mother's voice issue forth from
the volcano, amid a spout of flames.

The eruptions continued implacably. In 1631, after six months of
light earthquakes and seismic activity, an eruption killed 4,000 villagers and 6,000 farm animals; several farmers were struck by
lightning. Forty thousand refugees flooded into the already overcrowded and unhealthy Naples. The lava flow smothered the still
buried Herculaneum beneath a new layer fifteen feet thick. Neapolitans who survived that brutal eruption demonstrated their gratitude
to the Madonna and to the beloved Saint Januarius (San Gennaro)
by painting votive signs which showed their homes and, in the
background, Vesuvius erupting.

A desire for a more rational explanation had already been
sparked in 1538 by a singular event at Pozzuoli, a few miles south of
Pliny's seaside villa. In the course of a single night a miniature volcano named "New Mountain" (Monte Nuovo), had emerged from
the sea as an islet close to Baiae on 28 September. The event captured
the interest of scholars all over Europe.

In 1767 a particularly devastating eruption took place on the night of 20 October. As a ruby-red sheet of lava several miles wide washed slowly down the slope and destroyed everything in its path, Hamilton stood watching from a distance and making observations. Shortly his fascination turned to alarm, for he knew that the king and queen of Naples and their entire court were enjoying a hunting holiday at the royal palace which Charles had built by the sea at Portici. They were all uncomfortably close to the volcano, as were, incidentally, Herculaneum and its museum including the surviving papyri. Hamilton rushed to warn the king:

> The noise and sulphur increasing, we removed from our villa to Naples and I thought it proper, as I passed by Portici, to inform the court of what I had seen and humbly offered my opinion that His Sicilian Majesty should leave the neighbourhood of the threatening mountain. ...
>
> The confusion at Naples this night cannot be described; His Sicilian Majesty's hasty retreat from Portici added to the alarm ... The mob set fire to the Cardinal Archbishop's gate, because he refused to bring out the relics of St Januarius.[4]

Fortunately, the cardinal gave in and personally conducted the skull of San Gennaro in a carriage to a bridge between Naples and Vesuvius, the Ponte Maddalena. "And it is well attested here that the eruption ceased the moment the Saint came in sight of the mountain", Hamilton concluded laconically.

In fact, Hamilton may have entertained an impious doubt or two about the saintly effects upon volcanoes because he was already becoming an expert on the workings of Vesuvius, about which he sent regular reports to the Royal Society in London. Not long afterward Hamilton personally accompanied King Ferdinand and Queen Maria Carolina to see the dramatic lava flow by night high upon Mount Vesuvius. A gouache by Fabris shows, against the night sky, Hamilton and the Neapolitan royals silhouetted against the vivid red of the exploding volcano.

Hamilton's colourful later life tends to overshadow his work as a vulcanologist. But he was a pioneer who successfully predicted two eruptions. He became the first to announce that the volcano which buried Pompeii was not strictly speaking Vesuvius, but a second, curved volcanic mountain wrapping around it to the north, Monte Somma. He established definitively that the source of an eruption is not near the surface, but deep beneath. And he showed that volcanic cones grow through the accumulation of layers of ash and lava flows.[5]

In 1776, a decade after his arrival to Italy, Hamilton published a
collection of his reports on vulcanology in a book, *Campi Phlegraei*,
from which the above extract was taken. Illustrating it were drawings Hamilton had made as the volcano altered its shape plus forty
of Peter Fabris's watercolours, still sold in book stores throughout
Naples.

An interest in volcanoes led naturally to a desire to see their effects.
Thus Hamilton was on hand at Pompeii just when workmen
exhumed a group of charred and deformed skeletons of victims of
the AD 79 eruption. While there he also saw fine painted ancient
vases emerging from the lapillae at Pompeii and elsewhere in the
gulf coast area. From collecting rocks Hamilton now passed to
vases. Hamilton was familiar with ancient vases; they were discussed by Winckelmann in *History of Ancient Art*, which had
accompanied Hamilton to Naples from London, and eventually
Hamilton would own 1,500 of them. But, as with the volcano, he
was intrigued by what lay behind them. Specifically, who had
painted them? Here was a new intellectual riddle he could ponder
to his heart's content.

A painted pot by Euphronios may sell for a million dollars or
more today, and to our eyes its value seems obvious, but this was
not the case before the discoveries from the Vesuvian sites. Medieval
Italian farmers finding painted pots in tombs thought they were
magic vessels, made by the gnomes who notoriously dwelled
underground.

In Hamilton's day, painted vases imported from Greece or made
in coastal Italy had already been turning up in tombs for centuries.
Those found in central Italy were normally called "Etruscan", an
identification established in an influential Etruscan-boosting book
printed in 1723, *De Etruria regali*.[6] Because the Vesuvian towns had
been under Etruscan rule for a time, vases there too were called
"Etruscan".

These were not without value, for no less a figure than Lorenzo
de' Medici made a point of celebrating the Etruscan civilization as
superior, to the point that he had a philologist "prove" that his
name had an Etruscan origin (it was in fact Neapolitan). Lorenzo
collected Etruscan artefacts and in general promoted the worthi-
ness of the Etruscans and their art, and this helped establish the
Etruscan mystique. In 1726, when the Accademia Etrusca of Cor-

tona was formed, both Winckelmann and the Roman engraver Piranesi joined.

As the 18th-century Enlightenment advanced, some of the vases of southern Italy began to be recognized as works of Greek art. This, together with the seemingly limitless supply, stimulated collectors' interest, especially in Naples.

In the small world of foreigners at Naples, Hamilton's collection, kept in a special, secluded room at Villa Sessa, was a favourite of visitors. Goethe's diary entry of 27 May 1787 says that the room held an amazing mixture: ancient bronze statuettes, lamps of agate, and even an entire small chapel, sculpted and painted—the product, the poet observed, of Hamilton's "haphazard buying".

> Seeing a long packing case on the floor with its lid unfastened, I was curious enough to open it and found two splendid bronze candelabra. … With a sign I drew Hackert's attention to this treasure and whispered to him whether they did not look exactly like those at Portici [the Hercunaleum museum]. In reply he beckoned me to hold my tongue; it was no doubt possible they might have strayed hither from the vaults of Pompeii.[7]

Hamilton's vase collection prompted others to begin theirs. After a visit to Villa Sessa, Dominique-Vivant Denon, just then working in Naples at the French embassy and helping the Abbé de Saint-Non prepare a guidebook, began his.

In 1766 for the first time two important collections of ancient vases were put on the market in Naples and sold for high figures. The following year the nearly fifty-year-old Winckelmann met the considerably junior Hamilton in Naples and visited Villa Sessa, where he saw a hundred or so of Hamilton's vases. Winckelmann was more accustomed to the grand salons of Rome than to the outdoor life. Still, he accepted Hamilton's invitation for a hike uphill to the sulphuric pebbles of the Valley of Hell, where they watched lava rivulets ooze from vents. Over the rumbling from the volcano belly the two rumbled on about Greek pots and cooked up a joint venture. Hamilton, apparently seeking funds to buy more vases, was making a catalogue of his vases with an eye to selling them (the catalogue was later seen by the pottery industrialist Josiah Wedgwood).[8]

Each vase would have to be described and the place where it was made specified. Their discussion of the origins of the vases continued in a letter, in which Hamilton and Winckelmann shared doubts that "Etruscan" was the correct denomination. In their view, painted vases being found in the Vesuvius area were far superior to the crude paintings decorating the walls of tombs in Etruria.[9] And because Greek writing and stories from Greek mythology appeared on the Vesuvian pots, a direct Greek connection seemed logical.

Relatively few vases from the 5th century BC had yet been found in Greece, so identifying them as authentic works of Greek painting boosted their value. Authentic paintings from ancient Greece were extremely rare, but both Winckelmann and Hamilton reasoned that some of the paintings on the vases were copies of works by the ancient Greek masters. Even where scenes seemed painted specifically for the vases, they appeared to be authentically Greek, free of the later Roman influence.

Third, they were available for collecting. Paderni still snapped up all important marble statues from Pompeii for the royal collection, but the vases were readily available, less costly than statues, easier to transport, and easier to sell. Hamilton appealed to Winckelmann to write explanatory notes for the catalogue.

The finished catalogue (the first of four) had fine illustrations showing the vase decorations, and one of the first important scholarly works on the subject.[10] And in their working together, Hamilton and Winckelmann "sharpened their sight to something better than all the hundreds of marble copies of statues in the galleries of Rome", in the words of Hamilton's most recent biographer, David Constantine.[11]

During this visit Winckelmann did not bunk down in the monastic lodgings of Padre Piaggio, but was a guest of Pierre François Hugues, the phoney Baron d'Hancarville, a Hamilton sidekick who promoted Hamilton's pots in hyping captions.[12] D'Hancarville, who had lived in Naples since 1763, oozed charm but had a distinctly shady reputation and once even cheated Hamilton in a vase transaction.

Winckelmann and his new host the faux Baron d'Hancarville got on like a house on fire. Winckelmann had become mildly infatuated with a young German baron in Italy on his Grand Tour, Riedesel, hunchbacked and ugly, but obviously fascinating and later a noted diplomat. The three decided to hold a picnic on Vesuvius. A dangerous eruption had taken place only the previous day, and the usual guide, frightened, refused to accompany them. A beating with a stick (presumably by d'Hancarville) changed his mind. With the reluctant guide and three servants somehow also inveigled into

16. Pierre François Hugues, Baron d'Hancarville, was co-author of William Hamilton's first catalogue of ancient vases from the Vesuvian area. Their catalogue promoted the collecting of ancient vases and inspired industrialist Josiah Wedgwood to manufacture copies. Sketch by Dominique Vivant Denon, 1776, British Museum, London.

being of the party, Winckelmann, the baron and young Riedesel set out. Upon reaching the lava fields, the foreigners stripped off their clothes. Buck naked, they uncorked jugs of wine and roasted pigeons over the burning lava.[13] The gossip in the hovels at the foot of Vesuvius must have been equally scorching that evening, as the guide showed off the bruises from the beating and the servants snickered about the naked lunch *al fresco*.

Hamilton too picnicked on roast wild game, but at the sumptuous outdoor hunt banquets organized by King Ferdinand. The hunt involved hundreds of dogs. The beaters in the woodlands included some 2,000 soldiers, gamekeepers and peasants decked out in green-and-gold uniforms. Forty or fifty boar would be killed. Together Hackert and Goethe's artist and travelling companion Wilhelm Tischbein (1751–1829) painted a famous scene showing King Ferdinand at the hunt; it hangs in Villa Wolkonsky, the residence of the British ambassador in Rome.

In 1768, not long after the Vesuvian pigeon roast, Winckelmann became the prey, hunted down for his gold coins. The collaborative catalogue was not written. His murder in Trieste left Hamilton the sole authority in Naples whom cultivated visitors could consult about Greek vases from the excavations at Pompeii, Capua and elsewhere in the Neapolitan territory.

On balance, others had begun to challenge the Etruscan origins of the ancient vases, but Winckelmann, the Prussian who revived interest in Greek-influenced classical arts, had lent his prestige to the view that these were Greek. Hamilton, with his connections within the British establishment, then helped to launch a passion for vases among collectors and antiquarians there. Their views were further broadcast in France by the still younger Vivant Denon, who would build the Louvre for Napoleon.

Subterranean Pompeii and the tombs of other nearby towns were there for the raiding; Hamilton himself conducted his own Vesuvian excavation.[14] No one was policing the sales, despite Charles's law of 1755; an illustration from the period shows an antiquarian's shop in Naples stocked full of Pompeian pots, bronze urns and small ancient marble busts on offer for sale. A man, presumed to be Hamilton, tall and slender, with his austere profile, stands serenely among the cluster of distinguished connoisseur gentlemen watching as the future Duke of Sussex reflects upon the purchase of a vase fragment.[15] Portraits back in London from that period show the wealthy collectors like Charles Townley seated in their libraries amid a jumble of the antiquities they had acquired in Rome and Naples.

But the whiffs of democracy were also affecting the antiquarian world. In a preface to the first catalogue on Hamilton's vase collection, d'Hancarville had written that an objective was to encourage application of the Greek painting and design to industrial design. And in fact, Josiah Wedgwood had just launched production in the factory he named Etruria at Stoke-on-Trent, Staffordshire, inspired by his seeing, in London, Hamilton's first catalogue of Pompeian vases (see Chapter VII).

In this small but cosmopolitan Neapolitan world, Sir William, vulcanologist, collector and sometime dealer in antiquities, had become a sort of foreign deputy king. As a sign of approval from home, Hamilton was knighted in 1772 and became a member of the Society of Dilettanti in 1777. Besides his myriad outside interests, his diplomatic role was of growing importance, given the mounting fear in Britain of the French. Naples, however seedy, was a potential British ally.

Hamilton's agreeable private life ended when his wife died in 1782. Though heir to her considerable fortune, he was unhappy by all accounts, and perhaps all the lonelier for being the most famous Englishman in Italy, in love with the Mediterranean world, but lacking anyone with whom to share that love.

Enter Emma. As fascinating as Cleopatra, more beautiful, if woefully less educated (Cleopatra spoke six languages, Emma could barely speak or write in proper English), Emma Lyon was born around 1761 at Great Neston in Cheshire, England. Her father was a blacksmith. She left home in her teens for London, where she seems to have worked as a hostess in some sort of public house; current scholarship denies the common tale that Emma had ever worked as a prostitute in a brothel. In any case, this curvaceous teenaged beauty with a mane of auburn hair was still not twenty when she became the mistress of a young man or two about town. Through him, or them, she bore a child who was put out to board.

In the meantime she had met a handsome, charming, young aristocrat named Charles Francis Greville, who happened to be the nephew of Sir William Hamilton. Greville had fond expectations of becoming heir to his childless and fond Uncle William, but in the meantime had no money of his own. Figuring that portraits of Emma (now calling herself Emma Hart) would bring in good money, he went into business with painter George Romney, who used Emma as his muse for many portraits, some in classical poses.

The classical theme of the paintings raises the question of how much Emma learned of the classics at that time. In one Romney painting she appears as Diana the huntress—a true picture if one thinks that Diana was sweet and sexy and hunted in a pink tunic. By all accounts this earlier Emma was captivating and at the same time earnestly, generously, loving of her man.

When Greville was offered the chance to marry well, he knew better than to risk compromising his new circumstances. Anxious to rid himself of Emma, he coaxed his solitary uncle in Naples into inviting her for a lengthy visit at the Villa Sessa. Emma's ingenuous letters, with their bad grammar and spelling, show she believed that she was being sent to Naples to improve herself at the knee of her lover's erudite uncle.

Emma gathered her considerable forces and eventually she added William Hamilton, volcano watcher and lover of antiquities, to her collection of lovers. They lived formally apart if in the same house for years; she had her mother join her for the sake of appearances. There Emma became Hamilton's star attraction—a bauble with a classical spin.

Emma Hart had already posed for Romney many times in attitudes of neo-classical female pulchritude. For Hamilton and his guests Emma began to put on amateur theatrical one-woman pageants. With appropriate shawl drapery and a loose cascade of hair, she would assume the poses of a maenad (the word means ecstatic Dionysian or Bacchic dancer) from the many appearing on Hamilton's beloved Greek vases. These performances came to be called Emma's "Attitudes", writ with a capital A.

Goethe, among others, admired Emma's performances,

> nothing like you ever saw before in your life. She lets down her hair and, with a few shawls, gives so much variety to her poses, gestures, expressions, etc., that the spectator can hardly believe his eyes ... The old lord idolizes her and is enthusiastic about everything she does.[16]

In her Attitudes Emma became in effect an actress in an art form novel in its time. Her audience knew the tales of the ancients by heart; when she would strike a pose, in their mind's eye they would see the whole story evolve, just as saying, "Frankly, my dear, I don't give a damn", evokes the entire relationship between Rhett and Scarlett. Emma's Attitudes, today viewed as an innovative form of theatre, brought her fame in her own right and inspired imitators.

How could the lonely old lord and collector Sir William fail to desire to add Emma to his collection? If marriage to her was the price, so be it. Five years after Emma's arrival in Naples Hamilton sought permission from King George III to marry her. And on 6 September 1791 the maenad who had pranced about the sixty-one-year-old lord's drawing room in Naples, trying to look like a figure on a Greek pot, became Lady Emma Hamilton. The wedding took place at St George's Church, Hanover Square, London.

While in London for the wedding the sixty-year-old Hamilton, ever canny, found a moment to sell a collection of Pompeian bronzes to the connoisseur and collector Richard Payne Knight and one of gemstones to Sir Richard Worsley.[17] He also attended a meeting of the Society of Dilettanti, whose president gleefully handed him twenty-five newly-minted copies of Hamilton's collected essays on the Priapic cult at Naples, *The Worship of Priapus*. The Society's minutes show Hamilton was asked to distribute copies "among such Foreigners as he may think worthy of them and likely to do honour to the Priapeid system."

"Sir William says he loves nothing but me," Emma boasted in a letter to her former lover, Hamilton's nephew Greville: why, friends asked. "Sir William Hamilton has actually married his gallery of statues", sentenced Horace Walpole.[18] As Lady Palmerston wrote to her brother Benjamin Mee two years after the Hamiltons were married: "Sir William perfectly idolises her and I do not wonder he is so proud of so magnificent a marble, belonging so entirely to himself".[19]

The better to show off his magnificent marble of flesh and blood, Hamilton had a six-foot-tall box built, open to one side and painted black within a gilt frame. It was rather like a standing open coffin, and in it the young Emma performed. She struck her evocative (and perhaps innocently erotic) poses for the delight of all visitors, and of her watching, managing, December husband. Emma's stage appearance was as if magically severed from her otherwise generous, loving and quotidian sloppiness.

Once Hamilton must have winced just as she lay down and rested her head upon one of his ancient vases. Seeing his distress, Emma roused herself to shout, in Cockney, "Doun't be afeared, Sir Willum, I'll not crack your jaug". It rather broke the spell, a visitor wrote.[20]

Hamilton was not so distracted by either art or personal passions that he had forgotten the volcano, and indeed he was now paying Padre Piaggio twenty pounds sterling a year for keeping a diary of Vesuvius. Besides writing daily reports on Vesuvius, the calligrapher-priest was still toiling away at the papyri and his *macchina*. For the Grand Tourists pouring into Naples, he had become part of the circuit. Seeing the ancient, burnt scrolls of the Herculaneum library was as essential a rite of picturesque travel as a boat tour of the Pantheon when the Tiber flooded Rome. After touring Naples in 1771, Irish poet Anne Riggs, Lady Miller, reported to a friend in France, "No room of the Cabinet of Antiquities at Portici is visited with greater interest than that where the library is preserved. It has a vast collection of manuscripts on shelves".[21]

In a back chamber of d'Elboeuf's old villa at Portici on the grounds of the Reggia, visitors watched as, with quill and *inchiostra da chino*, the Genoese Piaggio made elegant, perfect copies of the mysterious letters that were barely visible, black ink upon charred black backing, on the papyri successfully unrolled. Beside him his ragged young clergyman assistant, Vincenzo Merli, toiled over the *macchina* to unroll more, inch by painful inch.

A Swedish traveller, Jacob Jonas Björnsthäl, has left a meticulous account of his visit to Padre Piaggio. Curiosity about the papyri was lively, and travel diaries circulated throughout Europe with notable speed. Bjornsthal's letter was published not only in Swedish, but in German, Polish and Italian.

> He [Padre Piaggio] transcribes the original with such skill that you can hardly tell his copy from the original, and all this without his understanding Greek. He engraves it onto copper plates by himself. Moreover, he imitates every sort of writing, including printed, as it is written …
>
> He is quite disappointed in that until now nothing has yet been published about these papyri, and he cannot have the honour of seeing them and his handiwork come to light for the good of the world. Now he is growing old and can be rightly disappointed about his work, which horrified me the first time I saw it.[22]

Disappointment was too weak a word. Padre Piaggio was heartbroken. He had been summoned to Naples in 1753, on a visit expected to last only a few months. Overcoming enormous obstacles, he became the first to unroll an ancient scroll from Herculaneum; after one year of work he had proudly handed it over to the scholars of ancient Greek for translation.

Three decades later he was still there, still bent over the *macchina* he had devised for unrolling the papyrus scrolls. And he was still frustrated.

The scrolls themselves came in for lavish praise. The same court ministers and Accademia scholars who had disapproved of Padre Piaggio's non-destructive methods lauded the scrolls as "monuments". In an address to Charles III visiting Portici, a Neapolitan monk named Mazzocchi rapturously described the scrolls as "pieces of Paradise". (This same monk, however, wanted the scrolls cut into small sections for convenience and assailed Piaggio for insisting that the scrolls be kept intact.)

"In all these years, now going on to thirty", Piaggio wrote in a letter to Pasquale Carcani, the Accademia secretary who kept the Pan and she-goat statue group locked in his private chamber, "not one of those whose duty it is to take some cognizance of our work has bothered, ever, ever to come to take the smallest look at these most unfortunate of 'monuments'".[23] Piaggio specifically attacked the Roman artist Camillo Paderni, still curator of the Herculaneum collections, for selecting the "very best scrolls ... [which were] cut up like melons, till they were reduced to powder and then dumped into the latrine".[24] Padre Piaggio then wrote a letter of complaint to Prime Minister Tanucci.[25] He received no reply.

The folly of chopping the scrolls into smaller pieces is evident to anyone who has seen the papyri. In them, tiny, barely visible writing

17. This satirical 18th-century cartoon mocks the venal antiquarians of Rome, queuing to sell ancient coins. Despite the Neapolitan crown's efforts to thwart looting of the Vesuvian sites, countless Pompeian artefacts slipped onto the market in Rome and Florence for export abroad. Vatican Library, Rome.

appears grey or black on black. Recomposing the pieces would have been a formidable task; the many already chopped apart present staggering difficulties today. Padre Piaggio's opposition helped to save the papyri for posterity.

Most of all, as Piaggio complained in other letters to the seemingly deaf authorities at court, he resented the relentless pressure to speed up the unrolling. Piaggio's pace was partly determined by his having a single assistant. Moreover, the scrolls had been made incredibly fragile by the intense pyroclastic heat produced by the eruption; that same heat had both charred and preserved the papyri. To speed up the unrolling risked tearing the papyrus and watching it crumble to dust.

To this a Neapolitan underling retorted, in a letter to the authorities, that during one week Padre Piaggio was seen at his desk only three days. Some north European visitors joined the chorus of his critics. "Everyone who takes culture to his heart deplores the slow pace with which they proceed to examine these manuscripts", the Englishman Charles Burney complained in his travel journal in 1771.[26] This negative comment, based on minimal knowledge, was published in the London edition of Burney's diary, which then was issued in Germany and France.

Piaggio also protested bitterly at the slow pace of the Neapolitan scholars translating the text. Instead of analysing the whole manuscript, he wrote, they would seize upon a minute scrap, base upon it a long dissertation, and then expensively publish that commentary, useful only "for wrapping anchovies". One such scholar kept a papyrus scroll in his home for a decade before giving up and admitting he could make no sense of it at all.[27]

A different level of trouble arose even when a few of the papyri were finally read. Piaggio unrolled and copied the first papyrus in 1754 and sent it to the Accademia for translation from the original Greek into Italian. Now known with the catalog inventory number as Pherc. 1497, this was Book IV of *On Music*, by a Greek philosopher who was influential in Rome in Julius Caesar's day, Philodemus. By 1761 three more scrolls had been unrolled and read. These too were by Philodemus: *On Rhetoric* (Pherc. 1672) and Books I and II *On Virtues and Vices* (Pherc. 1675 and Pherc. 1427 respectively).

Here the problem was that Philodemus was less famous than Virgil. Many were disappointed that the manuscripts which could now be read were in Greek rather than Latin. In particular, the title of the first commentary by Philodemus, "Against Music", was belittled because it seemed to argue a ridiculous thesis.

Instead of easing the pressure on the unfortunate and lonely Padre Piaggio, the Neapolitan establishment responded by urging him on to more speed. If only he would hurry, something better than disagreeable Greek texts by an unknown philosopher might yet turn up. By then, the generation of art restorers, conservators and excavators who had opened Pompeii had grown old. When Pasquale Carcani, the prime mover of the Accademia Ercolanese, died in 1783, the Accademia itself succumbed. No official scientific body for the study of its antiquities existed in Naples after that date.

In 1785 Padre Piaggio was still at work nevertheless, still unrolling his daily half inch, still transcribing, and still writing letters of complaint. In his small room nothing had changed. That 15 August, the secretary of the French embassy in Naples summarized the situation of the papyri in a report to his ministry in Paris. Of the 815 scrolls known to have been dug up at Herculaneum, 200 had been destroyed by an "ignoramus" trying to open them with a chemical cocktail (he presumably meant the amateur alchemist, the Duke of Sansevero) and the remaining fragments dumped into the sea. "Of the four or five hundred which remain", he wrote, "the four which they are recopying now are better preserved, but still show multiple gaps".[28]

The same French diplomat went on to describe the technical difficulties Padre Piaggio faced in unrolling the papyrus scrolls:

> More than two-thirds are impossible to unroll. They are crushed. The leaves form a compact chunk of charcoal. Of the other third, many have been ruined, and only the inner portion is good. Still others were damaged when opening them was barbarously attempted with a knife. All that which was copied with such effort after more than twenty years offers little from which we can learn. ...

The "barbarous" knife slashings of the papyri were, sad to say, the work of Paderni.

The French diplomat's evaluation echoed the general opinion of Neapolitan and foreign scholars visiting Naples at that time, that after thirty-one years, "little" of value had been achieved. Piaggio's work was dismissed as useless. Popular as Piaggio's room was among visitors for its curiosity value, an aura of failure enveloped the Herculaneum Library like a pall.

Others in Europe were still curious about the scrolls' content, but Naples remained reluctant to make revelations to outsiders. In 1788 the French scholar monk Barthelemy returned to Portici. Camillo Paderni showed him only one, twenty-eight-line scroll column. As Barthelemy recorded,

> I read it five or six times, and under the pretext of a need, I went back upstairs. I mentally compared my copy with the original, and I found the means to rectify my two or three errors. ... I sent it immediately to the Académie de Belles-Lettres, but asked them not to publish it, out of fear of compromising Mazzochi and Paderni.[29]

Comfort came from a strange corner, however. The reluctant bride Maria Carolina of Austria, unhappy wife to the wastrel King Ferdinand, became a frequent visitor. She sat quietly beside Padre Piaggio for hours on end, apparently soothed by watching the almost imperceptible progress in unrolling of a papyrus scroll. From the building where Piaggio worked she also liked to watch "the wild doves flying around the building. Tamed, these doves sweep in from the woods to build their nests here and there inside the walls", as Piaggio wrote.[30] Also crowding his small room, were the frescoes stripped from the walls of Pompeii: "Paderni has brought the pictures here. They do take up a great deal of space".

The king too made occasional appearances. For Piaggio in his endless war against Paderni this was serious cause for celebration. The king "always stood up beside my machine, never seeming to want to sit out of fatigue, nor move until the time the footman came to fetch him". To the Neapolitan royals in the twilight decades of the century of the Enlightenment, Padre Piaggio's little room at Portici, however cold in winter and hot in summer, must have been almost the only retreat in which they could seek quiet and repose.

Outside that hushed centre of monastic industry, of Greek calligraphy and unfamiliar philosophy, the revolutionary whirlwind was mounting. In 1776 Britain lost its American colony to revolutionaries, aided by the perverse French. France itself was skittering toward its revolution of 1789.

From Spain, the ageing Charles III sent concerned letters. Maria Carolina willfully ignored his advice from that alien (to her) turf. On 23 November 1776, Ferdinand wrote to his father to complain that his wife was forcing the Spanish appointee Bernard Tanucci out of power as prime minister. The elderly Tuscan appointed by Elisabetta Farnese half a century before was a last link between Naples and Spain.

In his letter to his father Ferdinand played the pathetic role. "I shall try to stop her, although she threatens me about everything, she says that she will make me see just who she is, who her parents are, and that for us it's a big favour and luck to have her in our family."[31]

In 1777 Maria Carolina successfully ousted Tanucci, who must have been relieved to see the last of such a peculiar court and return to Tuscany. Tanucci's departure paved the way for the coming forty years of chaos in Naples, the conclusion of which was foreign domination.

CHAPTER VII

Dirty and Other Pictures

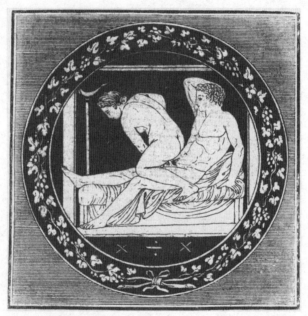

18. Pompeii erotica

Fleeing the celebrity that followed publication of his novel *Young Werther*, Goethe and his friend Tischbein reached Naples in 1786. Goethe wrote copious diary entries about the city, its food, the volcano, the ruins, and Emma's Attitudes. Tischbein painted; in the end he would remain in Naples a decade, appointed by the crown to direct the fine arts academy, the Accademia di Belle Arti.

Even before publication of his diary, Goethe's very presence in southern Italy attracted others. Goethe had been a member of the Musenhof at Weimar, the artistic circle of Anna Amalia, Duchess of Saxe-Weimar and a niece of Frederick the Great. In a letter to her, Goethe mentioned a certain "marvellous place" at Pompeii, "worthy of marvellous Thoughts … From it you can see the sunset over the sea". Inspired, the duchess set out for Naples, her itinerary planned by Tischbein. At Pompeii she located the precise "marvellous place" just outside one of the ancient city gates: a handsomely carved stone bench beside the tomb of the priestess Mamia. Already, Desprez and Piranesi had sketched the tomb; now Tischbein painted Amalia, seated upon the bench and gazing at the great gulf. Upon her return to Weimar, she had the bench copied as an architectural souvenir for her garden (today a public park, where the bench can still be seen).

The volcano itself was elevated to architectural caprice, part of the vogue for fake antiquities to adorn the gardens of the stately home. In the garden of his huge estate, Leopold of Anhalt-Dessau, a Prussian nobleman, installed a volcano on an islet in a lake. For parties, he had his servants light a fire in the phoney crater, from which smoke soared. "Lava" flowed down the cone, an effect created by water dribbling over red glass panels, illuminated from behind by torches.[1]

Until that time the city of Naples had been symbolized in folk arts by its huge Sant'Elmo Castle, always depicted from the sea. The eruption seen by Sir William Hamilton had created a new genre of thanksgiving votive paintings showing Vesuvius, and overnight the volcano was elevated to the symbol of the city.[2] These paintings became souvenirs, even as formal nocturnal views began to be painted by visiting foreign artists such as Joseph Wright of Derby.

Joseph Wright (the "of Derby" is added to distinguish him from a contemporary American artist of the same name) seems to have witnessed an eruption during his years in Italy (1774–5). During the course of the next two decades, Wright painted thirty dramatic pictures of Vesuvius, as well as a view of Virgil's Tomb and of a dramatic shower of fireworks in Rome. A true child of the Enlightenment, Wright was fascinated by the nature of light and atmospherics, which he studied in order to improve his depictions of it. To this end he belonged to the Lunar Society of London, a circle of scientists who met each Monday on the week closest to the full moon, whose members included Dr Erasmus Darwin, Charles's grandfather, and ceramics manufacturer Josiah Wedgwood.

Like Wright, Wedgwood made a pilgrimage to Pompeii, where the vibrant colours and skilful production of ancient cameo glass vases inspired this pioneer industrialist to develop his own production. In so doing, Wedgwood became the first to adapt the taste of the aesthetes like Hamilton into products for the masses.[3] In

London, in addition, Wedgwood saw Hamilton's catalogue of the ancient vases, which delighted Wedgwood, as he said later, for their style and spirit, their "elegant simplicity". He had them copied in his factory, albeit without "absolute servility", he added.[4] (The same catalogue drawings of Hamilton's vases were also utilized for craft production at Sèvres and Berlin.)

When Wedgwood inaugurated a great new pottery factory in 1768, its first line of six pots had decorations in red on black showing scenes from antiquity. All six came from Hamilton's catalogue, most of which were vases from Pompeii.[5] The line was nevertheless named "Etruria". Fine ancient vases were already being found in tombs in Etruria, the Tyrrhenian coastal area north of Rome. Many were imports from Greece, but were assumed to be of local production, as indeed some were. Hamilton himself helped to establish their Greek origin, and Wedgwood later acknowledged the vases were Greek, as in his catalogue of 1779:

> It is evident the finer sort of *Etruscan Vases*, found in *Magna Graecia*, are truly Greek Workmanship, and ornamented chiefly with Grecian Subjects, drawn from the purest Fountain of the Arts; it is probable many of the Figures and Groupes upon them preserve to us Sketches or Copies of the most celebrated Greek Paintings; so that few Monuments of Antiquity better deserve the Attention of the Antiquary, of the Connoisseur, and the Artist, than the *painted* Etruscan Vases.[6]

One particularly fine vase of deep-blue glass with white cameo designs, known as the Barberini Vase for the Roman papal family that had previously owned it, was bought by Hamilton and resold to Lord Portland. Fascinated by the renamed Portland Vase, in 1786 Wedgwood acquired reproduction rights to it, with Hamilton's help, and worked for three years to create a satisfactory copy.

Through all this frenzy of art, architecture and commerce the Neapolitan court under King Ferdinand I had remained remarkably lethargic, but in 1781, thirteen years after Wedgwood had introduced his Herculaneum-inspired ceramics, the Neapolitan royal factory at Capodimonte manufactured an eighty-eight-piece porcelain dessert service celebrating Herculaneum. Standing atop the centrepiece was a statue of Ferdinand himself, together with his late father, King Charles, portrayed as patrons of the archaeological excavations.

As a present to George III of England, Ferdinand then ordered manufacture of a set of *biscuit* porcelain dishes decorated in the manner of the "Etruscan" vase vogue launched by Hamilton and Wedgwood.

Through its own arts Pompeii was also speaking for itself, and what it said did not please everyone. In discoveries that to this day condition the attitudes toward Pompeii worldwide, objects of an obvious sexual content were found, shocking to many, titillating to others. The conclusion seemed inescapable. In Pompeii, erotic pictures were not a vulgar exception, they were the rule. All this fought against the uplifting image the Bourbon-Farnesi desired.

Although the 18th-century erudites were familiar with risqué ancient poetry, and possibly had seen vases with obscene motifs and the wall paintings of Etruscan tombs, in which light-hearted banquets were underway and the sex implicit, nothing like this had ever been seen, and surely not in such quantity. From the ruins emerged both mildly erotic and blatantly pornographic scenes, painted on walls and on vases, designed in mosaic tiles on floors, vulgarly scribbled onto street-front walls. Gigantic free-standing phalluses were found, and bizarrely erotic objects—terracotta lamps, bronze hanging charms, sculptures, even furniture. Some suggestive Dionysian scenes were dignified by their mythological associations—but then from the ruins came a series of ithyphallic bronze ragamuffins bearing trays, presumably meant to serve as bread holders for the dinner table. When lapillae were scraped away in a dining room, the floor mosaic in black-and-white tesserae showed a sea scene in which couples and groups of three copulated, in boats.

A favourite theme in wall paintings was the satyr creeping up behind a nymph to catch her by surprise. In a few cases the nymph, her veil ripped away, turns out to be a hermaphrodite, to the satyr's theatrical dismay, and the observer's amusement. Some wall paintings showed homosexual sex and, because African motifs were popular, pygmies enjoying a picnic orgy under a tent.

A peculiar *objet* resembling a wind-chime, found at Herculaneum in 1740, is an elegantly wrought tintinnabulum of bronze. It depicts a man whose hooked helmet and protective strap identify him as a *murmillo*, a type of gladiator, doing battle against his own gigantic phallus, transformed into a panther.

Naples itself had come to seem so lively that, in one of his books, the Marquis de Sade (1749–1814) used the temple to Venus at Baiae as an appropriate setting for an imaginary orgy. To earlier generations of Grand Tourists, Baiae had inspired only lofty thoughts of Virgil's Tomb. And until the findings at Herculaneum and Pompeii, ancient Rome had not been seen as a producer of visual pornography, but as a font of majesty and wisdom, inspired by the reflections of the eloquent Cicero, the meditations of Marcus Aurelius and the austerity of Cato.

The news of these discoveries travelled quickly. During his tour of duty at Naples, the diplomat and trained engraver Baron Dominique-Vivant Denon stole time from organizing drawings of travel sights for the Abbé de Saint-Non, to make a series of drawings of the erotica based on the paintings and artefacts of Pompeii. Under the title *Priapées et sujets divers*, Denon's drawings were published in France and circulated among cognoscenti. While serving as chargé-d'affaires in Naples after 1782, Denon received commissions for drawings from Sir William Hamilton, who turned over his collection of wax phalluses from Isernia to the British Museum in 1784. One Denon drawing depicts the white marble sculpture group from the Villa of the Papyrus, which had so shocked King Charles when first excavated in 1752. The statue had long since been locked away; Winckelmann was resolutely denied access, but somehow Denon had seen it.

Winckelmann, for one, knew that to understand the Pompeian erotica required analysing what such gods as Pan and Priapus meant in antiquity. Pan was a familiar figure in Greek sculpture, and when King Charles was shocked at Herculaneum by the statue of the woodland god Pan and the she-goat, he may not have known that among the vast treasures of his mother's inherited Farnese collection was an erotic variation depicting Pan together with Daphnis, the Sicilian shepherd boy. In ancient Arcadian legend, it was Pan who taught Daphnis how to play the flute; depicted together the two therefore symbolized lyric poetry and, in general, artistic creation. Carved in Greece, the Farnese group was famous because it was mentioned by Pliny in his encyclopedia. It had graced the so-called "garden of Love" (giardino d'Amore) at the cardinal's hillside estate on Rome's outskirts, the Villa Farnesina, until it was locked away in the Secret Cabinet of the Farnese palace at Campo de'Fiori in Rome, where it remained until 1770.[7]

The erect penis was understood as indicating intellectual excitement and a portrayal of nature (Pan) bringing culture to mankind. The two statues of Pan, therefore—the one in the cardinal's collection in Rome and the one hidden away in Naples—were readable as signifying at the same time pure lust and pure intellect, pure art.[8]

One man's dirty picture is another man's *divertissement*, however, and so in the libertine mood of the late 18th century many welcomed the erotica of Pompeii. The wealth of shocking and desirable pornography could hardly go unnoticed among the dealers, and also among forgers hustling their wares to the Grand Tourist collectors converging on Naples. Manufacturing ancient erotica became a lucrative business; Winckelmann himself reported seeing on the market skilful forgeries of Priapic figures from Pompeii in paint and sculpture. The most renowned of the forgers of ancient Pompeian erotica was Giuseppe Guerra, a Venetian working in Rome, whose clients included a Borgia family cardinal. The cardinal's lavish erotica collection included pieces subsequently purchased by General Joaquim Murat, Napoleon's brother-in-law, after he became king of Naples in 1808.

Winckelmann himself was curious about the Priapic figures, such as the myriad phalluses in bronze called *tintinnabula*, from which tiny bells dangled, to tinkle away perhaps as protection from jinxes and the evil eye. Winckelmann drew copies of several from Herculaneum and mailed them to a friend, G.L. Bianconi.[9]

What intrigued many was that, whereas some examples of the erotica found in the Neapolitan excavations were beyond doubt vulgarly pornographic, others, like the bronze table whose three legs formed elongated, ithyphallic figures, had other connotations. The tripod table, for instance, appeared to be a charcoal brazier, which suggested that it was intended for offerings: if so, it therefore held religious significance.

In the early period of Pompeian excavations, the same desire to understand the natural world that had caused Sir William Hamilton to study Vesuvius encouraged him to question the significance of the erotica discoveries. "I have actually discovered the cult of Priapus in full vigour at Isernia", he enthusiastically wrote to a friend in London in 1781.[10]

Unlike those surviving from antiquity, the phallus Hamilton had found in a church at the town near Naples was made not of terracotta, but of wax, suggesting that it was meant to be pitched into a sacred fire. The 18th-century gentlemen scholars understood fully that these were votive offerings that had religious significance. Priapus was what is known as an ithyphallic god, "ithy" meaning straight. His cult dates from prehistory, and perhaps pre-human history; "the association between ithyphallic display and protection of territory is also found among primates".[11] According to historian James Davidson of the University of Warwick, England, in antiquity the Greek concept of power through penetration was an extension of the sexual relationship—violence itself and "an absolutely central

19. This elegant Greek statue group, found in the 1750s at Herculaneum, shows the priapic woodland god Pan gazing lustily at a she-goat. A scandalized Neapolitan court kept the marble sculpture hidden, but its notoriety spread, contributing to the Vesuvian cities' reputation for dissolution. National Archaeological Museum, Naples.

concern, governing not just the zone of sexual relations, but the whole of ancient Athenian, or ancient Greek society".[12] And in fact, typically, Priapus was a service god who acted as watchman in a garden, and the phallus a symbolic weapon for safeguarding property. Priapus would punish any intruder; hence his frequent portrayal as an ithyphallic herm.

To the Etruscan-influenced culture that had shaped Pompeii, the phallus, by representing the creation of life itself, also seems to have represented the afterlife. This interpretation is suggested in several Etruscan-era objects found at Pompeii, such as one upright stone phallus nearly three feet tall. On its side, written in the Etruscan language, are the words of a wife grieving for her dead husband. This marker was his gravestone, and the phallus symbol held specific religious significance, beyond making offerings to a woodland or money-showering god.

During the Dionysian rites at Alexandria in Egypt, the life-giving phallus was celebrated in procession and carried on a float. Later, ithyphallic came to refer to the singsong metre of the hymns to Dionysus and Bacchus, and hence to the metre of generically licentious poems. Of Greek origin, these poems circulated in Rome and in Italy's Hellenistic south, including Pompeii.

Priapus was scorned in Rome in the 2nd century AD, in scathing words written by satirical poet Juvenal. In processions to Bona Dea, the goddess worshipped by central Italian tribes, wrote Juvenal, "... the flute stirs the loins, and the *maenads* of Priapus sweep along, frenzied alike by the horn blowing and by the wine, they whirl their locks and howl. What foul longings burn within their breasts! What cries they utter as the passion beats within."[13]

The *maenads*, in Greece, were in origin mostly upper-class women who escaped from their customary semi-prudish state to go into the mountains once a year to worship Dionysus—rich housewives on a binge, more or less. The ritual fused social life and religion, and included a wild and cheerful letting-down of hair. Associated with this was snake handling (which, by the way, persists in one church not far from Naples for one day a year), ecstasy, music, dancing. A contemporary equivalent of this blend of the social, religious and ecstatic is found in some US churches, where worshippers sing hymns, clap hands, talk politics, pray, enter a trance-like state and speak in tongues.

In another of his later variations Priapus brought wealth, and Romans accordingly made offerings to him, to coax his favour— hence the phalluses of terra cotta outside Pompeiian shops. Even today Priapus as a god is not entirely lost; the garden gnome or dwarf of kitschy taste is an echo of this ancient and once-loved protector of gardens, who has been sanitized for polite society through a cultural castration.

Publication by the Society of Dilettanti in London in 1786 of Hamilton's study, *The Worship of Priapus*, was promoted by an English friend, Richard Payne Knight. Born in Herefordshire, Knight was a self-taught scholar like Hamilton. He first visited Italy in 1767, when he was barely seventeen. In Rome Knight began collecting the ruin-studded, gilded landscape paintings of Claude Lorrain. On a visit to Naples with the artist Joseph Hackert a few years later, Knight discovered the landscape, arts, and easy life of the Campania. Having funds and the temperament of the quintessential connoisseur,

Knight joined Hamilton in exploring, exploiting and explaining the Vesuvian sites, and especially Pompeii, whose excavations were churning out new marvels almost daily.

On advice from Hamilton, Knight began a collection of Pompeian antiquities; later he purchased Hamilton's collection of Pompeian bronze statuettes and objects, which went to the British Museum upon his death in 1824. Until the Napoleonic blackout years Knight would continue to live in Naples off and on, gradually becoming "the ruling spirit" of the elite Society of Dilettanti in London.[14]

A youthful poem by Knight intimates what may have gone on behind the closed doors of these connoisseur expatriates. In his poem Knight expresses regret for having wasted time on "gentlemen jockeys" in London and admits frankly, "Ungovern'd passions led my soul astray ...". Even so, he added, the jockeys' morals were superior to those of certain "gentlemen picture dealers".[15]

From Naples in 1781, Knight himself wrote a letter to the Dilettanti entitled "On the Worship of Priapus in the Kingdom of Naples" (30 December 1781). In it he mentions his own collection of priapic relics:

> I had long ago discovered, that the women and children of the lower class, at Naples, and in its neighbourhood, frequently wore, as an ornament of dress, a sort of Amulet, (which they imagine to be a preservative from the *mal occhii*, evil eyes, or enchantment) exactly similar to those which were worn by the ancient Inhabitants of this Country for the very same purpose, as likewise for their supposed invigorating influence; and all of which have evidently a relation to the Cult of Priapus. Struck with this conformity in ancient and modern superstition, I made a collection of both the ancient and modern Amulets of this sort, and placed them together in the British Museum, where they remain.[16]

The London picture dealers were not the only ones with questionable morals. In 1767, when Winckelmann was fifty, he went on a volcanic picnic—there is no other word to describe it—with Pierre François Hugues, the gifted art historian who called himself, apparently falsely, the Baron d'Hancarville.

At the time d'Hancarville was Winckelmann's host in Naples. He combined amateur scholarship with professional charm so successfully that, when he first arrived in Naples in 1763, he was befriended by the youthful Sir William Hamilton, still married to his ailing first wife Catherine. The eminent British envoy to Naples and fellow scholarly connoisseur had d'Hancarville write the introduction and captions to Hamilton's catalogue of ancient Greek vases—though much later Hamilton would claim that d'Hancarville once cheated him of payment in the sale of an ancient vase.[17] The lives of the three men, Winckelmann, d'Hancarville and Hamilton were entwined; Winckelmann just then had agreed to write captions for a new catalogue of the ancient Greek vases that Hamilton was acquiring in Naples from dealers and from his own small personal excavation.

In Rome in 1766 Winckelmann had tutored the younger brother of the British Queen Charlotte, Prince George August von Mecklenburg-Strelitz. The young prince then travelled to Naples, where he was welcomed into the Hamilton circle. This royal connection had helped draw Winckelmann into the world of the Hamiltons in Naples. Winckelmann, now on his fourth visit there, was nervous. "Because of his critical account of the excavations at Herculaneum, brought in by Hamilton in 1764, he came rather apprehensively, fearing a beating of even assassination."[18] Nothing untoward happened there, however, perhaps—this is the conjecture of Hamilton's biographer David Constantine—because of Hamilton's protection. In any case, Hamilton promised Winckelmann some help in promoting English sales of Winckelmann's *Monumenti Antichi Inediti*.

The project with Hamilton was never completed. Sadly, within the year Winckelmann would be murdered in a Trieste inn during a tryst with a Tuscan youth who stabbed Winckelmann to death in order to steal a gold coin.

By the time of Napoleon's defeat, the association between the evidence of wanton sexual ways at Pompeii and the volcano's wrath was firmly fixed. The message was simple: pagan sexual misbehaviour brings geological punishment.

Because the volcanic eruption coincided with the dawn of the Christian era, some believers found it obvious that a just Christian god would rain down showers of burning rock upon people who placed ithyphallic statues in their gardens and in front of their bakeries on a public street. Citizens who placed phallic statuettes as bread holders on their dining tables, and read dirty stories by Ovid by the light of phallic clay lamps, deserved what came to them. This implied that the volcano was manipulated by God. Whatever Sir William Hamilton had tried to prove, many would never believe otherwise.

The mood at the end of the century was expressed by a stern English traveller, a certain Mr N. Brooke, in 1799. The revolutionaries of Naples had claimed Pompeii as the property of the people and had just thrown open the doors of the former royal erotica cabinet. "Had it belonged to me", thundered Mr Brooke, speaking of the statue of Pan and the She-goat, "I would have had it thrown into the volcano whose lava flows had already swallowed it once before".[19]

As the decades of the Victorian era advanced step-by-step with the expanding excavation of Pompeii, the discoveries of more obscene graffiti, more blatantly obscene bronzes and lamps churned up by the excavators, scarred the reputation of the dead city. In sermon and art, naughty sex and Pompeii became inseparably linked, and in his dictionary of 1864, seven years after the first known use of the word, Webster defined "pornography" as "licentious paintings employed to decorate the walls of rooms sacred to Bacchanalian orgies, examples of which exist in Pompeii". The association of pornography and Pompeii became a constant, part of the permanent image of Pompeii.

This mind-set can be misleading. In one famous instance archaeologists working at Pompeii came upon a terracotta phallus, eighteen inches long and jutting from a building wall. Inside, they decided, was a brothel. Beside the phallus was the inscription, *"Hic habitat felicitas"* (here dwells happiness). Happiness and phallus, it seemed to say, were one. Once excavated, the building turned out to be an ordinary bakery, and the phallus a charm intended to bring good luck and wealth, perhaps too to ensure that the bread would rise properly and not burn. These large good-luck phalluses, which have been found on building walls in many a Roman city, and not only at Pompeii, were popular with shop owners, and may also have been placed on a wall outside the family store to protect it from the envy of rival shop keepers.

In a sign of the change of mood in the early 19th century around the beginning of the reign of Queen Victoria, an engraving in architect William Gell's book of drawings of Pompeii shows a bakery that had a phallus projecting from a wall near the great bread oven. The phallus, however, is politely indistinct, more or less obliterated.

Today, Pompeian erotica is examined with the sort of clinical eye that would have delighted Winckelmann, Hamilton and Knight. More than them, however, scholars analyse not only the anthropology and ancient Greek mythical background, but the implications for the social organization of ancient Roman life, including the arts and the role of slaves.

Among the recent discoveries, for instance, is that the Kamasutra-like pictures in the various public buildings and private homes of Pompeii were painted by local decorators from a series of matrixes handed-down from a decorators' album, exactly as if it were a book of wallpaper designs. Variations of the positions appeared and reappeared in dozens of places: in prostitutes' hovels, in the special back rooms of taverns, on the mosaic of a dining room (*triclinium*) of a house, in the alcoves of half a dozen private homes, in several public and private bathhouses, and even in the grand master bedrooms of the great houses. They have also found a hotel bill that included the costs for the services of a "*puella*".[20]

Scholars from Italy addressing the issue today also make careful distinctions about the purposes of the erotica. Some paintings, such as the overt pornography in baths, various houses, and the brothel at Pompeii,[21] seem intended specifically for sexual arousal. Others hint at sex, or, when explicit, seem meant for nothing more than larky amusement in a summer garden. And one bronze object found at Pompeii and identified as Egyptian in origin shows a reclining child caressing an enormous phallus, which cuddles beside him like a teddy bear, perhaps to protect him while he slept.

Recent studies show that Pompeian pornography, in addition, reflects class distinctions. The sex shown on walls of common brothels and taverns is crude by comparison with the refined Venuses and hermaphrodites in the sex alcoves of private homes, where the decorations were relatively more playful and less *lumpen*. Marriage in ancient Pompeii was largely a political and economic liaison, and in these sex alcoves the master of the house entertained regular mistresses and perhaps more casual lovers. Some of these alcoves were situated directly off a posh dining room.

In other instances the situation of the sex alcove in the plan of the house suggests that servant wenches and young male slaves as well may have been obliged to be prostitutes. This may have been the case in the opulent House of the Vetti, where next to the kitchen the cook's room is decorated with hard-core wall paintings. The prostitution trade may have been vertically integrated; the male household slaves were expected to seek the services of the prostituted female slaves, on income-produced property owned by the *dominus* (master).[22]

Prostitution was not illegal; on the contrary, half a century before the destruction of Pompeii, the emperor Caligula (AD 12–41) imposed a tax on it. In the past, scholars studied it on two levels: as supposedly sacred, a theory given less credit today, and as entirely secular. That of Pompeii was the latter, and today scholars like Antonio Varrone study it as a unique window into the social history of ancient Rome at the height of its wealth.

The public brothel of Pompeii, which occupies a triangular lot in the heart of town, had five rooms, or alcoves, downstairs, and five upstairs. Besides the brothel, suggestive graffiti have been found in ten other Pompeian sites, many located near the brothel. The homes of several wealthy Pompeians, who included magistrates, were located nearby, but so were other shady taverns with back rooms for sex, so that, according to Italian archaeologist Antonio Varrone, a pioneer in such studies, "While Pompeii did not have a red-light district, there was a certain concentration". One such shady tavern was the so-called House of the Wounded Bear, named for a wall painting, which had a restaurant with a fountain (*nymphaeum*) and a suspect back room. A long inscription found there speaks of drinking Falernian wine—that wine Lord Lytton has his characters drink in *The Last Days of Pompeii*.

Other prostitutes plied their trade in single tiny rooms entered directly from the street. What also appears to be a brothel—if so, only the second found in the history of archaeology—is in the town of Puteoli, Pompeii's wealthy port city rival further up the coast. Whereas it has no graphic evidence, its layout with two separate entries and a cubicle, presumably for a guard of sorts or clerk, suggests it was indeed a brothel.

When the brothel of Pompeii was closed for restoration in late 2004, Professor Varrone and others were able to examine more closely than ever in the past its alcoves, walls and ceiling beams, upon which a total of 136 graffiti inscriptions have been found. Many of the inscriptions were simply names (a certain Felix left his signature in three separate places), but fifty-three were names of men, twenty-nine of women. Most (thirty-nine) were in Latin. Interestingly, in this city whose culture fused the traditions of early Oscans, Greek colonizers, and Etruscan and Roman settlers, thirty-four names—nearly half of the men's names, that is—were Greek.

Among the names of women, four-fifths were identifiably those of slaves; the remaining one-fifth of names (examples are Veronica, Fabia, Myrtale, Fortunata and Victoria) were from a higher class and are presumed to have been brothel customers. "We believe that women were clients. In addition, couples who had nowhere else to go may have rented the brothel rooms, as if it were a motel", Professor Varrone explained.

One curiosity about the inscriptions is that many are elegantly executed, indicating a relatively high degree of literacy and education among the customers. Most but not all are simply vulgar, such as the typically crude inscription "FUTUTA SUM HIC". But another seems rather sweet, boasting, "Daphne is mine". And in a parody of

Caesar's *veni vidi vinci*, a customer declared, "HIC EGO CUM VENI FUTUI/DEINDE REDEI DOMI" (Here I came, I had sex, then I went home.)

The pictures over the doors of the five downstairs rooms of the brothel provide a curious contrast between fantasy and reality. In addition to the explicit sex, the luxuries depicted would delight any travelling amphora salesman. One sees, in paint, movable beds made of finely carved wood, strewn with pillows and draped elegantly with striped linen covers over the mattresses. By contrast, inside the cubicle was the reality of stone beds and a stone pillow, whose discomfort was alleviated by, at best, a thin mattress of wool or straw.

True luxury was visible in the peristyle fountain gardens of the stately homes. Here the erotic sculptures scattered among the greenery, including the notorious Pan and the She-goat, were light hearted and intended to amuse.

For the educated there was even visual social satire, as in the small terracotta oil lamp that warns, in witty fashion, against fatuous intellectuals. Before a seated man engrossed in reading a book stretches his own elongated phallus, from the end of which a light burns. The oil lamp, then, illuminates both fake book and real room—though not, it is to be understood, real life, when the distracted intellectual becomes so lost in his book that he forgets the purpose of his phallus.

CHAPTER VIII

Running from Revolution

20. Wall painting from Pompeii

The tide of rebellion was rising. The indifference of King Ferdinand of Naples to the affairs of state made an important ally of Naples nervous: Austria. In 1778 the Emperor Joseph had succeeded his mother, Maria Theresa, to the throne in Vienna. Shortly afterward Joseph sailed into Naples to pay a call of duty upon his sister, the queen of Naples, Maria Carolina.

The queen who had said she would rather be drowned in the sea than marry the king of Naples had been obliged to marry him and was notoriously unhappy, not without good reason. In secret diplomatic reports back to London, His Majesty's envoy Sir William Hamilton described the king of Naples and the Two Sicilies in blunt and dismaying terms:

> King Ferdinand's habit of dissipation has taken such firm root there is scarcely a possibility of his ever applying seriously to business. ... The chase in winter and parties of sailing or fishing in summer call out His Majesty every day at Sun Rising and keep him out till it sets ... fatigued with the dissipations of the day.[1]

Ferdinand's fondness for the more idle amusements, as compared with governing, was confirmed by an English visitor, Hester Piozzi:

> The king rides and rows and hunts the wild boar and catches fish in the bay and sells it ... as dear as he can—but gives away the money ... He

dances with the girls, eats macaroni and helps himself to it with his fingers and rows against the watermen.[2]

The two Habsburg siblings, one an emperor of Austria and the other the queen of Naples, met on board Joseph's ship riding at anchor in the shimmering waters of the bay. Joseph warned his sister that the turmoil being created by aggressive France risked spilling over into all of Europe. The Kingdom of the Two Sicilies was unprepared to defend itself, he warned her.

"You have no navy. You must build one", the emperor advised his sister.

"How?" Maria Carolina asked. In the frequent absences of the lazy king, the queen ruled by right, as Elisabetta Farnese had. She must hire a capable naval officer, her brother said, to come to Naples to build a navy. He had just the man in mind, John Francis Edward Acton. His mother was French, but his father was English.

John Acton was known as a brilliant and innovative officer who had served well in both the French and Spanish navies. Just then Acton sailed under the colours of Tuscany, whose Grand Duke Leopold II was another brother of Joseph and Maria Carolina. Leopold agreed to release Acton to his sister the following year. Already Sir William Hamilton was a shadow governor of Naples. Acton would become its shadow king.

With her bony face shaped like a shoebox, Maria Carolina became Acton's kingdom. He jumped from commander of the revamped fleet to foreign minister and then prime minister. Beginning as Maria Carolina's wise counsellor and friend, he also became her lover—not the first, but the one Maria Carolina loved best and for the coming decade trusted most. In a famous Hackert picture of Ferdinand prominent on horseback in the foreground at the great hunt, Acton hovers in the background a few steps away from Maria Carolina.

Observing this kettle of fish at close hand was the talented engraver Baron Denon, just thirty-one years of age when he was posted to Naples in 1778 in the diplomatic service of France. For seven years in Naples Denon juggled diplomatic duties and work on the Abbé de Saint-Non's landmark illustrated guidebook to the Naples area—and on his own copies of Priapic ritual objects.

None of this was easy. As earlier at Herculaneum, the Neapolitans continued to insist that they alone were entitled to present their treasures, their way. Foreigners were still forbidden to take notes or measurements of antiquities; in 1774 a French architect, P.A. Paris, was obliged to draw the floor plan of the newly discovered Temple of Isis at Pompeii from memory.

Now the stakes were higher as Britain and France became commercial rivals in the Mediterranean. In a secret dispatch to the Foreign Office, Denon reported that Maria Carolina dominated the entire court and, of great concern for the French, "writes frequent secret letters to her brother in Vienna". This rang alarm bells. In theory, the Kingdom of Naples still had a special relationship with Spain. In practice, her writing "frequent secret letters" intimated that Maria Carolina's first loyalty lay with her native Austria. Denon described the queen as "fragile"; still, to keep the peace, Ferdinand signed whatever she desired, Denon added.

Denon relished such gossip. John Acton was detested at court, he reported. The kingdom was cash strapped, and so Maria Carolina took a "beautifully worked" brooch in the shape of a ship—a gift from Ferdinand when she had given birth—and had it melted down and sold for the gold it contained. In addition:

> The Queen says explicitly that which she should keep to herself. Once when her son misbehaved, she chided him before other people, saying, "It must be agreed that I've been unlucky in sons. Heaven gave me two of them, and both imbeciles whom (heaven) should just take right back. If it did, I wouldn't lose much, I'd marry off my older girl to my brother, and take the Kingdom of Naples back to my home."[3]

"My home"—the Habsburg court in Vienna.

Denon's relations with the queen and Acton gradually soured, and the artist had to be recalled—though not before spending an evening with the Hamiltons at Villa Sessa, where he made two sketches of Emma in her Attitudes.[4]

Anti-French sentiment having forced Denon to leave Naples, the artist and former French consul dawdled en route to Paris, making a long detour first to Venice and another to meet Voltaire. Both visits would later stand him in good stead. With him in his luggage was his personal collection of Pompeian pots, assembled during his seven years at the court of Naples.

In Paris, Denon showed his upward mobility by joining the prestigious Academie Royale. He also ingratiated himself at Versailles. Exhibiting a blend of commercial savvy and connoisseurship worthy of Hamilton, Denon sold his entire collection of ancient Neapolitan painted pots to Louis XVI.

The king's acquisition helped to popularize further in France both the Neapolitan sites and the collecting of ancient Greek vases from southern Italy. In the twilight years before the French Revolution, Herculaneum and Pompeii became an aristocratic vogue in France. Indeed, the country's love affair with antiquity had nearly become a fetish. France was adrift, to quote German historian Hagen Schulze, "in a dream of Greece as a Baroque Arcadia".[5]

In that brief moment before heads rolled, no one really believed that a revolution could take place in Paris. That same Abbé Barthelemy who had scribbled in the secret of a privy at Herculaneum to outwit the guards set aside his studies of ancient scrolls and Aristotle to attend a frivolous costume ball inspired by Herculaneum. Servant boys outfitted as Greek slaves flitted about with carafes of wine. The abbé himself was decked out in the long Grecian tunic called a *chiton*.

At Versailles the women of the dying regime wore their hair swept up in Grecian style—*à la Diane*, it was called, inspired by the huntress goddess. So coiffed, crowned with a wreath of laurel, the Austrian queen of France, Marie Antoinette, younger sister of the queen of Naples, donned a Grecian tunic for a party at the Trianon Palace. At the party she played a lyre like one of the dancing girls from the painted Herculaneum vases in the royal collection brought to Paris by Denon. (Decades later Jane Austen's women were still wearing these hair styles copied from the French, in turn copied from the paintings of women on the Greek vases and panel paintings of Naples.)

All that smacked of antiquity was chic. Streets were renamed for Cicero and Spartacus, and French parents named their children Lucretia, Brutus and Cato, for the greats of ancient Rome. "Am I really in Paris?" asked a sardonic visitor from Germany, Johann Heinrich Campe. "Only a few days ago these toddler Greeks and Romans all around us were French."[6]

From salon and street, the vogue penetrated the households of the new middle class. At the Paris Salon in 1775 a watercolour by Joseph-Marie Vien of a wall painting from Herculaneum was exhibited under the title, "Priestess burning incense on a tripod table". Strolling through the Salon, a French banker named Eberts saw the drawing and was captivated—not by the priestess, as Hamilton and Denon might have been, but by the simplicity of the tripod table. He arranged to have it manufactured and successfully marketed as L'Athenienne, the "Athenian Table". As a brochure promised, it was movable and could hold dinner platters, plants, flowers, goldfish, embroidery, and so on.

Napoleon shifted the paradigm of post-Revolutionary France from Arcadia to empire, from L'Athenienne to the imperial power of ancient Rome. Coupled with the French Revolutionary message of democracy, the French (and not only the French) willingly bought into this revised view of antiquity, which included its militarized grandeur. The desire to celebrate antiquity and to appear to be part of it at court and in the household quickly blossomed into the desire to *possess* antiquity. Ownership became an implicit part of its re-elaboration.

In March 1796 Napoleon led the French army into the north of Italy. The looting of Italian museums was a goal foreseen from the outset; before leaving on this first Italian campaign, Napoleon asked Paris to assign to his army "three or four noted artists to choose what's best to take." The artists were sent along with authorization to collect "all those monuments of the arts and sciences deemed worthy of our museums and libraries".[7]

Pushing down the Italian peninsula, Napoleon snatched up duchies and principalities and their classical artefacts and Renaissance works of art, trophies later displayed in museums all over France. The systematic pillage of Italian art began in the north. The first requisitioned plunder came from Elisabetta Farnese's Parma, then from Modena, Milan, Cremona, Bologna, Mantua, Verona and Venice. Everything was removed, but especially antiquities. The take was so abundant that in 1797 a French arts commission was set up specifically to evaluate the French seizures in Italy.[8]

Continuing their southward plunge, at Arezzo in Tuscany the French troops were billeted in the Church of San Francesco, where their lances left deep scars in the paintings of the fresco cycle by Piero della Francesca, *The Legend of the True Cross*. In Genoa the same soldiers seized medieval parchments—Muslim as well as Christian—which they used as torches to light their tobacco pipes.

Rome fell in mid-1796, and the pope became a prisoner of France. From the Vatican the French seized one hundred paintings, statues and other prized objects. Off to France went three large-scale and famous ancient statues: the Apollo of the Belvedere; the Laocoon group, and the Pallas of Velletri. This last, a powerful statue representing Minerva or Athena, had created a sensation throughout Europe when found in a vineyard at Velletri, the town near Rome, just three years before.

A sepia ink and watercolour sketch, dated 21 Floreal Year V (April 1798), shows the French convoy of artworks setting out for Paris.[9] With the dome of St Peter's Basilica rising in the distance, eleven covered wagons proceed due north along the Via Flaminia. To one side is the Tiber River; to the other, the great cliff of the Saxa Rubra. So heavy is the loot that each wagon-load of treasure must be drawn by ten mules.

One wagon was laden with early manuscripts, illustrated medieval parchments, and centuries-old books, together with the library's catalogue. These had all been removed from the Vatican Library, founded in the early Renaissance. Not all of it ever made its way back to Italy. The missing portions include a part of the Vatican Library catalogue.

Next step: an invasion by land of Naples.

In mid-1791, King George III had granted Hamilton's request to marry the twenty-six-year-old Emma. The newlyweds dropped by Paris en route to Naples. There, Sir William and his triumphant bride were received by Marie Antoinette. Being received by the queen of France was a social coup for Emma, but far more important, it is believed, for Marie Antoinette. The French Revolution had taken place two years before, and Marie Antoinette's purpose may have been to send her sister in Naples a letter via the Hamiltons; if so, this would have been the last letter Marie Antoinette ever sent her more fortunate sister.[10]

Marriage had given Emma legitimacy, and on returning to Naples, the second Lady Hamilton, commoner and cast-off mistress, became the confidante of Queen Maria Carolina. For the next nine years, or until the Neapolitan royals had to flee Napoleon's army, the two most famous foreign women in Naples were as thick as thieves. "We sit together two or three hours every evening", Emma gabbled in another letter to her former lover, Hamilton's nephew Greville. "Sometimes we sing". The king joined in the singing occasionally, but—as Emma said honestly—"it was bad, as he sings like a King"(!).[11]

The music was changing.

Maria Carolina found an excuse to put further distance between herself and her husband, if this were possible, when a letter surfaced proving the king's involvement with a certain notorious local woman. Now fully justified in despising her husband, Maria Carolina, a mature woman in her late thirties, assumed the reins of power, with the powerful backing of her brothers in Austria and Tuscany.

In 1788 Ferdinand's father, Charles, the kindly old king who had ruled Naples for a quarter century, died in Madrid. His death ended an era and froze the Neapolitan kingdom's relations with Spain. By the time Acton became prime minister, the Spanish connection was severed. Even then, however, few of the senior rulers of Naples were even Neapolitan, and this created simmering resentment.

Emma remained firmly at the queen's side as her closest female confidante. And behind Emma was her husband, Sir William Hamilton, representing the might of the British economy and its navy. This support was particularly important for southern Italy, strategically desirable, but also vulnerable because of its long coastline.

Not least, Maria Carolina had the support of her admiral (now her prime minister) Lord John Acton. The half-English Acton and Hamilton were almost as close as the two women. This was useful, for Hamilton's duty was to keep the Foreign Office abreast of political-military affairs, and Acton was as good a source on the state of Neapolitan defences as London could desire. The tortuous and entwined love affairs, moreover, had helped draw Britain, the ally of Naples, into an alliance with Austria for the first time in history.

As the century wound down Naples appeared the equivalent of a British colony with an Austrian accent. This could only aggravate relations with the French, Britain's sole rival in the Mediterranean. The distance was short from bedroom farce to deadly serious politics.

This was the atmosphere when a new visitor arrived: Admiral Horatio Nelson. The British fleet was fresh from its countless skirmishes with the aggressive French navy, attempting to reinforce its power in the Mediterranean. In need of reinforcements, Nelson sailed into Naples to ask the sixty-two–year-old Hamilton to persuade the Kingdom of Naples and the Two Sicilies to support the British cause with warships.

Hamilton introduced Nelson to Acton, who immediately agreed. This instant compliance freed Nelson for other pursuits. In Villa Sessa Admiral Nelson could not have ignored the thirty-four-year-old Emma had he wanted to. On stands were two sculptures of her head, and on the walls were eleven portraits of her, all commissioned by Sir William. They met at a beachfront villa furnished like a country cottage in England. Emma's affair with Nelson, who was still married, touched off a whirlwind of scandal in Britain even before she gave birth to Nelson's daughter, Horatia.

But Hamilton was not well. When Vesuvius erupted in 1794, Hamilton had hiked up to watch the event near the crater, where he had inhaled poisonous gases and collapsed. He had to be carried down the mountain on a litter. His health never recovered.

In the late 1790s, as the century which had dawned with a Europe-wide peace was hurtling toward its final violence, the love triangles of Naples therefore became on the one hand, Ferdinand and Maria Carolina and John Acton, and on the other, William and Emma and Horatio (this overlooks the hero's absent wife, of course). King Ferdinand seemed not to notice; he had his own Neapolitan mistress. As for Sir William, he limited himself to English phlegm and courtesy by feigning not to notice.

In January of 1793, a screaming, bloodthirsty mob had beheaded the king of France, Louis XVI. The shock this generated in Naples further cemented the southern Italian liaison, encouraged by Acton, with Austria and Britain pitted against the Revolutionary forces of France. Neapolitan warships sailed to join the British fleet near Toulon.

In the bloodthirsty mood of revolutionary France, this evidence of an encircling alliance endangered the interests of Marie Antoinette. The young Austrian queen had lived through the days of revolution in Paris but had been arrested, then released. But six months after beheading their king, the *citoyens* turned their wrath against her too, as symbol not only of Parisian fripperies, but also of the foreign encircling alliance thanks to her brothers—one the emperor of Austria, the other the duke of Tuscany—and her sister in Naples. All along, some in Paris believed, Marie Antoinette had been in league with Austria, Naples and—perhaps through her sister—the hated British. On 16 October 1793, she followed her husband to the guillotine.

The appalling news that her own sister had been beheaded fell on Queen Maria Carolina in Naples with the force of a bludgeon. Weeping, praying, hugging her children desperately, she vowed vengeance "to her last breath." But the risk was also to herself. Her sister's death showed that revolution could occur at home as well and overwhelm Naples. Seized by panic, the rulers of Naples—that is, Queen Maria Carolina—imposed a harsh crackdown on all those who were potentially dangerous to the crown: poets, philosophers, political free-thinkers. A tough new chief of police was appointed and, conniving with gangsters as well as Neapolitan nobles, built a vicious spy network.

Such harshness either killed outright or alienated from the Neapolitan crown the best minds of their time. The lucky were imprisoned, the unlucky were hanged in the market square. This beheading of the intelligentsia rewarded the lesser minds and the least cultivated, who carried on administration of the already overly centralized kingdom, to the further disadvantage of the tattered public weal, which included the Vesuvian sites.

All things French were evil, and the rampant anti-French sentiment took its toll upon the crown's pornographic collection. The French being libertines in sex as well as politics, in 1794 the erotica collection was for the first time severed from the rest of Pompeii's arts and artefacts and hidden away in a separate hall of the museum in Naples, Sala XVIII. Only visitors obtaining special permission could see it. Phallic objects ordinarily on view in other halls, including the belled phalluses (*tintinnabula*) meant to bring good luck, remained secreted away until after Napoleon's defeat; at that time they made a brief reappearance before being closeted once more until the doors were finally thrown open in the year 2000.

Under Napoleon's command a rag-tag revolutionary French army cut a swathe down the Italian peninsula, defeating first the armies of the independent state of Piedmont in north-west Italy and then of Austria, which ruled Venice, Milan and the rest of the north-east.

To defend the papacy and its state, Ferdinand manfully cast off his lethargy and led his troops into battle. They were briefly victorious, but soon routed. In 1796 Rome itself fell. Napoleon sauntered into the Vatican state, ordering its great treasures of antiquity transported from Rome to Paris. The pope became a prisoner of France. The Grand Tour came to an end; it would revive in a different form only after two decades had passed. Returning from defeat to

21. The wastrel Ferdinand I, son of the popular Charles III of Naples, was nine years old when he was made king and painted by Mengs. His careless sixty-five-year reign was marked by revolution, exile and scandal, and allowed countless foreigners to export Vesuvian artefacts. Prado Museum, Madrid.

Naples, Ferdinand found his kingdom in grave danger. The situation worsened with each passing day.

Sir William Hamilton saw the handwriting on the wall. Gloomily he warned London in 1798, "It needs no great penetration to foresee that in a very short time ... the Kingdom is lost".[12]

It was in these circumstances of fear, uncertainty and bloodshed that, in 1798, a booklet of the first Herculaneum papyrus scrolls to be unrolled and transcribed was published for the first time, half a century after the excitement of their discovery. *Herculanensium Voluminum Collectio Prior* brought to an end the need for visitors to pretend to have to urinate in order to make notes. One person was not there to rejoice. The previous year Padre Piaggio had died after forty years of toil on the scrolls.

Just then the French army was striding toward Naples from Rome, in a march requiring less than a week. The royal family and its greatest treasures, including Pompeian artefacts and the papyri from Herculaneum, had to be evacuated, and quickly.

Horatio Nelson directed the preparations for evacuation by British ships, with the help of a Neapolitan nobleman, Prince Francesco Caracciolo, who had become chief admiral of the royal navy when Acton became foreign minister.

All had to be arranged with the utmost stealth. The Neapolitan poor could not be expected to take kindly to the flight of their king and queen, abandoning a terrified and unarmed populace to defend themselves as best they could against the detested French invaders. Were knowledge of their evacuation plan to sweep Naples, the Neapolitans might vent their anger upon the royal family itself, which happened to include a newborn baby.

Hamilton had long since been stealthily crating his personal collection of statuary, objects and hundreds of ancient vases. It was agreed that he and Emma were to accompany the royal family on one of Nelson's boats to safety in Palermo, Sicily.

Maria Carolina and the king similarly packed up all they could in crates. This included the crown jewels, but also the Herculaneum papyri and the rest of the royal collection of hundreds of the finest (and most readily movable) statues and objects from Pompeii. Hamilton personally made an inventory of the objects removed from the royal palace and museum.

On the eve of departure a rumour swept the panicky city that the royal family were about to run for their lives. Darkness came early, and in the black evening an anxious crowd gathered outside the palace overlooking the sea. In an attempt to allay their fears King Ferdinand had to make an appearance upon the palace's first-floor balcony and pretend that all was normal.

It was 21 December 1798. A few hours after deceiving the crowd the king and his family fled on board one of Nelson's ships, which was riding at anchor at a safe distance from shore. Also on board were John Acton, along with the Austrian ambassador and dozens more from the community of foreigners who had set up in business to serve the Grand Tourist trade in Naples.

On Christmas Eve the ships set sail for Sicily. The dramatic crossing in high seas took several days before the little fleet of evacuees under Nelson's protection reached Palermo. En route one of the royal children, a boy of six, died. Maria Carolina, who had only recently given birth once more, fell into deep mourning at the death.

She roused herself on her arrival, to shower Emma with diamond jewellery for having saved all their lives. King Ferdinand gave Nelson the famous diamond-studded dress sword from Louis XIV which his father, Charles III, had carried into Naples sixty-five years before. Ferdinand's crown itself was lost during the flight to Sicily, and in later years, when a son of Ferdinand was eventually restored as monarch, he had none to wear.

A goodly number of Hamilton's pots made the trip successfully. In England two years later, when he was ill and desperately short of money, Hamilton sold the vases he had culled from the Vesuvian sites to the British Museum, where they can still be seen.

The pace of preparation for leaving Naples had been furious, but, for safekeeping, Hamilton had nevertheless loaded the vases he considered his finest aboard a second English ship, the *Colossus*, which was to carry those directly to England. But the *Colossus* sank in a storm off the Scilly Isles on 10 December 1798. Crates washed up onto a beach, but Hamilton maintained that the crates were so stoutly built that some vases must have survived. Little trace of them was reported until 1974, when some 30,000 fragments were found off Samson. They now belong to the British Museum, still reconstructing the vases on the basis of the few drawings made of them, in a giant jigsaw puzzle.[13] Most fortunately, due to confusion in assigning crated vases between the two ships, a number of his finest ancient Greek and southern Italian vases survived and were sold with the rest of his art treasures in London.

In Naples revolution followed the flight of the monarchs, and one of those plotting in secret with the revolutionaries was Vincenzo Merli, the silent and undernourished young monk who, dressed in rags, had since childhood served as the late Padre Piaggio's lone helper. All the better, then, that the papyri, at least, arrived safely in Palermo with the king and queen.

Naples fell on 2 January 1799. The monarchy which had already run away was replaced by the Parthenopean Republic. The first freely published newspaper ever circulated in the south of Italy declared that the excavations of Pompeii and Herculaneum no longer belonged to the crown. They were for the first time the property of the people of Naples.

The Grande Armée marched into Naples in early 1799. The Neapolitan royals had already scuttled off to safety in Sicily, having presumably entrusted to the early Christian martyr Janarius (San Gennaro) the destinies of their unarmed, leaderless people.

San Gennaro was then and is still now the most sentimentalized cult saint of Naples. Every year on his feast day for centuries the faithful have gathered in the cathedral Church of San Gennaro in downtown Naples, the Duomo, to watch the miracle of the liquefaction of the saint's blood kept in a phial. If the blood fails to liquefy, dreadful events are expected to ensue.

Marching into Naples, the French military leaders feared that the hostile Neapolitan clergy would somehow fiddle the blood to prevent its liquefying, which just might trigger a violent revolt against the invading army. The French commander solved the problem by holding a pistol to the priest's head until the blood liquefied. It did, obedient to a fault. San Gennaro might stop an eruption of Vesuvius, but he was not to stop the French.

During that year of liberty and fraternity in Naples, French soldiers found aid and comfort among local revolutionaries, who included a number of aristocrats, a contingent of Pompeian custodians, and Padre Piaggio's shabbily dressed, hungry, silent and underpaid assistant, Vincenzo Merlio.

In Naples the French packed up for shipment to Paris the great statue of Hercules from the Farnese collection. Fortunately, little else was seized during that brief French year, or until Napoleon's second invasion of Italy.

When the statuary from Italy arrived in France, it was displayed to Parisians in a parade which ended at the Place Vendome. From a high platform, Napoleon's Minister of the Interior, François de Neufchateau, blustered to the cheering mob that the arrival of the art treasures was appropriate. For, as he rhetorically informed the original artists and sculptors of antiquity, "*Oui*! It was for *la France* that long ago you created your masterpieces which *enfin* have found their real purpose. May you, the illustrious dead, rejoice, for at last fame is yours."[14]

Dominique-Vivant Denon also had reason to rejoice. Napoleon had appointed him as his new tsar of culture. The former chargé d'affaires at Naples, former Hamilton crony, and purveyor of classical pots from Pompeii to the French crown had outlasted the king who had befriended him. Thanks to the intervention of none other than Robespierre, Denon was appointed official engraver to the new France.

In a watercolour by the artist Benjamin Zix, Denon stands at the centre of a celebrity crowd in the Apollo Rotonda of the Louvre, presenting the plunder from Italy to *la France*.[15] The regime had changed, but the formula of promoting political power through the reflected glory of a past heritage (stolen) was the same as in the days of Lorenzo de' Medici and Elisabetta Farnese.

Zix's painting documents that the booty from Italy included a winged Venus, a muse playing a harp, a gigantic marble goddess (the Bona Dea of early Roman worship), an Athena, bas-relief panels from various Roman sarcophagi, and a kneeling figure in a finely draped Grecian gown. To the side is a gigantic, laurel-wreathed bust of a "Roman" emperor. This, at least, was new. It depicted Napoleon in his new guise.

After Italy, Egypt. In 1798 Napoleon led 400 ships bearing 44,300 men to conquer the country whose Ottoman rulers had kept it locked away from Europe for a century and a half. To entertain the troops billeted in Cairo, Napoleon ordered occasional stage performances. But instead of a Bob Hope cracking jokes, his was empire-boosting fare such as Voltaire's *La mort de Cesar—The Death of Caesar*.[16]

All was of a piece: Caesar, laurel-wreathed "Roman" bust, and an expeditionary force of scientists, artists and scholars, in emulation of Alexander the Great en route to India. They included 167 scholars, architects, draftsmen, and typographers capable of printing in the Latin, Greek and Arabic alphabets. As in the days when he worked for Saint-Non, official engraver Denon was put in charge of the squad of artists who were to record the sights and discoveries in

Egypt. Fifty years old at the outset of Napoleon's Egyptian campaign, Denon produced 150 sketches, often at risk to his life.

"Most of my drawings were made on my knees. Early on I had to make them standing up, and then on horse-back; not one was finished as I'd have desired", he later recalled.[17]

As in Italy, the French in Egypt seized those works of art which caught their fancy. Among these was the 762-kilogram black granite Rosetta Stone, found in a wall of the Rosetta fort in July 1799. Its trilingual vocabulary of equivalent words in Coptic, Greek and hieroglyphics permitted French archeologist Jean-François Champollion to decipher and read hieroglyphics, the first to do so.

Little more than a year later, England struck back. Lord Nelson defeated Napoleon in the Battle of the Nile and destroyed his fleet. He swept into Naples to celebrate with the Hamiltons. The English let go on to Paris the scientific drawings made in Egypt, including those by Denon, but kept Champollion's Rosetta Stone.

Back in Paris in late 1799, Napoleon appointed himself First Consul and created an institute of Egyptian studies. Denon was named its director. Setting to work, Denon published his illustrated journal of the Egyptian campaign, *Voyage dans la Haute e la basse Egypt*. Its much-admired sketches included one showing French scientists measuring the Sphinx. Forgetting Herculaneum, Paris gave itself over to Egyptomania.

In 1803 Napoleon appointed Denon his director-general of museums. Denon began with creation of the Musée du Louvre. In a speech in the Apollo Rotonda he lauded the requisitioned antiquities from Italy as "trophies of peace".[18]

The trophies would soon be joined by the ancient gilded bronze horses from above the entrance to the Basilica of St Mark in Venice— not coincidentally, Denon's home after leaving Naples.

CHAPTER IX

Napoleon's Family Affair

22. The French entry into Naples in 1799

In exile in Palermo, King Ferdinand claimed he was miserable. From a hunting lodge where he and his first-born son, Francesco, were staying in a bosky corner of the island, Ferdinand wrote to Maria Carolina, who had stayed behind in the comfort of a villa in Palermo:

> Everything disgusts me in Sicily. Yesterday I killed a boar in the woods at Cappellaro. But it doesn't matter, Sicilian boars are just not worth ours back home at Persano. …
>
> PS My beautiful bitch has given birth to four lively puppies. And by the way, our son Francesco has had terrible colic attacks and seemed on the point of death. The doctors are not sure they can save him.[1]

Forced to remain in the British protectorate of Sicily, a despondent
Sir William Hamilton warned the Foreign Office, in December 1799,
against "the general corruption of Naples & the infinity of defects in
Government."[2]

Hamilton, already weakened physically from having inhaled poisonous gases during the last eruption of Vesuvius, had gone into
debt. The enforced Sicilian sojourn had been expensive. He spent
liberally on his collections, but, like other diplomats of his day, this
was self-financing since he also dabbled in selling antiquities. But
the vases he had shipped to England had just gone down with the
Colossus, and setting up a new establishment in Sicily for Emma had
been costly. Perhaps too he was worn from the effort of feigning
ignorance of his wife's infidelity with the hero of the Nile—no easy
job now that she was pregnant with Horatia, her daughter by
Nelson.

One month after Hamilton wrote his despondent letter, Napoleon
was in retreat and the year of bloody revolution in Naples at an end.
In January 1800 the royals prepared to return home. Their year in
Palermo had left its mark upon all the exiles. It had made the sixty-
four-year-old Lord Acton bored with bachelordom, and of the bossy,
whining queen of Naples. He decided to marry, choosing as his
bride his cousin, a girl of thirteen. Already Acton and Maria Carolina had fallen out over politics. This was the final insult. She never
forgave him.

King Ferdinand, whom one would expect to be delighted at the
prospect of seeing Naples again, was not. In a dispatch to the Foreign Office in London of December 1799, Hamilton explained why:
at home the king could not with propriety "lead the same dissipated
life there, as formerly and He does not yet see such a military force
as He can rely on for His own personal Security. ... At Palermo his
Majesty diverts himself much the same as He did at Naples by going
from one Country House to another & shooting".[3]

The Foreign Office had its own notions of dissipated lives and
recalled Hamilton to London, after his thirty-five years of representing Britain at the court of Naples. He and Emma would never see
their homes in Naples again, never see Vesuvius or his excavation at
Nola. Nelson remained for the time being. He too would shortly
return home, where he would have to face his wife, but first he had
to settle scores with the defeated revolutionaries of Naples.

In Naples the Bourbon Restoration therefore began without Acton and without the Hamiltons. It would be brief; six years later Napoleon regained control of Naples.

Lacking Acton, the queen was truly on her own. She began with the launching of a brutal repression. Italian historians say that no one was harsher on the pro-French traitors and revolutionaries of Naples, no one more bloodthirsty, than Maria Carolina. Executions were held every Saturday in Piazza del Mercato, the market square, with beheadings for the nobles and the hangman for everyone else. The victims of the bloodbath included aristocrats like the intellectual aristocrat Eleonora Pimenthal.

Nelson captured Admiral Francesco Caracciolo, the man who had helped him arrange the court's midnight flight from Naples, for having later sided with the pro-French revolutionaries. In jail on board Nelson's ship, Caracciolo appealed to Nelson for time to bring witnesses to a trial, but Nelson turned a deaf ear. Caracciolo was hanged from the mast, his body tossed ignominiously into the Bay of Naples, where it was left to float until pious mariners buried it on the sand beach.

The French soldiers who had pillaged Rome and the north had done remarkably little harm to the archaeological treasures of Naples. The damage came from another quarter. When it became clear that Naples would fall in 1799, its art treasures, including the papyrus library, had been packed into crates with sawdust to prevent breakage and shipped to Palermo.

There they were forgotten. In the exiles' haste to return home, they left the crates behind in Sicily. There was particular anxiety for the missing papyri. Of the 1,800 charred whole and partial scrolls found in the Villa of the Papyri, just eighteen had been unrolled in the forty years of Padre Piaggio's work, and only a few more by his successor, a reportedly ineffectual Italian named Angelo Antonio Scotti.[4] Now, whoever was to pick up the pieces, first had to find the papyri.

Naples, with its wastrel king and his vindictive Austrian queen once again at the helm, was still an English protectorate, and the unrolling and reading of the Herculaneum scrolls was still eagerly awaited. The Prince of Wales (the future King George IV) stepped in, dispatching to Naples his personal chaplain, a cultivated English clergyman and calligrapher named John Hayter. Born in 1756,

Hayter had studied classics at Eton and Cambridge. Thus a new chapter began in the saga of the papyri.

The British Parliament signed a decree authorizing Hayter to hire a staff of, eventually, eleven assistants, including a number of Italians; Piaggio had worked with just one assistant. The Earl of Spencer contributed by allowing Hayter to sail as far as Genoa aboard one of the earl's cargo ships, the *Serapis*.

Three months after his arrival in Naples, Hayter was still seeking the missing papyri, which had been removed to Palermo for safety in 1799. He therefore went to Palermo, and for an irritatingly long period could find no trace. Finally the scrolls were located, still piled up on the wharves of Palermo, together with other treasures from Herculaneum and Pompeii and Renaissance paintings: "I went to the royal depots on the quay. Then to another warehouse where they were kept … We located them through Sir Arthur Paget. The court intervened, and so they came under my care." However, as Hayter then learned, in January 1802, some of the papyrus scrolls had already been returned to Naples. The cache he had found was only partial.

With the help of the new British consul who had replaced Hamilton as ambassador in Naples, these too were finally recovered. But there were new problems, as Hayter reported back to Britain:

> The ruinous expenses of a war against the common enemy have made it practically impossible for the Sovereign of the Two Sicilies, in the midst of so many problems, to have literary objectives and to dedicate [to the papyri] a part of his interest and his earnings.
>
> Indifference on all levels prevails, concerning research, the interests of knowledge and, in general, of erudition. Great treasures of ancient literature like the manuscripts of Herculaneum, even if written in classical languages, could not obtain the consideration of attention, nor even a thought.[5]

In addition, the Italians who had taken over the running of Piaggio's *macchina* saw Hayter as an interloper who earned far more than they did, and for the same work. Moreover, they claimed that the work was harder than in Piaggio's day because Piaggio had already winnowed out those in the best condition. (Those working on the papyri today in the Naples Library will confirm hearing the same objections made today.)

Hayter also clashed with the powerful new director of the Portici museum, Francesco La Vega, who had replaced Paderni.[6] Nevertheless Hayter could claim remarkable success. Thanks to the provision from England to pay eleven assistants, within five years 200 charred scrolls had been successfully opened. A painstaking and methodical Italian calligrapher monk from Messina named Arsenio Foti made a facsimile copy of each. Finally the long-awaited Herculaneum papyri could be read in earnest.

Then Napoleon returned.

Napoleon took special interest in emperors, empires and, especially, Rome. Ignorant of Winckelmann and his preachments about the serenity of Greek antiquity, Napoleon chose to emulate the grandiosity of Rome and make it his own, as can be seen in the neo-classical paintings being made by Denon's friend Jacques-Louis David. Napoleon saw himself a Roman emperor and had himself painted looking like one; he also contemplated rebuilding Paris along the model of imperial Rome.

By early 1806 Napoleon's army was on the move down Italy for the second time. It soon became clear that, after their six-year restoration in Naples, the Bourbon court would again have to scamper away to save their skins. That February the whole court, including John Hayter, fled to British Sicily for the second time.

Many years had passed since the king and queen of Naples had sat quietly by Padre Piaggio, to watch the scroll minutely unrolling and to listen to the cooing of the doves in the cote above. Their much-diminished Bourbon establishment, once more in residence in Palermo under British protection, nourished itself upon hopes that the Neapolitan population, whom they knew to be royalists in their heart of hearts, would rise in protest and overthrow the French invader. In consideration of the brutal repression for which Maria Carolina bore responsibility, that seemed unlikely.

And in fact it never happened: it fell to the Duke of Wellington to defeat Napoleon a decade later. Only Britain's victory brought about a second restoration of the Neapolitan royals. Making matters worse, the British at the naval base, who guaranteed the Bourbons' safety in Palermo, had wearied of Maria Carolina. They knew that the Austrian-born queen could never become a rallying cry to catapult the Bourbons back onto the throne of Naples.

Just as the Parisians had turned against Queen Marie Antoinette, the Neapolitans turned against her sister, Maria Carolina, whom they had come to despise. In the end it was she, not Ferdinand, who became the very "symbol of the Neapolitan monarchs' inability to keep up with the times", as a local historian has put it with some understatement.[7] However foolish (and he was), Ferdinand never quite lost his appeal to the Neapolitans. To them his misdeeds, down to his ineptitude, seemed human ones, not without charm.

William Drummond, the new English plenipotentiary who governed Sicily, quietly kicked Maria Carolina off the island. Her brother the emperor took her in. She died in Vienna, presumably of apoplexy, on 7 September 1814.

Napoleon's calling her "the only man in Naples" was perhaps the kindest assessment of poor Maria Carolina, the bride dragged kicking and screaming into the arms of a fatuous bridegroom with a big nose and a local mistress. Historians remember her as a mistress of intrigues, which included a Masonic plot, and harsh reprisals upon the revolutionaries.

This meant more than gossip. The Bourbon-Farnese dynasty would eventually be restored a third time, but her vindictiveness had left the kingdom itself intellectually weakened because its best leadership had been decapitated. Her heritage to Naples was to push it further backward in time and hence less able than ever to address its problems, including the new ones of the industrial revolution.

In any case, Ferdinand was not the only fool. Unfortunately for the progress of reading the scrolls from the ancient library of Herculaneum, in the haste to leave Naples in 1806 for the second exile, the scrolls had been left behind once more. All that Hayter had managed to bring to Palermo was a batch of Arsenio Foti's facsimile copies made from the papyrus scrolls already opened.

During all that time the Reverend John Hayter, the British king's chaplain and papyrologist lately of Cambridge, had whiled away the time. At age fifty, Hayter should have known better, but somehow he became involved in the kidnapping of the young daughter of the Baron della Tavola. To keep her from harm's way this quintessential Sicilian baron had secreted the girl in a remote convent. Perhaps in some kind of marriage-by-force plot with her brothers—a Sicilian custom which lasted into the 1950s—Hayter joined the brothers in the plot to spring her from the convent. This act of chivalry brought him an arrest on charges of abduction and seduction.

Fortunately for him, examination of the girl proved that she was still a virgin. The middle-aged Reverend Hayter dodged a prison term only by accepting lesser charges as an "accomplice" in the abduction. The English plenipotentiary Drummond, perhaps less man of the world than his predecessor Hamilton, was furious: "I suspect you had completely gone off your head … I am sick of the stories of your battles in the brothels etc. … I found it impossible to find a justification for your conduct. … You go from one muddle to another."

Drummond also claimed that Hayter had lied when he claimed unrolling 200 scrolls in four years in Sicily; they were "not even one hundred".[8] Furious with the libidinous Hayter, Drummond appropriated the facsimile copies which had already been made. He claimed them as the property of the British crown, to be sent to the Prince of Wales, Hayter's mentor. As King George IV, the prince donated them to Oxford University, where today's scholars still treasure them as Volume 9 of the Bodleian Facsimiles, thanks to Hayter's foolishness.

Buckets of rain poured down on 14 February 1806, as the French troops marched into Naples to claim it as their own for the second time. Because the British remained in control of Sicily, the First French division, this time under General Partouneaux, feared an English counter-attack. When it failed to come, Napoleon's brother Joseph arrived to take over the throne the next day.

For a decade while the vestiges of the Bourbon court sulked and stewed in Palermo, Naples and its territory would belong to France. A Bonaparte would roam the gigantic halls of the Royal Palace, enlarged and improved by Elisabetta Farnese and Charles III in honour of the Bourbon-Farnese dynasty of Italy. Napoleon now owned the world's richest sites for excavating classical antiquities: Herculaneum and Pompeii.

The late 18th century in Europe, when Napoleon first rose to power, was known as the "golden age of museums." Museums placing great art works on view had become the new cathedrals, the new temples; and in France the revolutionaries threw open the doors of the Louvre to the public for the first time. Dominique-Vivant Denon was its director.

Shortly after Joseph Bonaparte became king of the south of Italy, he ordered the crown antiquities to be placed into a great new public museum in Naples. At the time, the great archaeological treasures of the kingdom were divided: antiquities from Pompeii and Herculaneum were mostly housed in the museum at Portici (the old Villa d'Elboeuf), while the Roman portion from the Farnese bequest was in the hilltop Capodimonte palace.

With the help of a flotilla of French artists and *savants*, Joseph organized a grand new museum to show off both new and old collections. As a site he chose the old university building in the heart of Naples, today the state-owned Archaeological Museum of Naples. From afar Napoleon sent his brother Joseph useful tips on how to deal with the four million subjects of the south of Italy (the other two million of the kingdom were under British protection in Sicily). "Increase taxation. Show severity. Make examples. ... In a vanquished country it is not good to be humane."[9]

But in some ways Joseph was humane. He granted Naples its first written constitution nearly six centuries after the Magna Carta. He enacted five major economic reform bills whose provisions whittled away at the remaining privileges of the landed feudal aristocracy and of the Church.

In Spain, meanwhile, the Spanish Bourbons were ousted, exactly like their Neapolitan cousins. Napoleon summoned brother Joseph Bonaparte there in May 1808, after only two years in Naples. The empty crown of Naples passed to Napoleon's sister and his brother-in-law, Joachim Murat, the rough-hewn general who had fought beside Napoleon in countless battles. Murat was the sixth and youngest son of a small-town innkeeper. Sent to study in a seminary, he lasted three months before running away to enlist in the army, where he developed a taste for gambling, wenching, and the new cause of revolution in France.

This latter proclivity had him ousted from the loyalist army for insubordination. But when the revolutionaries won, those military men ousted from the army for revolutionary fervour returned as heroes. Rough revolutionary Murat scrambled up the ranks.

Along with Dominique-Vivant Denon, Murat accompanied Napoleon on the campaign to Egypt, where he was wounded. Ever after he continued as Napoleon's fiduciary; it was Murat who held the crown in the Church of Notre Dame, until Napoleon grabbed it and, placing it upon his own head, proclaimed himself emperor.

But that was in the future. His injury brought Murat to Paris for convalescence. There he courted Napoleon's sister Caroline, the sixth and cleverest of the seven Bonaparte siblings. In 1800 the couple wed, and Murat was given command of the French armies in Italy.

23. When Napoleon's favourite general Joachim Murat, portrayed here as a Roman hero, marched into Naples as king in 1808, his macho look and black curls captivated the street crowd. Murat and particularly his wife, Queen Marie Caroline Bonaparte, enthusiastically expanded excavations at Pompeii. Napoleonic Museum, Rome.

Murat cut a fine and manly figure when he marched into Naples on 16 September 1808. Lofty white plumes waved from his hat. He was tall and robust, bursting with animal magnetism. He had glistening black eyes and a mop of black hair whose unruly locks curled delightfully over a low forehead. Florid mutton chop whiskers heightened his macho-warrior look. To *il popolino*—the little people—crowding the streets, he might have been one of their own.

Beyond strutting about in white plumes, Murat wooed the crowds by withdrawing 26,000 ducats from the already depleted royal coffers and offering the money as an annual endowment for the Church of San Gennaro. Upon the altar he placed, in addition, a magnificently jewelled golden sunburst. Nothing could have done more to endear the Murats to Neapolitan hearts. For Murat, lique-faction was assured, without a gun. Unfortunately, Napoleon just then needed funds to finance his next war. He asked Murat for money from Naples, but the coffers were empty. On learning of Murat's generosity to the Church, Napoleon went into a rage over the waste of money on a saint.

Still, Murat was anointed king of Naples on 31 July. In his portrait for the occasion, painted by François-Pascal Gerard, he looks like a gangster dressed for a Mardi Gras ball—a peacock figure from cock-ade hat to satin slippers sporting birthday-gift bows. To woo the people, Murat had himself painted on a visit to the gigantic Hotel of the Poor, built by Charles III. Beside Murat stands his pretty young wife Caroline, a sylph in a simple, Greek-inspired *empire* white frock, on her head and shoulders a plain white shawl.

Caroline Murat was now queen of Naples. With their four small children, Achille, Letizia, Luisa and Luciano, the Murats moved into the Royal Palace in September 1808. This new chapter unfolding in her life delighted Caroline, whose pleasure in Naples appears to have been boundless. She had the children painted dancing a Nea-politan tarantella and then in individual portraits beside handsome stone urns from Pompeii. In gratitude to her emperor brother, she sent him a souvenir of Naples: a set of chessmen carved from black obsidian found on the volcano.

Writing to a woman friend in Paris in July 1810, nearly two years after her arrival in Naples, Caroline described her life:

> When I rise, I write to you and then I paint until midday, I don't know if I told you that a taste for painting has seized me. … All the time I do not spend sleeping I am on my terrace, which is truly charming … I dine there, paint there, receive my children there. … I have to sleep a lot. I've taken up the Neapolitan way of living—sleep, eat and *dolce far niente*.

The terrace where she took her sweet ease was shaded by an awning and ran the extraordinary long length of the Royal Palace. The ter-race overlooking the main port of Naples was lined with boxes of flowers, which can be seen as the background in a painting of Caro-line, in the permanent collection of the Metropolitan Museum of New York. In another painting, this by Count Jean-Baptiste Clarac

above: Pacini's seminal opera *The Last Day of Pompeii* (1825) concluded with a staged volcanic eruption. Its debut was at the San Carlo Theatre in Naples (San Carlo Theatre, Naples, engraving, circa 1820).

below: Excavation of the Temple to Isis at Pompeii in 1765 excited all Europe. In Naples in 1902 the temple became a vari-coloured marble table centrepiece (National Archaeological Museum, Naples).

A recent find at Murecine near Pompeii was this fresco depicting Calliope, muse of epic poetry. Typically she holds tablet and stylus, in an often-emulated pose (National Archaeological Museum, Naples).

George Romney painted this portrait of Emma Hart (later Lady Hamilton) in her home in Paddington, London (*Emma Hart in a Straw Hat*, 1785, oil on canvas, Huntington Library, Los Angeles).

left: Reviving a lost art, architect Nicholas Wood recreates the view from a triclinium (dining room) into the enclosed garden, or peristyle, of a fine Pompeiian town house (Nicholas Wood, London).

following pages: Russian artist Karl Briullov's terrifying vision of the destruction wrought by Vesuvius brought him, and Pompeii, enduring fame. Novelist Walter Scott watched Briullov at work in Rome, and when the painting went on view in Milan in 1833, it inspired novelist Edward Bulwer-Lytton (*Last Day of Pompeii*, 1833, oil on canvas, 4.565 x 6.51 m, State Russian Museum, St Petersburg).

An actual skeleton found by a Pompeiian gate inspired this moralising painting by Edward Poynter, often reprinted in Victorian schoolbooks. The stalwart sentry ignores the valuables under foot and dooms himself to death on duty (*Faithful Unto Death*, 1865, oil on canvas, 115 x 75.5 cm, National Museums Liverpool).

Sir Lawrence Alma-Tadema's depiction of Spring rites includes mischievous references showing that the procession is in honour of Priapus, the deity who gave fertility (*Spring*, 1895, oil on canvas, 178.4 x 80 cm, J. Paul Getty Museum, Los Angeles).

above: Workmen at Somma Vesuviana, scraping away at a wall of volcanic mud, were suddenly confronted by this uncanny marble ghost of a woman's face (University of Tokyo).

below: The team of Tokyo and Neapolitan university excavators found the statue, 1.1 m tall, still in its niche (above ladder). The palatial villa may have belonged to Caesar Augustus (University of Tokyo).

(and stolen from the home of art historian Mario Praz shortly after his death in 1982; the home is now a museum), Caroline appears seated on this same terrace, watching two of the little princes at play; Mount Vesuvius rises in the background, across the Gulf of Naples.

Caroline was also charmed by the biggest palace of all, the Reggio at Caserta which Vanvitelli had designed for Charles but which was first occupied by his son Ferdinand. Elisabetta Farnese's dream had come true, if only in part: "It is", Caroline sentenced, "the most beautiful palace one can imagine. Versailles is nothing in comparison."[10]

Now that Naples was a French possession French publications enthusiastically promoted it. J.J. Barthelemy's *Voyage en Italie* had appeared in Paris in 1801, a year after the first French occupation. Shortly before the second, Madame de Staël's extraordinarily successful novel *Corinne, où l'Italie* (1807) appeared, set in Rome, Venice and Naples. De Staël's heroine was based upon Emma Hamilton. Exactly like Emma, the fictional heroine Corinne finds inspiration in the women of antiquity; while dancing a tarantella, Corinne "recalled the dancers of Herculaneum". The character Corinne then launched other new ideas in the French arts.[11]

Ownership of the archaeological sites was the pride of the Murats, and Louis-Nicolas Lemasle painted Murat strolling regally through the House of the Diomedes at Pompeii.[12] Sons Achille and Luciano were painted at Herculaneum in 1815, with a torch-bearing guard accompanying the boys in military garb down the staircase to the Greek Theatre.[13]

In Murat's Naples the archaeological sites for the first time were thrown open to all comers. Artists and architects flocked there to paint and sketch without restrictions and, finally, to take careful measurements of the ancient buildings. The newcomers were not only French, but foreigners like Francesco Hayez of Spain, remembered today as one of the most admired painters of Naples. Some of the most evocative paintings of the Neapolitan seaside, its grottos and mysterious harmonies, date from those Napoleonic years.

At Pompeii the architects and artists were particularly taken with the vivid colours of the freshly excavated ancient wall paintings, hitherto seen only by the privileged few, and at a minuscule number of sites, such as the Domus Aurea and Hadrian's Villa in Rome. When the British returned en masse after the Napoleonic period, the followers of Robert Adam continued this discussion of the colours of ancient interiors.[14]

DETAIL DV PLAFOND

24. Architect François Mazoîs, who came to Naples during the fifteen years of French rule, made precise drawings of the ruins of Pompeii. His sharply detailed drawings, like this of a temple cornice, published by F. Didot in Paris in 1824, influenced the development of 19th-century neo-classical architecture.

The French artists at Pompeii during the Napoleonic decade were careful, accurate literalists whose watercolour drawings of the buildings and their interiors have never been surpassed. As atmospheric wear-and-tear and pollution have wiped away the originals, in many cases only the Napoleonic-era French works of art remain to show the glory of the originals seen during the newly opened excavations at Pompeii. Sometimes, of course, these were themselves copies of the lost corpus of ancient Greek painting. These French scholarship students' watercolours were so well made that their manufacture is, itself, considered a lost art—an artistic Pompeii, that is.

Exactly as it was to Elisabetta Farnese, the kingdom of Naples appeared to the Murats an opportunity to launch themselves as a new dynasty, destined to reign for evermore over the south of Italy. How then to make it appropriately grand? The road was already well trodden.

"The French sovereigns banked on culture for a total relaunching of the new Neapolitan 'nation'", according to Italian art historian Andrea Milanese, an expert on the important collection of Borgia family art and antiquities later purchased by Murat.[15] Their first steps were to organize an exhibition in Naples to introduce the findings from Pompeii to the general public and to pass the first law governing the management of the excavations. Alas, both the archaeological sites and royal palaces already appeared stripped of their treasures. To staunch the haemorrhage, the Murats took the important step of passing a law in 1807 prohibiting the export of antiquities and fine arts.

The excavations in Italy had become a Bonaparte family affair. Napoleon had shown the way in Egypt. A brother, Lucien, was excavating Etruscan tombs in central Italy. Now Caroline took charge of the excavations. As usual, the clearing of the archaeological area was under military command. Already, two theatres, three temples (one Greek, another to the Egyptian goddess Isis and the third to the Roman god of healing Aesculapius), a main entry gate to the city (today's Porta Marina), a "villa", and several important tombs had been uncovered. French General Jean Etienne Championnet launched new excavations to the left, facing the Basilica of Pompeii, near today's exit path. "She [Caroline] took a great interest in the excavations going on there and the number of workmen doubled and trebled during her stay in Naples. Many of the interesting objects dug up were used to form her own small museum", as Hortense de Beauharnais, wife of Louis Bonaparte, wrote in her autobiography.[16]

Under Caroline, François Mazois had come to live at Pompeii, where he began the illustrations for his book *Les ruines de Pompei*, the first ever written describing the city's architecture and urban plan, which he dedicated to Caroline. Deaf, Mazois had decided to become a painter and was one of the young scholarship students brought to Rome by the French government. He had met Winckelmann in Rome and came to Pompeii himself in 1808, shortly after Murat's arrival. His first sketches seem to have been made in a more or less clandestine fashion, but Caroline saw them and became his patron. Even when the French were ousted from Italy, Mazois managed to remain in Rome another sixteen years.

In the early 1830s, long after the French had been ousted from Naples, English archaeologist and member of the Society of Dilettanti, William Gell, praised Caroline Bonaparte Murat as inspiration for, as well as financial patron of, the French excavations:

> Under the particular and liberal patronage of Madame Murat (15,000 fr, we believe), in 1813 she instituted an excavation in the street which runs from the southeast angle of the Forum towards the theatre ...
>
> The walls around the city were laid bare. In Spring 1813 the greater portion of the Street of the Tombs was cleared. The Forum and Basilica were further cleared, and clearing of the great Amphitheatre had begun.[17]

Gell also lauded artist François Mazois's "splendid work of drawings of architectural details or ornaments."

The papyri, of course, had also fallen into the French heritage. In 1802, an influential French visitor, Auguste François Creuze de Lesser, toured Portici and its museum of antiquities from Herculaneum. Their condition was shocking, he related in his travel diary, published in Paris in 1806:

> What the museum shows off as the most curious but alas not the most useful thing is a conspicuous collection of rolled manuscripts, which owe to the chance of their having been burnt the privilege of still existing. ... The workers are slower still than their 'macchine.' On the other hand, they are badly paid. Thus after many years they have exhumed only two or three works which, in the height of bad luck, are absolutely unworthy. ... Perhaps new research will bring better results, but speedier.[18]

He still hoped, he said, that works by the Latin writers such as Tacitus would be found; if not, he predicted, all interest in the papyri "will be lost", a prevailing opinion. As an aside, he said snidely,

"In Naples everything one needs is not there or else is badly made".

This critical report was published in France while Murat was still there as mayor of Paris, and Caroline may have read his diary. Not long after arriving in Naples she visited the old papyrus workshop in a far wing of the Portici Museum and watched the men toiling to unroll the scrolls. She had their wages raised and also arranged for the hiring of two more apprentices. In 1809, one year after her arrival, she laid plans to publish an edition of the writings contained in the scrolls thus far unrolled.

Among the scrolls successfully opened was one of particular importance. Pherc. 817 (as it is now catalogued) happened to be the most important single text in Latin found until that time — an historical account of the Battle of Actium of 31 BC, which marked the transformation of ancient Rome from republic to empire. Caroline took the original of the scroll, which she sent to her brother; just so had Napoleon himself been transformed from consul, the Roman title he had first chosen, to emperor.

Searching for the scroll in recent years, the late dean of modern Italian scholars of the Herculaneum papyri, Marcello Gigante of Naples University, found it listed in the Naples city archives as "Papyrus n. 817 unrolled, with the original of Column VIII sent to Napoleon Bonaparte". With this scroll column Caroline sent her brother a drawing and an facsimile etching made from the original.[19]

Ferdinand had previously sent six charred and rolled Herculaneum scrolls in Greek to Paris in 1802. That gift was in fact a requisition. The French still occupied the north of Italy, and the papyri went to Paris as a pawn of the treaty that permitted the Bourbons their first return to Naples from exile. The French Academie des Sciences had attempted to figure a way of unrolling them better than Padre Piaggio's, but had failed.

Piaggio had, at least, a successor. In 1812, a boy of twelve, Carlo Malesci, the son of a skilled workman trained personally by Piaggio, entered the workshop at Portici as an apprentice. Carlo learned the craft literally at his father's knee. He would continue to work on the scrolls for the next sixty years.

While Caroline busied herself with archaeology, Murat sought acquisitions to fill the museum display cases found empty on their arrival in Naples. When King Ferdinand had fled to Sicily a second time in 1806, he had carted off fully half of the art and archaeological treasures of the Royal Museum. Some entire collections had never reappeared. To the Murats, Ferdinand's impoverishing of the museum was "barbarous".[20]

An important collection assembled by a cardinal of the Borgia family happened to have come on the market in Rome in 1804 after the death of Prince Stefano Borgia. This prestigious and expensive collection included, among other works of art, forty-eight objects of ancient erotica which had belonged to the Borgia princes. The king of Denmark sought to buy it, but his bid was refused by the pope on grounds that Denmark was a foreign power. Napoleon also reportedly toyed with the idea of purchasing the collection, a fact which may have egged on Murat.

Murat won, in an acquisition which involved politics as well as dirty pictures. His purchase of a collection celebrated for its scandalous pornography marked a change from the cultural politics of the deposed Bourbon-Farnese kings of Naples. The erotica collection of Pompeii stripped off from the rest of the archaeological treasures on view at the Portici Museum had been locked away in a special room for a decade.[21] Murat reopened it for the public. He also installed his purchases from the Borgia collection, including its erotica, in the Royal Museum in Naples in the summer of 1814.

Some of the Borgia collection erotica Murat purchased were authentic and remarkable, like a series of small stone dwarves from Ptolemaic Egypt. Seated or lying down, each dwarf is depicted holding an enormous phallus in his hands. While in Egypt with Napoleon, Denon had made drawings of several similar.[22] Others in the expensive collection are now recognized as forgeries, such as the rooster-headed herm with ithyphallus (a column topped by a torso, that is, with an erect phallus), which is being admired by a silly-looking hen and a duck. Another Murat acquisition presumed fake shows a sodomy scene involving a boy.

The Battle of Waterloo, 18 June 1815, put an end to French ownership. Caroline survived to live on in exile, but Murat, the rough-hewn French King of Naples, was captured on a Calabrian beach in October of 1815 while trying to escape from Italian royalist soldiers. The next day a firing squad shot him. His eldest son, Achille, who had been painted as a boy on the dark steps of the Greek Theatre of Herculaneum, went to the United States in 1821, became an American citizen and died in Florida in 1847.

Despite his crude appearance and cruel death, King Murat's legacy in Naples was not altogether negative. He had botanical gardens built, a museum of natural sciences and an astronomical observatory, completed in 1820. Murat also provided a grant so that a bright Neapolitan youth named Federico Zuccari could study astronomy at the more advanced Brera University in Milan. He guaranteed religious freedom and, shocking to the priests, divorce.

As a postscript, Murat had agreed to pay 50,000 ducats for the Borgia collection—a high price, and not in coin, but in mortgages on the kingdom's landholdings in the Abruzzo and in Calabria. Only 10,000 ducats had been paid when Murat was killed. Upon his return from his second exile, the restored Bourbon-Farnese monarch—King Ferdinand back again for a third round—found himself saddled with even more of the libertine pornographic items from antiquity, plus an enormous debt repaid only in 1821.

For his second restoration the newly widowed King Ferdinand returned to Naples with his children, the court, and papyrologist John Hayter. The décor of the royal palace at Capodimonte showed such marvellous improvements that young Prince Francesco supposedly exclaimed to his father Ferdinand, "If only you had been away another ten years!"

An English visitor touring the palace in 1823, the famously beautiful Marguerite, Countess of Blessington, agreed. "The residence owes all its comforts and its fascination to the excellent taste of Madame Murat, the ex-queen of Naples", she burbled. "She showed not a little taste in repairing and modifying the royal residences during her brief reign … impeccable examples of the Parisian style and luxury".[23] As the arrival of Lady Blessington shows, the British could now return. The golden age of the Grand Tour had passed, but a new class of British travellers would arrive—poets, writers, more artists and archaeologists like William Gell, able once more to visit Naples and its archaeological sites.

To celebrate his return, Ferdinand had a mammoth sculpture of himself, three times life-size, carved in white marble. An emulation of the Pallas of Velletri, which the French army had seized from the Vatican, it showed Ferdinand the Foolish in the guise of the Roman goddess Minerva, wearing her/his helmet. At Velletri decades previously, his father Charles III had successfully defended the pope from the French. The symbolism was obvious; today the mammoth statue overlooks the grand marble staircase of the Archaeological Museum of Naples. After restoration of his image, Ferdinand turned to issues of the public morality, if not his own. The ban on divorce was reimposed and would not be lifted until 1973.

In Paris, the fall of Napoleon finally brought to an end the extraordinary career of Dominique-Vivant Denon. Invited by the restored French monarch Louis XVIII to continue as director of the Louvre, Denon resigned. By the terms of the peace treaty, a briefly humble France agreed to return to Italy the antiquities and other works of art which Napoleon had looted, and which Denon had installed in the Louvre.

Restoration France kept, however, its seven papyrus scrolls from Herculaneum. In hopes that they could be read, in 1817 the French invited the now sixty-something (and presumably calmer) Reverend John Hayter to travel from Naples to Paris to give a demonstration of Padre Piaggio's famous *macchina*.

For Piaggio, a half-inch per day was the norm. But Hayter lacked Piaggio's patience. He twisted the knobs drawing the fragments taut, and twisted again, tighter still. The scroll split and then dissolved into dust. Neither the name of the text nor its author would ever be known.

In 1985, in tracing the other scrolls sent to Napoleon, Professor Gigante learned that five were still in the Louvre. Four were located, and two returned to Italy that September for unrolling via a modern technique developed by the Norwegian classicist Knut Kleve together with a fellow Norwegian who is an expert in book restorations, whom we shall meet later. Louvre inventories show that the final missing scroll is somewhere in its attic.

To date the last remaining "French" scroll has not been found. Like the missing portion of the Vatican Library catalogue, it continues to be a latter-day victim of Napoleon's wars.

CHAPTER X

A Dark and Stormy Marriage

25. The large theatre at Pompeii

Initially England's Romantic poets glorified ancient Greece, the French Revolution and Napoleon, all lumped together. When the revolution evolved into an imperial nightmare of aggression, the Romantics recoiled. Napoleon, as Wordsworth wrote plaintively in his poem "Home at Grasmere", has dashed "all Arcadian dreams,/ All golden fancies of the golden age".

During those dark Napoleonic years the British, all along the largest component of the Grand Tourists in Italy, were forced to bide their time in safety at home. But for the better part of fifteen years their passion for the Italian landscape and classical heritage had of necessity continued from afar. A young English artist named J.M.W.

Turner, inspired by Claude Lorrain's pictures of the classical landscape of Italy, with its iridescent pink-and-gold sky, longed to see
Italy but could not. In easier times a fellow student had actually
toured Naples and made drawings. Borrowing one of his friend's
sketches, Turner painted, in the manner of Lorrain, an entirely imagined dramatic view of Lago Averno, the famous lake at Naples
romantically associated with Virgil.

More ambitiously, Turner produced a splendidly large and
moody painting of Vesuvius erupting by night in 1817. He had still
not yet seen a volcano, least of all one in eruption; this too was created solely from his own imagination and a friend's sketches.[1]

The victory at Waterloo in 1815 reopened the Italian south. The
British and other foreigners began to return. Turner himself toured
Italy in 1819, to visit first Venice, then the Campania, where he
finally saw Vesuvius and painted the Gulf of Naples at sunset.

The wastrel monarch Ferdinand, King of Naples and the Two
Sicilies, could also resume ruling from the throne of Naples. It was
his third restoration, and Ferdinand sailed to Naples with obvious
reluctance; in Sicily, he said, the hunt was superior to that in Naples.
Besides, he had fewer obligations.

Home once more, Ferdinand had to contrive new amusements.
One was to send a number of the ancient charred papyrus scrolls
from the Villa of the Papyri to Britain's King George IV, in a swap for
a royal giraffe. The giraffe from England passed to the Naples zoo;
the gift of Herculaneum papyri, to a scientist in England named Sir
Humphrey Davy.

Davy knew that the calligrapher priest Father Antonio Piaggio,
who had worked for forty years in Naples, could unroll the precious, fragile scrolls a mere half inch daily. To speed up the unrolling
that would permit their being read, Davy planned a daring scientific
experiment utilizing a secret (or at least unspecified) "chemical
process". It failed when the chemicals Davy used entirely obliterated the writing on the scrolls. "It appears that the damp, having
penetrated both in ancient and modern times the ink, which was
nothing more than carbon and water, had generally disappeared
from those submitted to his process", English architect William Gell,
a new member of the Society of Dilettanti in London, wrote in somewhat apologetic terms.[2]

In 1818 Shelley became one of the earliest British visitors to see the
entire Roman forum of Pompeii, which had been only recently exca-

vated by the Italian archaeologist Michele Arditi. There Shelley found echoes of the presumed spiritual qualities of ancient Greece, still sought by the Romantics:

> This scene was what the Greeks beheld (Pompeii, you know, was a Greek city). They lived in harmony with nature; and the interstices of their incomparable columns were portals, as it were, to admit the spirit of beauty which animates this glorious universe to visit those whom it inspired. If such is Pompeii, what was Athens? ... I now understand why the Greeks were such great poets.[3]

Vesuvius was rumbling just then, Shelley recorded, a "subterranean thunder of distant deep peals [that] seemed to shake the very air and light of day, which interpenetrated our frames, with the sullen and tremendous sound". The ruckus did not disturb his picnic of dried figs, medlars, oranges and bread, which Shelley ate seated in the columned portico of the Temple to Capitoline Jove in the great public Forum at Pompeii.

Munching, Shelley also reflected, as he wrote later, that the signal "excellence of the ancients" lay in their public architecture. Here he left the Romantics behind to anticipate the coming Victorian era:

> Their private expenses were comparatively moderate; the dwelling of one of the chief senators of Pompeii is elegant indeed, and adorned with most beautiful specimens of art, but small. But their public buildings are everywhere marked by the bold and grand designs of an unsparing magnificence. ... It is wonderful to see the number and the grandeur of their public buildings.[4]

In future decades, wealthy Britain would borrow the presumed ancient Roman virtues for their own new architecture, which would transform the look of cities throughout the Western world.

This second golden age of travel to Italy was again a rite of passage, but more democratic than in the 18th century. The gentlemen still arrived, but so did travellers from other classes, including more women, and all in abundance. Writing in January of 1824, Franz Horny, an art dealer in Rome, predicted the arrival of 15,000 foreigners to Italy that year, in a boon for local artists and dealers in antiquities. As Horny wrote home to England, "He who travels has money, and they almost all desire to take home a souvenir of Italy, especially landscapes, according to their possibilities".[5]

Which landscapes? Gone were Poussin's Arcadian Greek ideal, the gilded complexities of broken column, nymph and hilltop temple; gone too Piranesi's tortured effects. For the moment grandeur and inspiring myths were still painful reminders of the Napoleonic wars. This revulsion, however, rendered the Italian landscape all the more visually interesting. Vesuvius and the Pompeian ruins were popular, but drawn and painted with more spontaneity, calm and naturalness than previously—more informally, as art historians put it. The natural scenery of the gulf, painted in an unpretentious manner, attracted visiting foreigners like the Belgian artist Gilles-François-Joseph Closson. Their drawings and oils of the ruin-scattered Italian landscape made the land itself more fashionable.

The Blue Grotto of Capri, first painted by German landscape artists in the 1830s, became a popular subject. Meantime the home-grown Neapolitan genre painters went on pandering to the revived tourism with scenery of Vesuvius and the gulf, which they depicted with masterfully shimmery effects of water.

The press of the new tourism would soon take its toll on the site. Dickens, visiting Pompeii at mid-century, created a character in *Little Dorrit* who carried home from an Italian tour souvenir "morsels of tessellated pavement from Herculaneum and Pompeii, like petrified minced veal".[6] (In 1998 a group of French tourists who had just helped themselves to similar tesserae from a mosaic at Pompeii were blocked by police.)

Even in London the members of the Society of Dilettanti were rubbing elbows with like-minded lovers of art and antiquities from different political parties and social classes.[7] Broadening their geographical reach as well, the Dilettanti scholarships for study and research were offered for Greece itself, although still ruled by the prickly Turkish Ottomans, as well as for Italy.

The single most influential of the early post-Napoleonic visitors was British artist William Gell, who was sent to Rome as the representative of the Society of Dilettanti, which had previously sent him to Greece. Visiting Naples, where he eventually bought a house, Gell reported that at Pompeii, in a famous *domus* where a skeleton had been found clutching a cache of gold coins, the guards had doused the painted walls with "frequent wettings … so as to freshen the colours for the observation of the curious". But these dousings to entertain tourists had "loosened great part of the fresco from the wall, until few traces remain for future revival".[8]

Gell's impact upon Pompeii was extraordinary. His architectural drawings of the site and his imaginary reconstructions introduced Pompeii to the English-speaking world. In addition, he introduced Edward Bulwer-Lytton to the site. Gell's tutoring taught the secrets of Pompeii to the novelist.

Born in 1777, Gell had attended Jesus College, Cambridge, before studying art at the Royal Academy of Arts in London and had been a member of the Society of Dilettanti since 1807. For the Dilettanti he had helped in the negotiations which forced Louis XVIII to return to Italy art treasures "despoiled by Napoleon", according to an official report of the Dilettanti.[9] The Dilettanti were now financing archaeological projects, and in 1812, shortly after the Elgin marbles reached London, the Dilettanti sent Gell to Greece, where a new archaeological expedition was to begin.[10] Before he left, club members warned him against the "pestilence and insurrection" in Greece and gave him a special kitty for greasing the hands of the locals.

Freeing Greece from the Ottoman Empire was a Romantic *cause celebre*, and on his arrival Gell found Lord Byron already there. Theirs was a small world, and the poet and passionate libertarian found a few words about both Gell and the Dilettanti Society in a jest:

> Of Dardan tours let dilettanti tell,
> I leave topography to classic Gell.[11]

In 1820, the architect/archaeologist Gell (now Sir William, thanks to his work in Greece) settled permanently in Italy, occupying a house with a small garden in Rome and "a beautifully situated and elegantly arranged villa" in Naples.[12] He had become the Dilettanti Society's official "minister plenipotentiary" and the de facto successor to Winckelmann and Hamilton at Pompeii. Each month Gell wrote the Society a scholarly report describing the latest archaeological discoveries—a diary also laced with gossip about the reliably colourful doings of Neapolitan high society.

Since Winckelmann, Gell noted, "no work has appeared in the English language upon the subject of [Pompeii's] domestic antiquities, except a few pages by Sir William Hamilton".[13] He remedied this rapidly. Four years after his arrival the first edition of Gell's remarkable illustrated book on Pompeii appeared, *Pompeiiana, The Topography, Edifices, and Ornaments*. It was the first scientific description of Pompeii to appear in half a century and the first in English.

Most important of all, it was available to the public, and Gell was among the first published writer/artists to benefit from this. London was the centre of the publishing industry in the West, but technology had kept print runs minuscule until 1801, when the British invented a mechanical method for making paper. It was the first change in printing since the Middle Ages, and within two years six miles of paper could be manufactured a day. The cost of paper for a book, previously twenty per cent of the total, fell to eight per cent.

More innovations followed rapidly. In 1802 the plaster mould stereotype was perfected, enabling type impressions to be used a second time. The hand-operated iron-frame press appeared in the mid-1820s, and within two years hourly print runs quadrupled. The drop in publishing costs tripled the number of print shops in Britain overnight. Copyright rules were eased, distribution systems improved, and private and public lending libraries expanded accordingly.

Crucial to Gell, and to Pompeii, the previous, antiquated technology had limited the circulation of images. Until 1800 illustrations were normally printed from copper-plate engravings, from which no more than 300 copies could be made.[14] Even scholars and students had little opportunity to visualize the ancient world.

The advance which most propelled Gell's book (and Pompeii) into broad public knowledge was the invention of the steel-plate

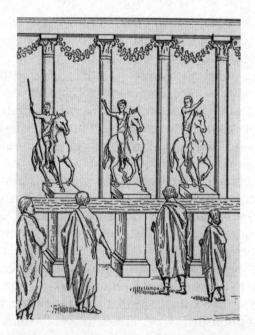

26. Pompeian citizens in the forum read an edict pinned to equestrian statue bases. Copied from a wall in the house of wealthy widow Julia Felix, the drawing, was published in New York in 1899 in Augustus Mau's *Pompeii, Its Life and Art*, which helped popularize Pompeii in the United States.

intaglio, which allows pictures to be reproduced by the thousand in exquisitely fine linear detail, with cross-hatching and stipple.[15] Gell's illustrated *Pompeiiana* could be printed and reprinted again and again, and was. In his careful text he reconstructed the history of the discoveries. His illustrations included eighty-one evocative views of Vesuvius and the ruins. He also included his own imaginary recon-structions of the interiors of houses and temples at Pompeii, and finely drawn, fold-out maps. Some of the illustrations were by archi-tect John P. Gandy, co-signer of the book, but Gell was responsible for most, which he made using a *camera lucida*, a lightbox like the one built in the 17th century by that Vesuvius enthusiast Kircher.[16] Gell's success inspired others, and reproductions of other, earlier engravings from Pompeii were rushed into print. They too became a fashion in Britain.[17]

More than elsewhere in Europe, the British public were readers, and at the time of the publishing revolution Britlish literacy was rel-atively high, including among industrial workers. By the 1830s some thirty per cent of the lower classes were considered "readers", as opposed to merely literate. As a result, during the decade after 1815 publishers marketed some forty British travel diaries, letters and guides dealing only with Italy.[18]

The new technology had also changed the content of what people read. In the Romantic decades (conventionally, 1780–1820), poetry— concise, using little paper, often politicized—was foremost. But mass production helped turn Sir Walter Scott's novel *Waverly* (1814) into a best-seller, the world's first. Followed by the equally popular *Ivanhoe* (1818) it launched the historical novel as a popular genre in English literature. Italy had always lent itself to historical drama, and so Scott toured first Rome and then Naples in 1832, the guest of none other than William Gell. Exactly like Shelley, they picnicked amid the ruins of Pompeii "at a large table spread in the Forum."

Gell had already been in Naples for five years when a Sicilian composer, Giovanni Pacini, wrote an opera called *L'Ultimo giorno di Pompei* (The Last Day of Pompei, in the singular), from a libretto by Leone Andrea Tottola, the librettist for Rossini's *La Donna del Lago*. The new Pompeii opera was first performed in 1825 at the San Carlo Theatre in Naples. It was a typically southern Italian potboiler of seduction and vendetta, but the finale brought down the house. It was the first volcanic eruption to be staged in history.[19]

A young Russian named Karl Pavlovic Briullov, studying paint-ing in Rome, was another visitor to Pompeii. Briullov was a handsome auburn-haired youth who was born in the year of the Neapolitan revolution, 1799. His father, an Italian sculptor, had emigrated to Russia, where Karl grew up and studied painting at the academy. Coming to Italy at twenty-four, Karl became one of a group of Russian artists in Rome. He almost certainly saw a performance of the Pacini opera after hearing his architect-artist brother Aleksandr's enthusiastic descriptions of touring the Naples archaeological sites in January 1826.

In the summer of 1827 a wealthy Russian countess took Briullov with her on a tour of the Italian south and then commissioned a painting from him. Exactly like the Pacini opera, it was to be called *The Last Day of Pompei*. It was not the first: in 1821 the English artist John Martin, one of Gell's collaborators, had painted a dramatic, large-scale scene of *The Destruction of Pompeii and Herculaneum* (now in the collection of the University of Manchester).

In preparation for the painting, Briullov studied the letters Pliny wrote to Tacitus describing the death of his uncle. He visited the ruins of Pompeii in 1830, where he watched the excavators at work and took advice from his brother and from a noted Italian archaeologist, Michelangelo Lanci. He prowled the corridors of the Naples Museum to study the wall paintings and other ancient artefacts.

In 1829 he had begun daubing color onto his huge canvas, but for a year he put it aside. Then he threw himself into frenzied work on it once more, becoming so fraught that his fellow Russian artists in Rome later related that they would have to go to his studio and drag the exhausted Briullov away from the canvas. In the end, the painting required five years to complete, developing from obsession to masterpiece. At one point the countess gave up hope that it would ever be finished and withdrew her financial aid. Briullov found a new patron, another Russian. Sheer size contributed to its drama; at 4.565 by 6.51 metres the painting covers an entire large wall; put another way, it is the size of an average living-room floor.

Word of the gigantic project spread, and as the painting neared completion in 1832, it became fashionable to drop by Briullov's studio to admire it. Sir Walter Scott arrived, to sit gazing at it for a full hour.

The painting was formally exhibited in Rome in 1833 and was greeted as a stunning success. Fires and lightning illuminate the desperate faces of the doomed Pompeians—and also illuminate the small cross worn by the cowled figure on the lower left corner, Briullov's invention, there having been found no trace of Christian symbol at the real Pompeii. From Rome the painting went on tour, including to Milan, before it went finally to Russia. Everywhere crowds gasped at the sight of its groups of figures, staggering as they seek escape from the inexorable horror.

The painting not only made Briullov's career, but also launched an entire school of Russian historical painting. He was now famous in Russia and abroad for his *Last Day*, to which poems were written; Nikolai Gogol called it "one of the most important events of the 19th century" in his magazine *Arabeski*. Briullov was invited to join three academies in Italy and one at home. The tsarina of Russia gave him a diamond-encrusted ring. Even today the Italian art historian Fernando Mazzocca recognizes it as "the single painting which had the most resonance in the 19th century".[20]

In Milan in 1833 a visiting English aristocrat saw and admired Briullov's painting, on exhibition in the Accademia Brera. Edward Bulwer-Lytton, writer and politician, was touring Italy with his wife while working on a book set in Italy, *Rienzi*. The tour was also intended to shore up his disastrous marriage. Seeing the painting changed his life. It was an inspiration, according to a memoir written by his son.

Lord Lytton, as the Victorians called him, was born in London in 1803. His father, a general, died when he was four, and later, from his mother, he inherited Knebworth, a Tudor estate with a rich library. This library and his Oxford-educated tutor provided him with a solid grounding in the classics. "My father wrote prose, both in Greek and Latin, with much fluency", Lytton's son recalled.[21]

Following a period in Paris, Lytton returned home and fell in love with a devastatingly beautiful woman of twenty-six, Rosina, from an old but penniless Irish family. In need of money for marriage, Lytton published under a pseudonym a satirical novel called *Pelham or the Adventures of a Gentleman*. Others followed, for an eventual total of twenty-three plays and novels, including *Paul Clifford* (1830), which famously begins, "It was a dark and stormy night".

He was intelligent: the novellist and future prime minister Benjamin Disraeli noted in his diary in 1833 that Lytton was "one of the few with whom my intellect comes into collision with benefit".[22] Despite the grand house and popularity, money was always in short supply. Lytton worked ever harder, and in 1831 he entered the House of Commons while also becoming editor of the *New Monthly Magazine* and writing a new novel, *Eugene Aram*, published in 1832. But Rosina seems to have disliked the crude sort of company encountered in politics and journalism. Their stormy relations worsened.

In 1832, Rosina and Lytton set sail for Italy on a trip intended to mend fences. In a museum in Milan, Lytton saw Briullov's enormous and striking painting showing the destruction of Pompeii in AD 79. Already ancient Rome fascinated him. This painting of Pompeii suggested a new dimension.

That winter the couple reached Naples, "beautiful, enchanting, delicious ... the only city in all Italy which is quite to my heart", as Lytton wrote to a friend.[23] Lytton spent the chilly but sunny late winter days at Pompeii in the pleasant company of William Gell

27. Touring Milan, British novelist Edward Bulwer-Lytton saw a dramatic painting of Pompeii by Russian artist Briullov. Inspired, Lytton rushed to Naples, where he began writing the evergreen best-seller *The Last Days of Pompeii*. Vesuvius contributed to the book's success by erupting in the year of its publication, 1834. Knebworth House.

(Rosina later claimed that the men had female company as well). During those weeks and months, when Mount Vesuvius wears a white shawl of snow, Gell introduced Lytton to the ruins of the houses later used as settings for his book, which he called *The Last Days of Pompeii*.

In the Temple of Isis, whose stunning wall paintings are in what is now the National Museum, Lytton imagined secret trickery found behind the altar, trickery described at length in *Last Days* but perhaps more akin to the liquefaction of the blood of San Gennaro. As had Shelley and Madame de Staël, the two Englishmen walked through the Forum, the baths, and the great public building called the Basilica. As his characters took form, Lytton chose the houses in which they lived: the newly excavated Villa of Diomed, the House of Pansa and the House of the Tragic Poet. In a tavern—and Pompeii offered a delightful choice—he imagined a scene of gladiators swilling down wine and gossiping. In the joshing, rough crowd were female gladiators whose "long and snake-like arms" he described as ill suited to hugging a man.

Rosina did not share her husband's passion for archaeology. She rather disliked Naples. Her English maid had said, "Mr. Bulwer out of contradiction seems to enjoy the bad beds and bad dinners". To this Rosina added her own comment, "I am getting quite thin upon lemonade and lamentations. Poets ought to be strangled for all the lies they have told of this country." Remaining in Naples while Lytton gave himself to archaeology, she consoled herself by dallying with a local prince.

On his return to England from Naples in early 1834 Lytton had already completed three-quarters of *Last Days*. The novel coached by Gell and written in a fury of Vesuvian inspiration and rage against his wife was published that July, to immediate success. The dedication was to Gell, not Rosina. And in fact the second honeymoon had been a failure. A separation agreement was signed in 1836.

Disraeli added his authoritative voice to the chorus of praise that November:

> You have done more than all the erudite delvers have done. We can enter the city when we choose. ... join the pugilists at the tavern, and take a look at the female Amazon with any of them. I was present at the tremendous tragedy of nature—a trembling spectator, I watched the artists till I was overcome by the phantasma, and was glad to find myself once more in the solitude of my armchair.[24]

Last Days was, after Scott's *Waverly*, the second best-selling novel the world had seen. It reaped the immense benefits of the advances in printing and distribution; the book was not only borrowed from lending libraries, but, in an economy edition, it was sold from news-stand stalls in the brand new railway stations. The public adored it, as Lytton's good friend Lady Blessington wrote on 13 October 1834:

> It is in everyone's hands. Hockham told me that "he knows of no work that has been so much called for" (I quote his words), and the other cir-culating libraries give the same report. The classical scholars have pronounced their opinion that the book is too scholarly to be popular with the common herd of readers—but the common herd, determined not to deserve this opinion, declare themselves its passionate admirers … Fonblanque told me to-day that he never heard a work so universally praised as Pompeii. … Gell will be proud of the dedication, and no wonder for it will send him direct to posterity by a railroad instead of leaving him pottering about …[25]

From Pompeii Lytton received commemorative gifts still visible in their glass case in his study at Knebworth: two skulls from the exca-vations and a wooden writing tablet with stylus.

Inspired by Briullov's painting, advised by the archaeologist Gell, Lytton had looked at the ruins and, through his craftsmanship, imagined Pompeii as if new and whole once more. On a canvas as huge as Briullov's, he peopled his historical novel with believable characters who lived in the houses Gell showed him. The novel skil-fully exploits Gell's maps and reconstruction drawings of Pompeii while offering a vivid description of the volcanic eruption worthy of Briullov. Cannily, Lytton had also incorporated the enjoyably seamy side of wanton Pompeii, cheek-by-jowl with the piety of main-stream religion. Then he added religious overtones—that cross worn in the corner of Briullov's *Last Day* painting—in which the evil of pagan priests (not Greco-Roman but Egyptian) is contrasted with Christian virtue. All races along in a breathtaking style toward a horror-movie ending that mingles self-sacrifice with Christian redemption.

Like Wedgwood's pottery and Adam's libraries, Lytton's was a carefully selective use of antiquity. The book is salted with direct quotes from the recognizable heroes of a British classical education, like Cicero and Aristotle (in case they were not recognized, Lytton identified his sources in footnotes).

The essence of the plot is that Glaucus, a kindly and cultivated Greek youth, befriends a well-born but mistreated blind slave girl who lives in a tavern and sells flowers in the street. Blind Nydia, bent over her flowers, sings like an angel. Naturally, she falls in love with Glaucus, who fails to notice her infatuation; and in any case their class differences would make their love impossible, certainly in the eyes of the British author. Well-intentioned Glaucus arranges for wretched but smart Nydia to become a servant to his well-born fiancée, Ione.

Their lives are torn apart by the machinations of Iona's improbable guardian, an evil Egyptian priest from the Temple of Isis named Arbaces, personification of that moral turpitude which will shortly destroy Pompeii through the geological action of the volcano. Arbaces's power derives from the trickery he passes off as miracles in his temple. Eventually Arbaces connives to have Glaucus condemned to die in the gladiatorial arena.

Good Christians can only whisper warnings against the bad old gods like the one Arbaces represents. As one of the Christians, Nazarene, points out to a pagan temple-goer, "Jupiter himself is a parricide and an adulterer, and you make your prayers to an adulterer! ... you worship murderers".

The eruption allows sight-challenged Nydia to save the day. It was Lytton's genius to conceive of the idea that she alone, who has always walked in darkness, can find her way through the pitch black of Pliny's darkest of dark nights and thus lead her beloved and his girlfriend to safety. Amidst atrocious destruction, crashing roofs and searing flames she locates Glaucus and cries: "Arise! Follow me! Take my hand! Glaucus, thou shalt be saved!" He is—through Nydia's death, for him. Saved too are the now Christianized slaves of mean old Arbaces, who of course dies a suitably horrible death.

This subject matter was brand new in Pompeian literature. Lytton wrote little of grandeur, nothing of philosophical studies of Greek tyrannicide. What he did write were elaborate and accurate descriptions of Pompeian housing arrangements, interwoven with detailed word pictures. Here is Lytton blowing away like a whale, describing a tavern where a fight is breaking out: "Meanwhile, the gladiators, lapped and pampered, and glutted upon blood, crowded delightedly round the combatants—their nostrils distended—their lips grinning—their eyes gloatingly fixed on the bloody throat of the one and the indented talons of the other." No one before Lytton had attempted to describe the face of a gladiator for the general reading public.

Wine, women and song are writ large. Glaucus attends a banquet where he is served, "Delicious figs, fresh herbs strewed [sic] with snow, anchovies, and eggs, were ranged [and] small cups of diluted wine sparingly mixed with honey", along with a "silver basin of perfumed water, and napkins edged with a purple fringe." In Chapter Three Glaucus and his fun-loving, wealthy and irresponsible young male friends reclining on couches talk wine-snob chatter:

> "Taste this Lesbian, my Pansa," said Sallust; "it is excellent."
>
> "It is not very old," said Glaucus, "but it has been made precocious, like ourselves, by being put to the fire:—the wine to the flames of Vulcan—we to those of his wife—to whose honour I pour this cup."
>
> "May this cup be my last, but it is the best wine I have drunk at Pompeii!"
>
> "Bring forth the amphora," said Glaucus, "and read its date and its character."
>
> The slave hastened to inform the party that the scroll fastened to the cork betokened its birth from Chios, and its age a ripe fifty years.
>
> "How deliciously the snow has cooled it!" said Pansa. "It is just enough."
>
> "It is like the experience of a man who has cooled his pleasures sufficiently to give them a double zest," exclaimed Sallust.
>
> "It is like a woman's 'No,'" said Glaucus: "it cools, but to inflame the more."

Our world-weary sophisticates carry on with more dining upon wild boar, Ambracian roast kid, oysters (the best, they remark, come from Brindisi at the heel of Italy). Then, as the musicians swing into a "wild Ionic air", come the desserts, "A variety of fruits, pistachio nuts, sweetmeats, tarts, and confectionary tortured into a thousand fantastic and airy shapes".

Such sensuality and subliminal prurience were justified by the contrast between impure pagan and pure Christian thought. The Isis parishioners are scorned as "an ignorant and sensual herd ... men reeking with all the filthiness of vice." Their description also makes them sound inviting; as the high priest Arbaces coaxes his acolyte: "I will lead thee also to pleasures of which the vulgar do not dream ... the sweet night". An acolyte makes a slip of the tongue. "By the gods—", the youth says. "What are the gods to us?" Arbaces snaps, narrowing his "serpent eye".

Heady stuff for porridge-fed, cold English schoolboys in their lines of dormitory beds with rain drumming down the windowpanes. But as his Christian counterpart warns in Chapter Thirty-three: "Tremble!—even now I prepare the hour in which thou and thy false gods shall be unveiled ... I speak from the inspiration of the True God, whose servant I am ... ere thrice the sun has dawned, thou wilt know all! Dark sorcerer, tremble, and farewell!" The Christian somehow knew the volcano would act up.

After the success of *Last Days* Lytton was made a peer in 1866; choosing the title "Baron Lytton of Knebworth", he inherited what had been the family home since 1492. He remained close politically and personally to Disraeli and friend to Charles Dickens, to whose magazine Lytton contributed a short story called "All the Year Round. A Strange Story", filled with a vein of Gothic mysticism.

As Lytton stayed close to home, *Last Days* moved abroad. It reached New York almost immediately after publication in London and Boston in 1837. American editions were published in coming decades in Philadelphia, Ithaca, Hartford, St. Louis, and Reading, Pennsylvania.

The first translation was into Italian. John Auldjo, to whom the novel *Devereux* was dedicated, arranged to have *Last Days* translated and published in Naples in 1835 and then in Milan. The Naples sales were brisk. At Pompeii, as Auldjo wrote to Lytton,

> Will it not gratify you to know that people begin to ask for Ione's house, and that there are disputes about which was Julia's room in Diomed's villa? Pompeii was truly a city of the dead; there were no fancied spirits hovering o'er its remains, but now you have made poetical its very air, you have created a new feeling in its visitors. In the dusk, wandering through the deserted streets, the rapt antiquarian startles at the rustling of the vine leaves, and fancies he sees the shade of Arbaces the Egyptian beneath the luxuriant festoons; or the peasant girl tramps her way home, singing her evening song, pictures to himself Nydia feeling her way through the Forum and singing, "Come buy my flowers."[26]

A French edition followed in 1839, with 120 copies sold. Then came Polish (1842), Dutch (1846), Danish (1856), German (1880s), Spanish (1897), and Swedish (1909). In the 1930s it reached east Europe, with Latvian, Hungarian and Czech editions appearing. And in the meantime the earlier editions in English, Italian, Danish and French continued to be reprinted.

In his imaginary restoration of the dead city to a fictive life, Lytton carried Pompeii beyond the realm of Arcadians and artists, architects and classicists and the rich Dilettanti. The city ever after belonged to anyone who could dream and gasp over a novel or thrill to the movies made from it, in any country.

Lytton had shown Pompeii as the quintessential city of love and sin—a battlefield between the virtuous and the wanton, where a volcano stepped in on behalf of the Christian God to punish evil. His powerful imaginings quickened foreign interest in Pompeii—an interest that would never lose its submerged undercurrent of the sexual, the sensual, and the Christianized, punitive volcano.

More in general, at the time when Briullov's painting and Gell's drawings were being circulated in Europe and *Last Days* was published, the ancient city was still a novelty for the general public. The British were shocked by what they saw and read. They interpreted the dead city as a metaphor for the individual trapped in calamities beyond his control, and even a reflection of the turmoil of the failed Napoleonic revolution. Other authors of the period developed a dark literature, whose themes of premature burial, natural calamity and universal extinction derived directly from the new and greater public knowledge of Pompeii, in the analysis of the perceptive American literary scholar Laurence Goldstein.[27]

These dark writings, the opera, the novel and other history novels boosted interest in Italy and its sights, from Pompeii to the source of all the trouble, Vesuvius. Overnight both became best-sellers among tourists; in 1838 the volcano attracted 7,000 visitors, an extraordinarily large number for the period.

More arrived the following year, when they travelled there via Italy's new railway, its first, which ran at the foot of Vesuvius between Naples and Portici, near Herculaneum. Its construction required a tunnel, which raised a chorus of protests from Neapolitan men fearful that in the tunnel darkness female visitors risked undesired attentions.

The larger interests of tourism prevailed. The tunnel remained.

CHAPTER XI

Rebels in the Ruins

28. Painting of a carpenter's workshop

During their decade of dominion over the kingdom of Naples, the French fostered what was an extraordinary novelty: an orderly, logical approach to the excavations of Pompeii. Credit for this goes not only to Murat, but to the able Italian, Michele Arditi, whom he appointed director of antiquities.

Without Arditi, English archaeologist William Gell would have had little to go on for his topographical drawings of Pompeii. Without Arditi, Lytton would not have had the houses whose descriptions captivated readers of *The Last Days of Pompei*. And without Arditi, Shelley would have had no picnic in the civil forum, for before Arditi it had never been excavated.

At Pompeii Arditi also brought to light temples, two theatres, a section of aqueduct and a 400-yard stretch of road lined with funeral monuments just outside the Herculaneum gate. This immense amount of work provided the broadest vision of the city seen to that time.[1]

In a discovery which went on to captivate millions, just outside the Pompeian gate facing Herculaneum Arditi's workmen came upon a skeleton in full armour—a sentry who had remained at his post even in the face of certain death. Hearing about that finding made an enormous impression upon Lytton, whose fictive lovers see the Herculaneum Gate sentry as they try to escape:

The lightning flashed over his livid face and polished helmet, but his stern features were composed even in their awe! He remained erect and motionless at his post. ... There he stood, amidst the crashing elements: he had not received the permission to desert his station and escape.

The sentry faithful at his post became a prototypical hero, celebrated down to our own day, as we shall see.

Ferdinand I, the King of Naples and the Two Sicilies, had been less heroic. He had cut and run from Napoleon twice, leaving an unarmed populace to fare as best they could. But Murat's execution on a Calabrian beach in 1815 had restored Ferdinand to the throne for the third time.

Neither hard times nor two seasons in exile had improved the scatter-brained monarch. Ferdinand had been back in Naples barely five years when a serious political revolt broke out. In consideration of the harsh repression after the 1799 revolution in Naples, the rebels showed great courage.

The rebellion of 1820 was organized by conspirators who came to be called "Carbonari" (charcoal makers) because their network was reputed so clandestine that they could only live deep in a forest, like true charcoal makers. The rebels demanded a constitution. Ferdinand refused. The revolt was put down brutally, bringing peace, if only momentarily.

When Ferdinand died in 1825, he was succeeded by his dull and pious son, Francis I, who reigned only five years before he too died. This brought Francis's young son to the throne in 1830 as Ferdinand II. In the north of Europe peace and prosperity had returned, and the economy there was expanding. Nearing mid-century the great cities of the north, especially in Britain, were hives of industry and bold public works. Indeed, more public buildings were under construction in Europe than ever previously in history. Among all these London held the record.

But the south of Italy remained stubbornly semi-feudal and agrarian. The southern aristocrats went on living from rents collected from ever poorer tenant farmers. After 1840 the hunger and poverty of the countryside were again swelling the numbers of people living in Naples without finding work. Capital investment was minimal, and even north Italians spoke with concern about "the southern question". The growing political resentment would shortly translate into violent political rebellion, including in the south.

Archaeologist Michele Arditi died in 1838, and the court at Naples lost interest in the excavations at Pompeii, save as a convenient source of prestigious gifts to bestow upon fellow sovereigns.

For over two decades Pompeii would otherwise be left largely to itself, a poaching-ground for both rough brigands who still dwelled upon the slopes of Mount Vesuvius, and for courtly dealers of antiquities who resided in Naples and Florence.

Cultural and teaching institutions faltered. Those intellectual revolutionaries who had escaped the hangman's noose in the market square of Naples in 1799 and 1820—the men and women who might have ensured an enlightened management of the kingdom's heritage—had long since fled abroad. In their stead a benighted bureaucracy gave full play to its arrogant ignorance.

All this took its toll upon Pompeii. There being no central plan, as the workmen proceeded digging now here, now there, they dredged up ton upon ton of volcanic debris, which they left in scattered heaps on the site. More excavating meant more and bigger mounds of debris, interrupted by an occasional excavated patch. The presence

29. In the middle of the 19th century, French artist Alfred Guesdon soared above Pompeii in a hot-air balloon to draw the ruins, with the Greek theatre in the foreground. Engravings like this by J. Jacottet, based on Guesdon's drawing, helped attract thousands of middle-class foreign tourists. Pompeii no longer belonged to the elite.

of these rubbish hills compromised future excavations, for before
any orderly digging of the site could begin, they had to be removed.

In fairness, as the historian of Italian archaeology Marcello Barbanera points out, the concept of large-scale archaeology did not yet
exist. The German school of archaeology was relatively more
advanced, but it had yet to excavate the sanctuary at Olympia in
Greece and the cities of Pergamon and Troy. Indeed, although under
Napoleon some systematic excavations had been conducted in
Rome, until Mussolini's day even the Forum area remained largely
buried beneath medieval and Renaissance buildings.

And yet Naples showed some small stirrings of change, particularly in the arts. Under the old regime, a candidate desiring entry
into the Naples fine arts institute was given specifications on how to
draw or paint a certain rock, down to the most tedious detail. This
system efficiently winnowed out the gifted and imaginative.

But as Europe skidded toward 1848, the brighter young artists of
Naples invented their own new ways of depicting their world. They
rejected the shimmering, magical landscape style learned from
Hackert, which they scorned as folkloric, in favour of a less ethereal
and more realistic depiction of the countryside—its farm cottages,
country views and ordinary people in the narrow streets and fields.[2]

Their small rebellion was echoed in politics. In the late 1840s, or at
about the same time that the British were buying cheap industrial-
era copies of *The Last Days of Pompeii* at railway station book stalls, a
cell of Carbonari revolutionaries began meeting stealthily in the
ruins of Pompeii.

Their leader was a brilliant youth from the Puglia region of southern Italy named Giuseppe Fiorelli. The man who would become the
most important archaeologist in the second flowering of Pompeian
excavations was the son of an army sergeant. In his teens Fiorelli
earned his living collecting bills for a manufacturer of asphalt. A
family friend was a scholar specializing in the study of antique
coins. He became Fiorelli's mentor, and at twenty Fiorelli published
his own monograph on the subject. The book gave him immediate
recognition as an archaeological prodigy, and he was hired for a
low-paying and lonely scholarly post at Pompeii.

Fiorelli was a child of his times, and he dreamed of unification of
an Italy freed of all foreign dominion. Many of the custodians'
fathers had fought in the revolution of 1799. Meeting them secretly
in the temples of Pompeii, young Fiorelli organized an armed Carbonari cell of anti-royalist custodians. They signed a pledge which

described themselves as "accustomed to a taciturn life amidst the squalid left-overs of people who had disappeared from the earth eighteen centuries ago". Inspired by the faithful soldier at the gate, the custodians of Pompeii were preparing for battle.

> Shortly twenty men will have the training to load two cannons and aim them at the destruction of the enemies of the fatherland ... in the shadow of that soldier left to guard the Herculaneum Gate of this city, who was found dead at his post, having put honour before life.[3]

In this revolutionary cell Fiorelli was not alone. Francesco De Sanctis, director of the excavations since 1845, openly favoured unification of Italy, or *Il Risorgimento* (the word means "Resurgence"). In a pamphlet De Sanctis linked the ancient Italian heritage to nationalism for the first time, by declaring that "the study of the ancient glories of the Greeks, the Latins and the Italians demonstrates a love of nation".[4] Subsequent Risorgimento leaders would seize upon this presumed link.

Insurrections began in 1848, and in Italy alone nearly 2,000 died. This, the third rebellion since 1799, also failed. Fiorelli and De Sanctis were both sent to prison. Behind bars, the twenty-four-year-old Fiorelli passed the time by transcribing ancient inscriptions from Pompeii. The custodians spirited into his cell daily progress reports and sketches of the ongoing excavations, which he recorded meticulously in a diary. When he was released from prison ten months later, Fiorelli found a typographer willing to print his prison diary of Pompeian archaeology, the *Giornale degli Scavi*.

When the scholars of the Naples Academy heard about the forthcoming publication, they furiously reasserted their right to be the sole source entitled to issue reports on Pompeii. They reminded the king's police that Fiorelli was a notorious rebel, who had armed and trained the site's custodians against the ruling monarchy. Any archaeological reports he wrote would be politically tendentious. The police agreed. For the second time they broke into the rooms where Fiorelli was correcting proofs, which they seized and destroyed. Fiorelli was fired from his job at Pompeii.

As luck would have it, these terrible final years of a dying regime—years of prison, hunger, and terror for Fiorelli—were unexpectedly relieved by a quirky stroke of luck. It happened that the brother of the king was a count from Siracusa named Leopold. A free-thinking playboy and patron of the arts, and himself a frustrated artist, Leopold maintained his own lively court in the deep south of Italy. Archaeology was fashionable, and Leopold longed to open his own excavations at a promising site, Cuma. To do so he required the services of an archaeologist. Overlooking Fiorelli's spell in prison, Leopold hired him.

With an elegant young widow from England, who was touring Italy after a stay in Greece, Leopold cooked up a hoax designed to test Fiorelli at Cuma. The pranksters buried a souvenir ancient marble panel which the woman had bought in Greece, then had it excavated as if newly found.

> The digging began, and everyone was in a circle watching the excavators, when one announced he had found something. He pulled out the piece of marble. "Call Fiorelli," they all cried in chorus. Fiorelli came. He carefully examined the marble panel and said immediately, "But this could not have come from here—it's Greek."[5]

Fiorelli won the day—and more admiration from his new mentor, Leopold.

In 1846, while Fiorelli was plotting at Pompeii with the custodians, a new pope was elected, taking the name Pius IX. A journalist trumpeted the news: "A new era opens for Italy ... He will be Rome's fortune". But the very next year the revolutionaries laid siege to the Quirinal Palace, which housed at the time the pope and administrative offices. Fleeing Rome, Pius IX took refuge in the Kingdom of Naples and the Two Sicilies, in a grim fortress castle at the port of Gaeta, on the sea just inside the northern border. Ferdinand II and his family rushed to greet him on his arrival there the night of 11 November 1848.

The troubles continued, and Ferdinand was obliged to find quarters more appropriate for the papal party than a military fort. The choice fell on the Royal Palace at Granatello (the *Reggia*) at Portici, just south of Naples. Suites were renovated and furniture borrowed from other scattered royal palaces.

Ships carried the pope and his considerable staff to Portici on 4 September 1849. There he took up occupancy of six sumptuously appointed rooms overlooking the sea. The pope's brother, Count Maffai, occupied another six-room suite while three cardinals each had a room. The largest hall was outfitted with a throne for papal audiences. A carpenter knocked together twenty-four white chairs with gilt decorations and dozens of other pieces of furniture, as Reggia records show, down to the prices.

The pontiff's Neapolitan sojourn was brightened in October 1849 by a visit to Pompeii. By then one-third of the site had been excavated, or twenty-two hectares, albeit never yet systematically. As is recorded in the pontifical diary, *Diario della venuta e del soggiorno in Napoli di Sua Beatitudine Pio IX.P.M*, the pope reached the little Pompeii railway station at 8:30 in the morning, accompanied by dozens of Neapolitan nobles, Swiss guards in high uniform, and his private chef, the *scalco segreto*.[12]

To protect him, 1,000 men were mustered. They included the war veteran custodians still employed at Pompeii in this pre-Fiorelli era and a host of soldiers, who formed a tight ring which entirely encircled the excavation site. To save His Holiness from a long walk in the ruins, a cart was at the ready. This cart had presented problems. Within the walls the ancient roads are paved with giant slabs of volcanic rock, with high stepping-stones at crossings so that the Pompeians of Pliny's day could avoid stepping into muck and mud. All ancient Pompeian deliveries thus had to be made by the company holding the cart monopoly; only officially calibrated cartwheels could pass through notches cut into the stepping stones. To make sure that the papal cartwheels would pass, along his route the ancient stepping-stone blocks were simply removed. They were never replaced.

Like any tourist, the pontiff visited temples, houses and tombs. He paused to study the "stupendous mosaic showing the Battle of Alexander and Darius" (then still *in situ*, and today the showpiece of the Archaeological Museum at Naples). In the tradition of Pompeii he took a seat to watch the excavators at work. Predictably, as usual, the workmen dug among the lapillae from which popped up thrilling and marvellous discoveries (the prank Leopold and his English girlfriend had played on Fiorelli comes to mind). These gleanings were given to the pope for the Vatican collection of pagan objects. The pope's last stop at Pompeii was the famous gladiatorial amphitheatre, filled with local Catholics shouting "Viva il Papa! Viva il Re!"

There is a slightly sour echo. Several days later Pius IX visited Herculaneum, where he was offered more antiquities as souvenirs. However, no records were kept to indicate which objects came from which excavation, Pompeii or Herculaneum (not to mention the specific room or house), and so all but the most general provenance was lost.

Better housekeeping records were kept. When the papal party returned to Rome after a year in Naples, a careful list was made showing a dismaying quantity of broken crockery and other damages, "the effect of use during the long stay of the Very Holy Pontiff and his suite".[13] Everything from beds to wool blankets and chairs needed mending, the housekeepers complained.

Broken beds were the least of it. Such was the crescendo of political chaos in the Holy City, as elsewhere in the various Italian statelets, that in 1850, when Pius IX called the customary quarter-century Holy Jubilee year, he then had to suffer the humiliation of cancelling it. As time passed, Pius IX, who had been elected as a man with liberal views, turned more conservative and defensive. From this period of the final thrust for unification of Italy date his proclamations of the dogma of the Immaculate Conception (1854) and then of papal infallibility (1859).

The pope's host in Naples was Ferdinand II, who is described by Neapolitan historian Antonio Ghirelli as "picturesque but behind the times". In 1857 the king suffered a bayonet wound in an assassination attempt. Two years later he died from the injury.[14]

Succeeding him was his twenty-two-year-old son, consecrated as Francis II before the bones of San Gennaro in the Cathedral in Naples. It was perhaps ominous that this Francis could technically have no coronation. When his great-great-grandfather Ferdinand had fled Naples for Sicily for the second time back in 1806, the crown had somehow been lost at sea.

On the eve of the breach of the walls of Rome in 1870, Pius IX made a last-ditch propaganda effort to show the world that he was still in control. The new regime was trumpeting propaganda about its ties to the glories of ancient imperial Rome. By way of a reply the pope arranged a firework display atop the Pincio—that hillside rebuilt by architect Valadier during the Napoleonic era. In a brave attempt to show the continuing primacy of Catholicism, the fireworks burst into a gorgeous pyramid of multi-coloured lights showing six continents in a political hierarchy of authority. On the lowest and presumably most primitive level were Oceania, Africa and America. Asia, Egypt and the Middle East (conveniently considered a continent) occupied the middle ground. Then came Europe, which included the by then decade-old Risorgimento Italy. Atop the whole, as a reminder, was Saint Peter gloriously in his throne.

Brilliant and loud as they were, the fireworks were a last gasp. There was no resisting the unification of Italy. The papacy lost its immense properties stretching across central Italy. Its physical territory, which had stretched from sea to sea, shrank to less than one square mile.

Despite the failure in 1848 to unify Italy, the Risorgimento had remained a *cause célèbre* throughout Europe, celebrated by Romantics in paintings, literature and music. And then it happened. On 7 September 1860, Garibaldi triumphantly chugged into Naples. The hero of the Two Worlds entered the kingdom by train.

It was, for the Bourbon-Farnesi, the end of the line. Francis II, the fifth and last Bourbon-Farnese to be King of Naples and the Two Sicilies, lasted a mere two years (1859–60). Revolution swept Naples for the third and last time. Again the king of Naples had to run away to Rome, to become the guest of Pius IX.

On 22 September 1870, Italian troops burst through the walls of Rome. The French garrison protecting the pope fled. The monarch of united Italy was Victor Emanuel I, from the northern region of Piedmont. As if overnight Italy was cobbled together from disparate and formerly rival political entities: the kingdoms of Naples, Sardinia, Piedmont, and Tuscany; the duchy of Parma and Piacenza; the former Austrian holdings in the Veneto and Lombardy, and all but a patch of the former Vatican territories.

In the first unification of 1860 Turin and then Florence had been the capital. With 1870, glorious Rome could become the definitive capital of the new Italy. But not all the patriots wanted it. Arguments raged. The Eternal City was magnificent but hopelessly run-down and backward. The Roman Forum was still called Campo Vaccino— Cow Field. Great monuments lay half buried. Within its walls Rome was sparsely populated, so rural that the eminent German archaeologist Theodor Mommsen once lost his way among the orchards. Rebuilding, reviving, renovating would be costly, when money was already in short supply.

Moral reconstruction promised to be equally difficult. Some of the new political leaders believed that Rome, with its population of 500,000, was too southern, too lacking in the dynamism desirable for a modern nation. They despised the Roman underbelly of indulgences and cut-throat Curia appointees, its ignorant *popolino*, abject beggars, pickpockets and vendors of rosary beads.

Little indicated that relations between Church and State would soon heal. During the decade before Rome fell, the new regime had seized immense lands and buildings belonging to the Church. Understandably, the pontiff snubbed the government's offer of a peace treaty, preferring to remain a visible prisoner of Italy until his death in 1878; his successors continued to refuse a peace treaty with

Italy, negotiated only under Mussolini. How could two such enemies share the same capital?

Conversely some of the patriots feared that nothing the new Italy
had to offer could compete in Rome with the Church, with its centuries of splendour and coherently lofty mission unlinked to any new
idea of "nation". In a famous exchange Mommsen asked a prominent politician of the new Italy, Quintino Sella, "Just what do you
intend to do with Rome? One cannot be in Rome without having
cosmopolitan goals".[6]

In the end Rome was chosen. The patriots lay claim on behalf of
the entire country to the Roman heritage of grandeur and ancestral
glory, which they hoped would help to consolidate the infant state
as well as to counter the might of the Church. Mazzini promised a
"Third Rome", after those of Empire and Renaissance. It was, as an
Italian historian has put it, " an ideological shortcut."[7]

The addition of the Vatican territories in 1870 had brought a host
of other knotty problems. The fledgling government found itself
deeply in debt, in part because the sovereigns in Piedmont had over-
spent while Turin was capital. What funds existed went for priority
goals like education and aid to farmers. The already minuscule portion spent on the new nation's cultural heritage was actually
decreased. And of just what was that "cultural heritage" composed?
No one knew, for no catalogue existed. Nevertheless, for Naples,
unification brought improvements. Local intellectuals, previously
unable to obtain university posts because they lacked aristocratic
friends at court, could finally apply for them and win. Experimenta-
tion took place in the arts. Paintings and, now, photographs of the
Neapolitan landscape lightened in style and spirit. Neapolitan artists and musicians formed a mutual aid society that organized
exhibitions and performances, previously possible only after court
recommendations. As in the egalitarian year of 1968, no be-ribboned
official handed out prizes. Everyone was a winner, everyone equal.

Fiorelli was reinstated at Pompeii. Curbing the clandestine sales
of antiquities was difficult everywhere, and especially at Pompeii
because in the past the kings of Naples had dispensed custodian
jobs to homeless war veterans. Many, Fiorelli noted, were notorious
drunkards.[8] By night the old soldiers on the site told stories, boozed
and snoozed, while the brigands living on Mount Vesuvius ven-
tured downhill in the moonlight to help themselves to the pickings
of Pompeii. Fiorelli had the veterans fired and hired new men,
ordered to be more professional, and even to wear uniforms. This

professionalism was put to the test when an attractive foreign female tourist stood at sunset admiring a temple, and a custodian paid her unwanted attentions. Informed, Fiorelli ordered the custodian stripped of his uniform and forced to run the gamut of being kicked by the other assembled guards, one by one.[9]

In his first large-scale methodical excavating, Fiorelli opened 20,000 square metres in three *regioni* (as the sections of Pompeii were named). For the first time visitors could follow streets, and this enriched their experience of the past. Fiorelli excavated entire important houses, like the sprawling, finely decorated mansion called the House of the Vetti—still one of Pompeii's most popular buildings—located in previously unexplored areas. Insisting upon careful excavation, mapping and drawings, Fiorelli became the first since Domenico Fontana to try to protect the area under excavation from the devastation of careless workers' picks and shovels. He also had a miniature railway built, as in a mine, to cart away the old hills of rubble.

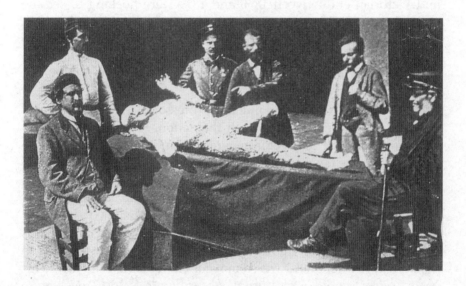

30. Giuseppe Fiorelli (seated left) devised the method of pumping plaster into cavities left in hardened pyroclastic matter by decayed organisms, revealing the shape of a body. Following Italian unification in 1870, the former hothead revolutionary became the director of Pompeian excavations and a national hero.

In 1853 an excavator at Herculaneum had dug up animal skeletons, and noted that they were inside husks that revealed traces of the shape of a decomposed animal. Finding one such half-hollow, Fiorelli had plaster poured inside it. The daily diary accounts relate that his helpers were stunned at the result when the hardened ash husk acted as a matrix for a plaster casting.

When a hollow was found containing a human skeleton, Fiorelli had plaster pumped inside the husk. Cracked open, the matrix revealed a casting of a body captured in the throes of death. Shortly, several dozen figures were cast—a mother clutching her child, a man raised on his elbow in a last gasp. The effect was horrific.

Until that moment, death and the macabre had been conveniently off stage and left to the imagination. Now the people who had died in the violence of the volcano had become visible and recognizable in their extreme agony. The castings (and eventually 1,700 such skeletons were found) shrank the distance between the deep past and today.

The castings also quickened the general public's interest in the macabre aspects of Pompeii. Already, the English middle class of the mid-Victorian era between 1855 and 1879 were flocking to see the more ghoulish of Madame Tussaud's wax figure exhibits in London. Fiorelli's agonized plaster figures from Pompeii coincided with both that vogue and with the birth of middle-class tourism, while offering, moreover, not waxen but real death.

After 1860, Fiorelli was appointed a Professor of Archaeology, and Pompeii was declared property of the nation. Henceforth it would be administered by a director-general of antiquities, who would be appointed in the new capital. The first was a Frenchman, the novelist Alexandre Dumas *père*. Dumas had followed Garibaldi's Sicilian campaign as a journalist, and in 1860 Garibaldi personally appointed him to direct Pompeii. Dumas envisioned a second French season at Pompeii and jumped in with enthusiasm, but was not appreciated by the new Neapolitan establishment (it included the hothead Fiorelli) and was removed. He remained in Naples for years, trying to open a restaurant. According to Ralph Trevelyan in his short and delightful history of the early Pompeian excavations, Dumas's main contribution to Pompeii was to catalogue the 206 pieces of erotica in the Gabinetto Segreto.[10]

The following year Professor Fiorelli took charge. Within months he had 500 workmen excavating Pompeii. Yesterday's terrorist revolutionary was today's national hero, and the same scholarly academy which had engineered the loss of his old job at Pompeii hastily elected him a member. In a lack of gratitude the feisty archaeologist dissolved the academy and started up his own.

In fighting a shooting war against the Catholic Church, the Risorgimento army had seized by force all but a postage stamp of Vatican territories. The fledgling unified state now had to build, from scratch, national civic pride and to cast off the old local loyalties to the eight former states as well as the cultural shackles of the Church. The leaders of the new Italy cut no slack in their ideology of anti-clericalism, and they began a desperate search for cultural symbols which could unify Italy spiritually.

In the end, they decided that only the lost Roman Empire could offer a secular model capable of contrasting the wonders wrought by Christian Rome. A first result was the government's passing of a law in 1873 which permitted the expropriation of churches and monasteries, including when necessary for archaeological excavations. This was in Fiorelli's mind when, in 1866—before full unification, that is—he created a new public museum of the history of Naples inside an old monastery, the Certosa di San Martino.[11]

When Fiorelli inaugurated a new archaeological site near Naples in 1872, the new King Vittorio Emanuele I was on hand with several cabinet ministers who were all photographed wielding shovels.[15] The message was simple: to dig Pompeii was to build Italy. Patriot Fiorelli was Italy's most revered archaeologist by then, a folk hero whose marble bust was placed in the Great Hall of the library at Naples in 1874.

The following year Fiorelli was summoned to Rome as protector of the antiquities for the entire new nation because, as a former director of excavations at Pompeii, Stefano De Caro, put it, "The new government needed to create new heroes who could at the grass roots level symbolize the cultural values of the young nation".[16]

Fiorelli was replaced at Pompeii by Michele Ruggiero. The two, Fiorelli and Ruggiero, had worked together there for thirty years. Ruggiero, too, was innovative, and under his direction conservation of the monuments—some now open to the elements for over a century—became a goal for the first time; Fiorelli's goal had been to demonstrate the whole urban structure, but he had never restored any of the buildings, some by then visibly deteriorated after being open to the sky for so long. Ruggiero had the stones used in restorations cut diversely from those *in situ*, to distinguish them from the original. Where water infiltrations were disintegrating painted walls, he taught restorers to detach a decaying fresco, bind it upon a solid backing inside a frame, and replace it in its original position on a wall so as to conserve it. Ruggiero also supervised such important excavations as the House of the Centennial (so-named to commemorate the 18th centennial of the destruction of Pompeii) and the House of the Silver Wedding Anniversary (this patriotically to honour the anniversary of King Umberto I and his wife, Margherita).[17]

One of the first cultural projects of the new state was to organize a touring exhibition of artefacts from ancient Pompeii. Fiorelli had remained a rebel at heart and objected that the security arrangements were inadequate. Unless they were improved, he said, he would go back to work as a money collector. "Our job is to protect our treasures, not watch them be destroyed", he thundered.[18]

In the general war between secular Risorgimento Italy and the Church, Pompeii became embroiled in a minor skirmish. In 1872 a young southern Italian named Bartolo Longo who had studied law at the University of Naples found a job managing an estate adjacent to the Pompeian excavations "without pay", as Catholic Church literature about Longo relates. This large holding belonged to a widow from Naples who had many children. Eventually the two married.

During his many trips to Pompeii on her behalf, Longo could not have failed to notice the countless visitors attracted to the pagan site by its arts, its pornography, the brothel, the bodies caught in the agony of death, the temples and the marble statues erected to perverse gods. Meditating upon this while collecting rents on behalf of his mature and wealthy bride, Longo realized that the pagan world was a wicked attraction which the local peasants living on their scattered tenant farms needed to combat. He set out to do something about it. And what better way than by saying the rosary? He organized a prayer group.

Longo had not always been so pious. Indeed, like Houdini and Arthur Conan Doyle, he had been for a time deeply involved in occultism; some suspected him of having witnessed black masses and such. To make himself more alert to the occult spirits he had once fasted to the point of grave intestinal illness—so says the Church literature—as the tangible result of his lack of faith.

But eventually the young lawyer saw the light and confessed his sins. As a born-again Catholic he vowed to propagate the saying of the daily rosary in the vicinity of ancient Pompeii in thanks for his salvation. To this end he acquired a painting on wood of the Madonna, bought in Naples off a cart. Next step: a fund-raising campaign among the local peasantry for building a chapel in which the rosary would be recited.

The folk-art Madonna was displayed for veneration in the modest new chapel in 1875. News arrived as a thunderbolt shortly afterward that the new Madonna of Pompeii had performed a miracle. Other miracles followed in short order. The chapel became a church, the purveyors of the objects of belief and worship set up stalls, the hostel keepers set up beds, and the modern town of Pompei (with one "i") was born.

The next stage was to connect the new Shrine of the Madonna of Pompei by train to the same Naples–Portici–Sorrento line which carried the visitors to the pagan excavations. This was accomplished even as the miracles multiplied. The Madonna acquired a crown of diamonds and a host of other precious jewels, given in thanks for prayers which had been granted. The dimensions of the expanding shrine reflected its growing importance among the faithful. It acquired a tall spire, a giant dome, and long passageways whose floors were paved with fine, polished marble. Hotels and restaurants sprang up.

Today its vast corridors are lined with votive paintings and drawings in crayon, paint and pencil, from a host of nations. One from New York City shows the beneficiary, seated in a crudely drawn automobile, and wearing a Goodfellas hat with a brim. An unseen machine gun pelts the car with bullets like hailstones, but the author of this sketch is seen unscathed, thanks to the Madonna of Pompei.

In a corner of this immense, domed shrine stand two obviously ancient columns, trophies from pagan Pompeii although their provenance is unmarked. (Columns from the Greek Theatre of Herculaneum also stand in the Naples Cathedral, incidentally.) It is a commonplace to say that the pagan columns in these places of Christian worship are reminders that ancient and modern worship, pagan and Christian, have coexisted in Naples for 1,800 years or so. They still do. In antiquity legends abounded of bleeding and/or sweating statues; today, Naples still offers the annual liquefaction of the blood of San Gennaro in the glass phial. Napoleon's generals had threatened it, and Pius IX had kissed it.

To return to the founder of the shrine, the lawyer Bartolo Longo made a good living running it. But such success eventually strained relations between Longo and the Vatican. As a Pompeian journalist told me, "The Church warned they would excommunicate him if he did not turn the shrine over to them". It is at least a fact that during Longo's lifetime the shrine, built on land tilled by the tenant farmers of Longo's wife, was transferred to the Vatican and is today properly known as the "Pontifical Sanctuary of Pompei".

By then the shrine's mammoth building complex had expanded to rival St Peter's Basilica in size. Every summer 30,000 worshippers walk there, in a pilgrims' procession stretching nearly two miles. And every year some two million of the faithful come there to pray—roughly the same number as visit the pagan site next door.

Bartolo Longo died in 1926. Not long afterward the greatest miracle of all took place. The Church in Rome formally beatified Longo, a first step toward his being proclaimed a saint. The house he built for himself at Pompei, a short walk from the excavations, was made a museum, the tiniest in the town he created from nothing, so bustling that it now boasts a McDonald's.

Even as the Italian Church fought for its primacy and existence in the post-Risorgimento state, the brave new world of entrepreneurial go-getting was being built in an industrial strip surrounding Milan and Turin. By the 1920s this was Europe's single largest concentration of industrial workers. But as the century came to an end, the government in Rome became embroiled in grave financial scandal. The Vesuvian excavations kept pace.

At Pompeii in 1894, the work of excavating was farmed out to private businessmen for the first time. A local contractor named Vincenzo De Prisco won the bid to excavate an important villa which had belonged to Publius Fannius Synistor at Boscoreale, a few miles from Pompeii. While excavating there for six years De Prisco unearthed a fabulous trove of over one hundred pieces of silver tableware and finely crafted banquet items. De Prisco seized it for himself and sold it to the Rothschild banking family for immense personal profit. (Today, the trove is in the Louvre.)

At the dawn of the 20th century a new scandal broke in the wake of the long archaeological campaign by another private contractor, Gennaro Matrone, in search of the lost port of ancient Pompeii. He never found the port, but during three years of excavations (1899–1901) numerous artefacts which had been found simply disappeared.

Long after 1870 the new state had remained splintered by incompletely welded and sometimes rival systems of justice, education and police. Different approaches and radically diverse laws had continued to apply to antiquities, their protection and ownership, in a legal bungle that facilitated archaeological theft. In addition, Italy's older and richer territories with long experience in managing art and archaeological properties, like Florence and Rome, had relatively advanced and sophisticated laws. Those with lesser heritage had developed fewer legal tools. Bringing the heritage laws into a unified whole proved neither quick nor easy.

Indeed, for a time unification actually eased the exporting of ancient treasures. Old and restrictive export laws applied in the more sophisticated territories, but elsewhere laws were lax. Dealers in strict territories simply shipped the artefacts to the lax, and from there they were easily exported abroad.[20]

Trying to halt this, between 1870 and 1900 the new central government debated seven different national laws aimed at limiting archaeological exports. Parliament could agree on none, and so the scattering of the Italian archaeological heritage continued.[21] But in the end the loss of the so-called Treasure of Boscoreale was such a galling setback for Pompeian and Italian archaeology that it spurred adoption of protective legislation, Italy's first, in 1909.[22] From that time on its antiquities would at last belong formally to the Italian nation.

As the end of the 19th century approached, Pompeii was no longer the city whose arts, statues and dirty pictures had been the playground and province of Europe's rarefied elite. The Italian and foreign visitors to Naples now came by steamship and railway. In 1880 a two-car funicular was inaugurated to sweep visitors to the summit of Mount Vesuvius, where they could peek into the crater and then recover over tea and sweet pastries stuffed with orange-flower flavoured ricotta.

To connect the funicular to the already ageing Naples–Portici line, a trunk line was built, incorporating a difficult, expensive, and steep cogwheel stretch. To popularize it and bring in revenue, Neapolitan songwriters Peppino Turco and Luigi Denzo were commissioned to write the song *Funiculì funiculà*. The first Neapolitan pop song to become a hit worldwide, it was played so often that German composer Richard Strauss, mistaking it for a traditional Neapolitan melody, worked it into a symphony.

The flux of middle-class tourists to ancient Pompeii had continued unabated. In the details of existence and in the hollows of hardened ash cast in plaster the tourists read the life and the death of ancient Pompeii, generally overlooked by the Grand Tourists and

31. Italy's first train line linked Naples and Portici, and brought foreign visitors like Mark Twain to Pompeii. After 1880, visitors were also whisked up the volcano by a funicular, publicized with postcards and a specially commissioned song, *Funiculì funiculà*.

collectors of the previous century. To the new generations of visitors Pompeii had become a person, a dog, a horse, a wooden door, a tool, the roots of vines and rose bushes.

Winckelmann's Pompeii had become Everyman's.

CHAPTER XII

Victorians in Togas

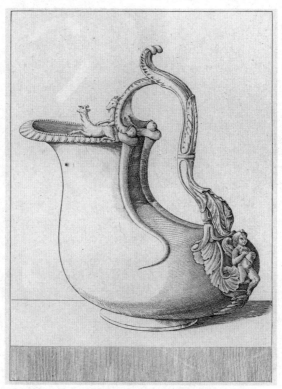

32. Engraving of a Pompeian milk jug

On the day *The Last Days of Pompeii* was published in 1834, author Edward Bulwer-Lytton was in Ireland. Fearing the fierce critics, he wrote to his friend Benjamin Disraeli, the politician, in London. "Tell me what you, your father, sister and mother think of it", Lytton pleaded. "I am no judge, but fear it won't please the women. They don't appreciate artful plots, and artful management."

He need not have worried. His artful concoction offered something for everyone, from sumptuous foods to sacrificial love. No sooner had his anglicized literary ghosts of Pompeii appeared on a printed page than they were household presences. Because the British publishing industry dominated the Victorian world, the novel broadcast its peculiarly British view of ancient Roman culture worldwide, first in English and then in dozens of translations. For the entire century to come the novel was read from Russia to America. Even after the novel wore thin, as if breeding spirit clones, his Pompeian themes recurred again and again in new forms, new technologies, affecting even Pompeii itself.

Until 1815 French domination of Italy had kept Pompeii out of bounds for fifteen years. Architect William Gell's pictures and his friend Lytton's novel were therefore for most people their first introduction to Pompeii and ancient Rome since Gibbon half a century before. All things French, including the libertine tradition left from the French 18th century, were rejected. Returning at last to Pompeii, the early Victorians found its overt pornography deeply offensive. Touring Pompeii in the 1840s, the famously starchy history don Thomas Arnold of Oxford deplored the dead city as worse than even what one would see in the ruins of Sodom and Gomorrah.[1]

Other early Victorians were enthralled at rediscovery of the extent and amazing variety of pornographic artefacts and images of which daily life at Pompeii was composed. Some rejected it, but other Victorians obsessively collected Pompeian erotica. They bought the shocking *objets*, which they kept tucked nicely away in a "secret" museum accessible only to well-born and wealthy males. In emulation, secret museums "were created all over Europe", such as L'Enfer in Paris and even the Private Case at the British Library in London.[2] All women were excluded. Lytton, however, had carefully ignored the explicit pornography of Pompeii. His blind heroine was captured by the evil Egyptian priest, but no one explained what had happened to her in captivity, even though in Pompeii or in the Secret Cabinet in Naples (not yet closed to the public), Gell and Lytton, strolling for weeks on end, had seen ithyphallic objects and obscene sculptures.

Only in an erotic subtext in his Chapter Ten does Lytton allude to them, however—but then he calls them "magnificent debauches". We then learn that the blind slave girl Nydia, whom we are told is a virgin, risks becoming a part of the debauchery. Nydia begs the rough tavern keeper who is her master not to send her to "*that unholy place ... those horrible feasts ...*", I shall call a policeman, she threatens. Don't even try, the tavern keeper retorts, or we shall take you there, "gagged". Eventually we learn that the orgiastic goings-on did not involve the pagan Romans or pagan Greeks, but—worse still, it is implied—priests of Isis.

Elsewhere, over a cup of wine, the devious Egyptian priest Arbaces rattles on about the forthcoming "whole nights of those magnificent debauches", which will offer a "snug carousal".[3] Lytton himself comments, after describing lovely Nydia selling her flowers and singing, "The ancient Italians were like the modern, there was nothing they would not sell, much less a poor blind girl".

Dastardly Arbaces seizes his ward, who happens to be Glaucus's fiancée. The girl faints. The mad, evil Egyptian priest carries her away, gloating:

> The law that gave me the person of my ward gives me the possession of my bride. Far across the broad main will we sweep on our search after novel luxuries and inexperienced pleasures. Cheered by my star, supported by the omens of my soul, we will penetrate to those vast and glorious worlds ...

"Possession", "bride", "novel luxuries", "inexperienced pleasures" (inexperienced for the bride, that is), and "penetrate"—this adolescent pipe dream, transposed to acceptable antiquity, contributed to the novel's enduring popularity in Victorian Britain. If Lytton's description of the volcano's eruption was written in a fit of fury reflecting Lytton's rage at the crisis of his marriage, much of the rest was by and for the student living in an all-male institution, with little occasion to see women, and none for a good meal.

The hypocritical moralizing of the Victorian world was beginning, and Lytton's *Last Days* would become a testimony to and component of it—universal and lasting. In 1871 Charles Haddon Spurgeon, one of the most popular of English preachers (his sermons drew thousands of listeners), visited Pompeii. He was in his forties and was profoundly shocked. Ever after in his sermons, which are still read today in the US Bible Belt as models, he utilized Pompeii as a proof of God's wrath against sinners.

Lytton's novel of 1834 also flowed into the Victorian passion for antiquity, a reflection of the aggressive politics of the age. Britain became more grand during the reign of Victoria (1837–1901), and the queen was transmogrified to empress—formally of India alone, but in reality, of the great new empire. Exactly as in Napoleonic France, the earlier passion for the arts and ideas of Greece veered toward Rome. Ancient Roman grandeur became the model, and Roman symbolism was subsumed into the British national spirit as its own.[4]

Like their peers of the previous century, Britain's architects had routinely studied in Rome, but their neo-classical architectural canon differed from what had gone before. The Victorian world desired majesty and grandeur on display, in enlarged versions of Roman temple and basilica. It was not simply that more space was needed for more office workers; quite literally the power brokers of Victorian architecture demanded a gigantic, Romanized stage setting that would exalt its builders. Even their exclusive clubhouses lining London's Pall Mall boulevard were given handsome neo-classical facades and atria.

The Victorians' rapturous adoption of imperial Rome showed in a host of other ways besides architecture: in their collections of antiquities, in their school curricula and in their paintings with themes from ancient history. Indoors, temple facades rose atop bookcases and sideboards. Sofas assumed the shape of Roman chaises. Chairs were puffed out in comparison with the Louis XIV style, their bulk marching in step with the massive scale of the architecture.

On the other hand, Lytton had also replaced the Grand Tour by being the first to transport Roman antiquity from intellectual passport for a rarefied elite to entertainment for an enlarged middle class, whose literacy and leisure time took benefit from both the industrial revolution and the spread of literacy enabled by Protestant Bible-reading. Thanks to Lytton, anyone of any walk of life could know Rome, no longer a fiefdom of the century-old club of snobbish Grand Tourists, the Society of Dilettanti.

The second element which helped keep the novel a favourite for over a century was its Christian message. In the plot of the book written in 1834, Christians are fed to the lions in the Pompeii amphitheatre. Following this is a happy ending of Christian redemption while Vesuvius roasts the pagans alive—just what they deserve for their appalling customs (this presumes that everyone knew that the pornography was there even if not everyone could see it).

The inspirational Christian message was pure fabrication on Lytton's part. The reason that no Christian reference was ever found

33. In the 19th century, Pompeian rooms were a rage for garden pavilions and dining rooms. Young Queen Victoria had toured Pompeii, and, to please her, in 1844 Albert had architect L. Gruner design this one (now over-painted) for Buckingham Palace. Buckingham Palace archives.

with certainty at Pompeii or any other Vesuvian site was simply because the eruption of AD 79 preceded the spread of Christianity in Roman southern Italy by 200 years. Nor were Christians or even the misbehaving pagans fed to lions at Pompeii; its amphitheatre lacked the subterranean facilities, found in the Colosseum in Rome, required for keeping lions. In short, Lytton introduced a false Christian message which sanitized Pompeii even as he fostered its reputation as Sodom and Gomorrah.

Such was its success that less than a year after the novel's publication, an adaptation by John Baldwin Buckstone was already presented at the Adelphi Theatre in London in December 1834 and another by Fitzball at the Royal Victoria Theatre in January 1835.[5] This was followed in 1858 by an Italian opera adaptation which made its debut at La Scala in Milan, with lyrics by Giovanni Peruzzini and music by Errico Petrella. Its title was for one of Lytton's characters, *Jone, o L'ultimo giorno di Pompei* (Ione, or The Last Day of Pompeii). Toward the end of the century English composer George Fox also attempted a new operatic version of *Last Days*, this one named for another of the novel's heroines, *Nydia the Blind Girl of Pompeii*, first performed in 1892. In America, too, Lytton's character Nydia, the self-sacrificing martyr, became a popular figure. Particularly during and after the Civil War, Nydia was presented as exemplary in US newspapers, which lauded selfless women who joined their men at war.

In 1855, on the eve of that war, American sculptor Randolph Rogers, who had come to live in Rome in 1848, carved a highly polished white marble statue of Nydia, 145 centimetres tall, (now in the collection of the Metropolitan Museum of Art). In the book Nydia saves her friends because only she can lead them to safety in the post-eruption blackness, and so Rogers portrayed Nydia leaning on a stick and with a hand clapped to her ear to listen.

Before this, Rogers, like Briullov, was unknown; afterward he was a celebrity. The statue became so popular that Rogers's workshop at Piazza Barberini in Rome produced fifty-two copies in two different sizes, which sold for the remarkable sums of either $2,000 or $800.[6] Americans were now touring Italy, and the workshop was an obligatory stop on their tours, even though Rogers himself apparently worked only in clay, leaving his Italian workmen the job of marble carving.

Similarly, Italian sculptor Giuseppe Moretti (1857–1935), who was born in Siena but went to the United States in 1888, sculpted a life-size bronze statue entitled *Nydia, the Blind Girl of Pompeii*. The statue, which seems to have stood in the statehouse of Alabama, is lost, but a drawing of it was found in Moretti's scrapbook in Alabama. Moretti, incidentally, the creator of war memorial monuments in various American cities, created the biggest iron statue the US had seen at that time, a fifty-six-feet tall, six-ton neo-classical Vulcan, god of the fire and of the forge, which was forged in Pittsburgh for the Chicago World's Fair.

Lytton's second character to acquire an existence independent of the novel was the stalwart soldier in ancient Roman armour, found at his sentry post in AD 79, ignoring the fires and boulders from Vesuvius raining down upon him. Aside from the novel, the faithful sentry was introduced to Americans by Mark Twain, who visited Pompeii in 1869 and described the site in *The Innocents Abroad*. Twain had scrambled up Mount Vesuvius to peer into the mouth of the volcano and wandered the alleys of Naples, whose folk cults of the Madonna and San Gennaro he found disgusting. At Pompeii, indifferent to the arts and artifices of the ancient Romans, he complained at stumbling on the large paving stones and cracked jokes about the skeletons that leave most visitors pensive; in the analysis of Professor Laurence Goldstein of the University of Michigan, Twain's devaluing of Pompeii by facetious humour made his readers laugh away the dead city, and with it, "all the magical importance that European writers from Winckelmann to Gautier had attributed to it".[7]

His debunking ended at the sentry, however, whom Twain called "that grand figure of a Roman soldier." Pompeii offers no finer moment than consideration of the sentry's example, he wrote: "We never read of Pompeii but we think of that soldier; we cannot write of Pompeii without the natural impulse to grant to him the mention he so well deserves. Let us remember that he was a soldier." By then, even the custodians at Pompeii knew the story of the stalwart soldier—not from archaeologists, but from Lytton's novel, translated as *Gli ultimi giorni di Pompei*. As they accompanied awe-struck visitors around the site, the custodians related Lytton's version.[8]

In Britain the sentry's inspirational role was exalted in a painting of 1865 by Sir Edward Poynter, who was Edward Burne-Jones's brother-in-law. For decades afterward *Faithful unto Death* was routinely included in British school textbooks as moral inspiration for the future leaders and administrators of the empire. Dark-skinned savages, the textbook picture showed, are about to massacre you, but you too will stand firm at your gate in the mud forts of India and Afghanistan. To the British Establishment of his time, Poynter's painting offered an ideal of masculine Stoicism, which countered the trend toward "creeping modern effeminacy".[9]

The Victorian architects built a fantasy Rome; the artists showed what happened there. Poynter, the artist of *Faithful unto Death*, belonged to a group known as the Greco-Roman school. Many of their highly realistic paintings are imagined extrapolations of daily life, based upon the vestiges of houses they saw at Pompeii and in the Naples Museum, and only there.

Initially the foremost artist of the group was Frederick Leighton, whom the young Poynter met while the two studied painting in Rome; both would become presidents of the Royal Academy and as such extremely influential. In their time these artists skilfully played on the ambitions of the late-Victorians, whose powerful leaders enjoyed seeing themselves in the superior frame of Greco-Roman

34. Up to ten thousand Londoners turned out every Sunday to hear British clergyman Charles H. Spurgeon preach. After touring Pompeii in 1872, he made the association of God's wrath and the doomed city a theme for some of his writings and impassioned sermons, still studied today. Spurgeon Archive.

antiquity. Their very Britishness, incorporating Rome, gave the
movement a nationalistic undertone parallel to the neo-classical
architecture of the time; and indeed this somewhat innocent and
ingenuous genre ended with the shock of World War I, although one
of their number, John William Godward, was still working in the
1920s.

The Greco-Roman school of artists painted in the bold colours of a
bold age. Gone were the Poussin-style classicized paintings,
inspired by the Roman countryside, with their tiny nymphs or
pagan priests in the foreground and, in the background, a romantic
temple poised against golden-pink sky. The Victorian Greco-Roman
artists had moved south, and a constant of their paintings are the
views of the shore and Bay of Naples, with brilliant cobalt waters,
transparent periwinkle sky and gaudy flowers; the isle of Capri
floats recognizable in the distance.

Sherlock Holmes explained why the British adopted the new colour palette: London was grime. "Stand at the window here. Was
ever such a dreary, dismal, unprofitable world? See how the yellow
fog swirls down the street and drifts across the dun-coloured
houses."[10]

The Greco-Roman painters' typical emphasis on technical virtuos-
ity was at least partly fostered by the arrival of that new accessory to
diary and sketchbook, the portable camera. Back in 1848 the Reverend George Wilson Bridge of England had photographed the
amphitheatre at Pompeii; for the first time in history the Bay of
Naples and ruins of Pompeii could be seen as they were, without a
painterly diaphragm. The photographs of Pompeii's ruins, Vesuvius

35. Pompeii was a favourite subject for early photographers. But most photographs, including those for stereoscopic viewing in parlours, showed
glorified views, unlike this rare early scene of sheep grazing in almost abandoned ruins.

36. Neapolitan-born artist Domenico Morelli was Italy's foremost in the
school of Greco-Roman history painters. Like Alma-Tadema, Morelli painted,
with near-photographic accuracy, lissome lasses in the archaeologically correct Stabian baths of Pompeii. Alinari Archives.

in the background, were then viewed in magic-lantern shows in the intimacy of darkened Victorian parlours.

Taking the new technology in their stride, the artists working in the classical genre incorporated photography as an aid. Not coincidentally, at a time when the Impressionists were experimenting with the gauzy effects of light, the works of the neo-classicists became more literal than ever, as if they were trying to out-do the photographers in both colour and detail.

The most famous and successful artist of the Greco-Roman school was Sir Lawrence Alma-Tadema (1836–1912), who followed Leighton and Poynter by a generation and made use of photography as a tool for archaeological paintings inspired by Pompeii. Alma-Tadema was obviously influenced by Leighton and company, but, more than them, he is esteemed as a precursor of the pre-Raphaelite painters. In his day his works sold for such high prices that he had emulators in Italy, France and Poland, where his most famous disciple was Henryck Siemiradzki. In Britain, the outstanding John William Waterhouse produced similarly Greco-Roman inspired paintings that put life and breath into antiquity. Waterhouse was born in Rome of English parents and moved to Britain, but such charming and tender paintings as his *In the Peristyle* (1874) and *Household Gods* (1880) were inspired by Pompeii.

In addition, a separate school of Alma-Tadema forgeries developed, some of high quality. A particularly accomplished and prolific forger (probably English) is known only as the "Master of 338". Alma-Tadema carefully numbered his opus with Latin numerals, but his painting CCCXXXVIII was rumoured lost, and the famous forger—whom some have identified as Arthur Hill—always signed with that number.

Born in Holland, Alma-Tadema was thoroughly schooled in classical languages and literature before becoming an artist. In the 1850s he moved to Antwerp, where he moved in a circle of archaeologists who included Georg Ebers, a noted German Egyptologist. Their friendship inspired Alma-Tadema to begin painting scenes from ancient Egypt. The shift toward the Greco-Roman world began in 1862, when, at age twenty-six, Alma-Tadema went to London to see the great International Exhibition, where the star attraction was the Parthenon Marbles purchased by the state from Lord Elgin. Shortly afterward he moved permanently to England.

Like so many of his predecessors, Alma-Tadema moved to Italy for a two-year stay in 1876. A tour of Pompeii, the city that was both

Roman and Greek, revolutionized the themes of his paintings. For decades afterward Alma-Tadema spent his winters painting in his London studio and summered in Naples. He was such an assiduous visitor that the Neapolitan Royal Academy of Art made him an honorary professor. Beavering away in Naples and in the halls of its Archaeological Museum, he studied sea, sky and the fountains, statues, tables, beds and vases discovered underground at Herculaneum, Stabiae and Pompeii, before returning to paint them in drab London. In addition, striving for authenticity, Alma-Tadema assembled a personal collection of 5,300 photographs of ancient monuments and archaeological artefacts, mostly from Pompeii.

Like Bulwer-Lytton, Alma-Tadema showed the lives of Pompeians of all walks of life. His Pompeians play music, recline on picturesque balconies against the sea, and loll about the public baths in archaeologically correct settings. His *In the Tepidarium* replicates the same hall of the Stabian Baths at Pompeii, whose colours had earlier inspired architect Robert Adam. In specific homage to Lytton, he painted two of the characters in the novel *Last Days of Pompeii, Glaucus and Nydia* (1867).

The near-photographic reality that was a hallmark of his finished oil paintings left his customers gasping with admiration, while drawing sneers from a few of his contemporaries. John Ruskin in Venice described a group of Alma-Tadema warriors carrying shields as "beetles looking for a rat". But what matter? For both smog and the era's constipated morality, Alma-Tadema offered the remedy of a fugue into an ancient Pompeian reverie of clear skies and flower-bedecked balconies, where gorgeous women (always young) flirt in the dishabille of Roman draperies.

Alma-Tadema's exquisitely recreated marble surfaces in particular sent his well-heeled customers over the moon with delight. Sir William Armstrong, having seen Alma-Tadema's *An Audience at Agrippa's*, asked for a similar picture. Alma-Tadema offered him an indoor scene of girls lounging in a room with typically Pompeian red walls. Armstrong rejected it; it had no marble. Alma-Tadema then decided to reverse a procession scene he had already painted intentionally showing only the backs of the toga-clad Romans. That way, "Marble will remain the main subject", he said, not without sarcasm.[11] It was Sir Lawrence now, for he had become a Knight of the British Empire, but as *Punch* commented, his KBE of 1899 should have been a KCMB, for Knight of the Cool Marble Bath.

In his salad days in Rome, Alma-Tadema had painted a girl, supposedly of ancient Rome. She was shown as if posing for a sculptor,
who was carving her in marble as the goddess Venus. The nude
model for the statue is shown full frontal view. The painting was
exhibited in England in 1877, shocking a bishop. "For a living artist
to exhibit a life-size, life-like, almost photographic representation of
a beautiful naked woman strikes my inartistic mind as somewhat if
not very mischievous", the bishop declared.[12]

Alma-Tadema remained mischievous, but took greater care
about it. His carefully dosed antiquity suited both Victorian lust
and the era's overt desire for decorum. Lounging at the edge of a
cold white marble tub, or languidly reclining on a bench with brilliant sky behind and a lover passing a note, Alma-Tadema's young
women wore bee-stung lips and flimsy robes that dipped to reveal
a nice show of plumply bare breast. His staple paintings of the
Pompeian bathhouse frolic dodged the copulations, group sex and
other erotica which he and every other Victorian male visitor had
seen on the mosaic floors and walls of the real bathhouses of
ancient Pompeii.

His sanitized antiquity held special appeal to American collectors;
nearly a third of his sales were to the United States. In general,
American collectors avoided authentic Pompeian artefacts. The
American railroad and banking tycoons who had amassed great fortunes were just then building important private collections and
endowing public museums. They spent fortunes buying Italian
antiquities and art, as Bernard Berenson's sales from Florence show,
but they specifically avoided acquiring objects from the real Pompeii, whose erotic statues and dirty pictures they considered
boudoir fare, down-market and frivolous.

As the director of the Whitney Museum of New York, Maxwell
Anderson, has explained, "A new nation bent on acceptance abroad
could ill afford to fill its salons with any but the noblest traditions of
the West. Rome, with its majestic public monuments and grand traditions, served the cause far better".[13] Acquiring Pompeian objects,
therefore, would have been subversive, undermining national pride.

The Alma-Tadema painting called *Spring* (1895), today in the collection of the John Paul Getty Museum, illustrates American taste in
the era. In the painting, women and children play lyres and dance
down a Roman street against a background of lush flowers and classical buildings faced with, naturally, pristine marble. The painting is
"exquisitely beautiful", said a contemporary review in the *Magazine*

of Art, specifically because in it Alma-Tadema had avoided "excessive merriment, drinking and lascivious games; all is perfectly respectable ...". That critic failed to notice the many clues in the painting which linked the procession to Priapic rites.

During the 1890s Alma-Tadema, who was more than any other artist identified with Pompeii, had actually come under criticism for his alleged failing to denounce in his paintings the depravity of the ancients.[14] More recent critics ignore his concealed sexual content, but see duplicity in Alma-Tadema's use of antiquity to describe his own era "in fancy dress". For all their photographic realism, said one British critic, his paintings arguably show that which does *not* exist and therefore are themselves a "skilful forgery" in a *tableau vivant* of an elaborately restored Pompeii.[15]

The real *tableaux vivants* of stories from antiquity still existed as a popular vaudeville staple. In 1906 a great beauty named Pansy "La Milo" Montague arrived in London from Australia to present her *tableaux* of elegant "silent and static representations of ancient statues." Pansy's performances evoked Emma Hamilton in her Attitudes, but Emma had been dead a century and times had changed. A critic for a women's journal panned poor Pansy for her "cold, white statues, for all the world like the statues that people neglect every day of their lives when they pass the National Gallery".[16]

Last Days, persisted, however, adapted for a summer fireworks event in 1888, a "pyrodrama", directed by James Pain, Jr. The storyline of *Last Days* was already well known, and the actors galloped through a simplified version with, in the background, a full orchestra playing and a grand finale of fireworks standing in for the volcano. After being tried out by the East River in New York, this imposing spectacle was performed in the park at Alexandra Palace on Muswell Hill in north London (where, incidentally, the world's first public television service was launched in 1936). Its last performance was inside the Crystal Palace in Sydenham, south London, in 1919.[17]

Europe's travelling circuses, legitimate heirs to the gladiatorial spectacles of ancient Rome, had been producing historical spectacles like the act called "The Lion-tamer of Pompeii" since as far back as the 18th Century. In 1889, the year after the pyrodrama, P.T. Barnum presented *Nero or the Destruction of Rome* at the Olympia Theatre in London, "a grandiosely realistic spectacle, classic, romantic ...".[18] The characters included, besides Nero, his tutor Seneca and his mother Agrippina. Many Italian musicians, architects, and directors worked on the production.

But let us cut to the chase. Act V of *Nero* starts timidly with a "Stupendous scene of Nero's Orgy", proceeding in a crescendo to "Grand Bacchanalia", "Stupendous dances", and "The burning of Rome", a theatrical precursor of the volcano's destruction of Pompeii. The happy ending brings a "Glorious vision of the dawn of Christianity in which angelic forms rise and descend taking to Heaven the souls of the victims".

But times and tastes were changing. In 1913, as World War I approached, the critic of the *Sun* newspaper in London dismissed Alma-Tadema as "the most ridiculed painter of the 19th Century".[19] Today his reputation, like Lytton's, has been restored, unlike Pansy's pageantry, which remained a failure because, as we shall see, better had arrived in cinema—historical statues that moved.

Even views of Pompeian eros had changed to become a positive virtue in a seminal and startling novella written in 1903 by a noted German author, Wilhelm Jensen, *Gradiva: ein Pompejanisches Phantasiestuck* (Gradiva, a Pompeian Fantasy Tale). The story intrigued Freud, who discussed it an article of 1907, "Delusions and Dreams in Jensen's *Gradiva*".[20]

The story tells of an ascetic young German archaeologist who has become so absorbed in antiquity that he has lost touch with real life. While touring Rome to admire its classical antiquities, he sees an ancient marble carving of a beautiful woman. Uninterested in real women of flesh and blood, he falls in love with this marble *mädchen*. As Jensen explains, "Archaeology had taken hold of him and left him with an interest only in women made of marble and bronze". (Ancient Pompeians would have put him on a sarcastic clay lamp.)

Continuing his archaeological pilgrimage, the youth visits that city of Sodom and Gomorrah, Pompeii. And in fact, while strolling down the Decumanus at the "hot and holy" midday hour, he finds himself face to face with his beloved. Her name is Gradiva, and she is no longer made of marble but of blood and, especially, flesh. Inner trumpets sound. He rushes toward her—to life, to love, to lust.

Boudoir Pompeii has saved a man from self-destruction.

Cinema was still being invented when the first blockbusters with sumptuous costumes appeared, earning good money. The early cinematographers plundered the circus history extravaganzas for the themes, characters and stories from antiquity, adapted for the new art form. The Italians immediately excelled. Their producers transferred the glorious and scandalous stories of Italian antiquity to cinema, churning out well-made silent film versions of *Quo Vadis?* (Henryk Sienkiewicz's 1896 novel about Rome, written while the author, a Pole, lived in Naples), *Giulio Cesare, Messalina*, and, still recognized as a masterpiece, *Cabiria* (1914).

Italian production was so outstanding between 1906 and 1914 that the period has been called a "golden age" for its cinema. Productions included *The Fall of Troy* (1910), *The Bride of the Nile* (1911), *Jerusalem Delivered* and *The Odyssey* (both 1912). Subtitles were translated and shipped out immediately so that the films could be sold in the USA and Germany as well as at home.

In cinema form the historical material differed from both the evocative stillness of a *tableau vivant* and the blowsy mayhem of the circus. Cinema added a new dimension beyond the specific subject matter, and this made it singularly well suited to archaeological themes. For cinema historian John David Rhodes,

> Film viewing begins with darkness; it is experience shown in light. Like archaeology, films reveal a hidden world—when you see the classical past in cinema, it's a version of the same experience an archaeologist has lived. There is a poignant resonance between past and present. And it is not a coincidence that the early movie theatres were in the form of classical temples.[21]

Vesuvius was made for cinema; little in moving pictures moved better than an exploding volcano. And in fact, before 1900 two silent films were made about volcanoes.[22]

Pompeii too was there for the picking, and the first cinema version of *Last Days* was produced in England in 1900 by Robert William Paul, directed by William Booth. Having no empire at the time, the Italians were uninterested in the stalwart soldier. To them Christian themes mattered, and so a pamphlet promoting the film promised a happy ending with "the punishment of the pagan sinners".

At the time, the novel *Last Days* had been selling for over six decades and had the benefit of having been on school reading lists for decades. Even those who had not read it knew its name. In terms of visual cinema it had the volcano, and, like Alma-Tadema's paintings, in it "women could be shown in dishabille within the framework of Christianity", in Rhodes's phrase.

The first Italian cinema version of *Last Days* was made by the Ambrosio studio of Turin, Italy's biggest film company, in 1908 and presented contemporaneously in fourteen cinema houses. Technical improvements in camera and projector allowed it to be unusually long, double the usual 180 metres of film. Directed by Luigi Maggio, the film showed lava splashing on spectators in the amphitheatre of Pompeii. Houses (toy houses, that is) were destroyed by lava, and boulders dropped from the sky, although Pompeii, which literally drowned in pebbles and volcanic ash, had not had lava flows.

Even in America the film was lauded as a "magnificent production", "a model". Its success (and it is still considered an early masterpiece) paved the way for production of a dozen remakes as well as for other films that fused antiquity and circus-like spectacle. Its audience went beyond Italy, for Italian silents were popular in Germany and in US cities with large Italian communities. Critics in America lauded the film.

The clones began in 1909 with a Milanese production by Saffi-Comerio. It was a love triangle story about a Pompeian gladiator, his girlfriend Nica, and the rich but cruel merchant who wanted to make her his slave. That same year Ambrosio followed its triumph with a new epic, *Nero and the Burning of Rome.* When it was shown in the USA, *Moving Picture World* lauded the movie's sumptuous parades, splendid costumes, acting, "and finally the great burning of Rome, with effects of marvelous realism".[23] Jumping on the bandwagon, other Italian silent history epics followed in the wake of the commercially successful Italian silent history epics *Quo Vadis, Julius Caesar, The Fall of Troy, The Bride of the Nile, Jerusalem Delivered,* and *The Odyssey.*

When imaginations flagged, *Last Days* was always there as a last resort. One Pompeii-inspired movie was made by a phantom Italian "Pompei Film Company", whose concoction incorporated footage stolen straight from the Ambrosio production, borrowed from a 1911 movie about the fall of Troy, and copied from a movie about the Middle Ages. This circulated even in America before disappearing as mysteriously as it had arrived.

Movies had grown longer, their effects more thrilling. Ambrosio itself made a remake of *Last Days* which premiered in August 1913. Cinema had turned more ambitious. The publicity promised that the movie would show "the sorrowful story of the Pompeians, the subject of the wrath of the volcano, their castigator for their sins." The critic for *La Tribuna* of Rome waxed delirious as he spelled them out:

> The chariot races ... the enchanting corners of the domus of Glaucus, rich with marbles, the tinkling fountains, the beautiful gardens and spacious terraces overlooking the moonlit gulf against the blue and silver sea ... the amphitheatre, the beasts, the gladiators' parade and their combat, ... the terrible visions of the cataclysm that in brief hours reduced into smoking ruins and buried under torrents of lava and

storms of cinders the enchanting city ... the collapse of temples and palaces, the populace's desperate race for safety, the vision of implacable Vesuvius vomiting its range and the death.[24]

Audiences, unaccustomed to such a degree of realism, were bowled over. *La Tribuna* of Rome called the Ambrosio film "a milestone in cinematographic art ... which transports us into a magical, remote world".[25]

The same month another Italian studio, Film Artistica Gloria, launched an ambitious rival version of *Last Days*. The film, a hit with audiences but now lost, was directed by Ernesto Maria Pasquali, and to differentiate it from Ambrosio's, its title was *Ione o gli ultimi giorni di Pompei*, with the name "Ione" in minuscule letters so that the title seemed to be Bulwer Lytton's.

The goal of the Italian silent film industry was to entertain. But when the costumes were stripped away, the films revealed, despite (and thanks to) their carefully crafted archaeological settings, a specific political message that reflected nationalistic aspirations. This gradually acquired importance because, in addition to the early Italian cinematographers' impact at home, they influenced foreign producers and audiences, especially in Germany, whose industry lagged a decade behind Italy's.

An ecstatic trade magazine review of the silent film version of *The Last Days of Pompei*, produced by Ambrosio of Turin in 1908, shows clearly the arrival of an incipient political message:

> Tears of joy streamed from my eyes, and I felt, as rarely in my life, all the sense of our national artistic strength! Our beautiful and glorious art lives! When we want to, we know how to make the foreigners pale before our burning, complete, full and finished art—we know how to show that beneath Italy's sky there lives always the genius and the love that we had when we were masters of the world![26]

Having seen that film's success, the self-acclaimed masters of the world produced more of the same, and in 1911, mission and epic movie met once more, when the Italian movie maker Cine produced a jingoistic historical epic about Italian knights on a crusade to save the Holy Land from the infidel Muslims. The film *Gerusalemma Liberata*, Jerusalem Liberated, reached British and US movie audiences as *The Crusaders*.

No sooner said than done. Within months Italy launched itself upon its first imperial adventure in 1,500 years. Italy declared war against Muslim Turkey and seized Libya, a Turkish protectorate.

Gerusalemma Liberata had served as a justification for the invasion of Libya to the extent that the movie had taken some of the sting from the ruthless invasion (at least for the Italians) by making it seem virtual warfare, *ante litteram*—an entertaining spectacle, seen from a distance.[27]

Italy had no monopoly on simmering nationalistic sentiments, of course. But the Italian cinema industry, in the avant-garde of the new medium, was also toadying to the sentiments of the political establishment.

In 1914, as Europe plunged into World War I, Itala Film produced an even bolder epic set in Roman antiquity, *Cabiria*, made by Giovanni Pastrone. This landmark of silent cinema was the most ambitious production of its time, and it celebrated the ancient Romans' invasion and subjugation of Carthage, the capital in antiquity of Italy's newly acquired colony, Libya. *Cabiria* was more than a movie, it was itself reality and transported audiences into realms "beyond the vulgar art of cinema, becoming instead history, becoming true history", as a film journal said.[28]

The underlying ideas about Italy's role as heir to its antiquity would have existed without cinema, but, building upon *Last Days*, the cinema broadcast them further—and paved the way for more, and not only in Italy. Immediately following World War I, Germany's late-developing, state-owned cinema industry managers adopted the ideas of the Italian history "kolossal" specifically and consciously because it was entertainment which incorporated a skilfully masked dose of propaganda, for which Italy had provided the model.[29]

CHAPTER XIII

"M" is for Mussolini

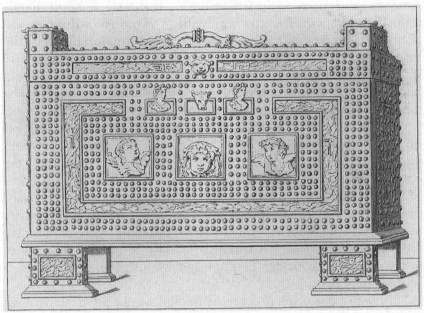

37. Pompeian strong-box, engraving

Even during World War I, Italians countered the real wartime history of pillage, plunder and death by watching movie-style history. In *La Tragica Fine di Caligola* (The Tragic End of Caligula, 1916), the mad emperor was an inadvertent commentary on the war to end all wars; in *Gerusalemma Liberata* (Jerusalem Liberated, 1918), and *Giuliano l'Apostato* (Julian the Apostate, 1919), history was entertainment.

Caligola bombed, but otherwise, because the captions of these silent ancient history epics were readily translated, exports were easy, and captivating advertisements for Italian spas and other tourism sites were inserted for good measure. But no celluloid fantasy could hide the truth of the postwar moral disillusionment and economic recession. Heightening this was, for the Italians, the knowledge that for decades negative images had circulated abroad portraying Italy as a nation of impotent dreamers, the Black Hand, organ grinders, and "mandolin players and emigrants".[1]

The history epics which had made Italy's reputation in the 1910s were a solace, but war had made them too costly to produce. Besides, like Alma-Tadema's Greco-Roman paintings, just then fading from popularity, they also seemed linked to lost pre-war certainties. Meantime, new-style films were flooding into Italy from America and from Germany, whose previously laggard movie industry bloomed after the war with government subsidies and ponderous propaganda. Italian cinema production tumbled steadily from the 415 films of 1920 to 254 in 1922, and on down to just forty in 1925. The Italian film studios that year were reduced to "a desolate landscape of ruins, weeds, broken glass, dust and rats", in the description of cinema historian Stefania Parigi.[2]

Coming to power in 1922, Benito Mussolini promised redress through "national rebirth". Beginning with this slogan he would launch a sweeping propaganda barrage called "la Romanità", the cult of Roman antiquity. Other and more devastating consequences of Fascism have, very properly, had priority in study and analysis, but it is also true that the radical expansion of its excavated territory as a showcase of ancient Italian glory indelibly scarred Pompeii, with consequences which continue to defy the best intentions of today's managers. Under Fascism and Maiuri, Pompeii became a hostage to politics.

For twenty-one years to come, Mussolini would wave the heritage banner of antiquity to legitimize presumed Italian racial superiority and, on grounds that the world needed more Italians, government subsidies of big families. Their great ancient heritage would help the Fascists to organize consensus and bring the Catholic Church on board as a prop. It would help to propagate a violent, military culture. It would promote the concept of a lifetime dictator and Italy's right to rule an empire acquired by force of arms. And it would help popularize racial laws which sent non-Romans to their deaths.

The Roman forums and Pompeii were the principal showcases for Italy's ideology of a presumed ancient superiority, and both sites suffered immeasurable damage from this. Fascist classicism, which used ancient Rome and Pompeii as visual rhetoric, compromised not only the sites themselves, but the related academic studies, and especially archaeology, for decades after Mussolini.

Napoli - Da Mergellina

38. "See Naples and die," the saying went. The sheer beauty of the gulf was promoted in this early 20th-century postcard, and even silent films had commercials inserted to publicize Italian spas and tourist sites like Pompeii, accessible by cruise ship as well as train.

It did not begin that way.

During the pre-war period a group of young Italian intellectuals calling themselves the Futurists turned their backs entirely on Italy's ancient past as retrograde. "We will destroy museums. Museums are cemeteries", thundered poet Filippo Tommaso Marinetti, author of the "Futurist Manifesto" first published in *Le Figaro* in 1909.[3]

To the Futurists, Pompeii, and hence all antiquity, represented passive death as opposed to active living, and in a Futurist pamphlet of 1915 Pompeii was described in a (bad) pun as "FUNERAL POMP". By contrast, war was active and aggressive, and armies were on the move. The Futurists supported the cause of purifying war. Adding sexual prowess to this concept, a boxed notice entitled *POMPEI 1915* informed readers that pacifists and neutralists have "genitals of stone or paint".[4]

In their paintings, drawings and pamphlets the Futurists promoted what was new, dynamic and swift—automobile, locomotive, airplane. They desired to make the arts and daily life more dynamic, down to promoting meals they hoped would invigorate the Italians, become dullards from eating too much pasta.

In the years before World War I, Benito Mussolini was the editor of an obscure and nastily aggressive Socialist newspaper in north Italy. With the Futurists he shared a taste for violence and violent language. In a famous passage written when he was twenty-seven Mussolini denounced Rome as a place of "parasites, landladies, shoeshine boys, whores, priests, bureaucrats … a vampire city that sucks the best blood of the nation".[5]

Although Mussolini had opposed the Italian invasion of Libya in 1911, in 1914, when he was thirty-two, he changed his mind and joined the Futurists in embracing the cause of war as vibrant, vital and energizing. At the time, Mussolini's likes and dislikes seemed beside the point, for even in 1919, when the pain of the Italian army's humiliating defeat at Caporetto was still fresh, his Fascist party had only 870 members. In the general political elections that year his strongest constituency, Milan, awarded him a mere 4,000 votes, too few to send a deputy to parliament. Only three years later he and his *squadristi* (armed punishment squads) had acquired sufficient strength to take over the country.

Becoming premier in October 1922, Mussolini made good use of his professional training as a journalist. Literacy was limited (only one in five could read in 1900), and so newspapers had limited readership, though as a preventive measure he abolished freedom of the press in 1926. It was Mussolini's good fortune that radio broadcasting became available throughout Italy in 1924.[6] Mussolini instinctively mastered the new means of mass communication, and his radio harangues were broadcast from loudspeakers set up in piazzas, thus reaching the most remote hamlet. Some of the *contadini*, knowing little of the outside world save for Mussolini's voice, believed that he was king. As no political force or means of communication had until then, radio unified Italy and rallied a media-ignorant people around their new leader, the Duce.

In the visual arts, Mussolini made good use of the Futurists' talents and sponsored their agenda of dynamism, modernity and virility. For Mussolini the Futurists were paid to produce bold wall posters, giant slogans painted upon building walls, and, in a nod to the country's biggest industry, ads for Fiat cars and motorcycles; one Fiat automobile actually bore the name of the Fascist youth group, Balilla.

Architecture offered an occasion for ideological strutting, and construction began on a host of new Fascist buildings associated with speed, such as train stations and post and telegraph offices.

The planning of whole new towns like Latina and Fertilia in areas of reclaimed land echoed Mussolini's borrowed Futurist ideology of modernism. Its masterpiece, so to speak, was a gigantic new Fascist administration building at Latina, just south of Rome. The squat, heavy building formed a mammoth "M", visible only from the air.

Mussolini had come to power with just one-tenth of parliament behind him, but it was one thing to attain power, another to remain at the helm, and in an extraordinary political about-face he declared in 1929 that the Futurists were "anarcoid and rebellious" (which they surely were; that had been the point when he was a rebel).[7] As it had been for the Risorgimento patriots, the classical heritage was there for the taking, and with many advantages.

From the outset Mussolini had made use of ancient Roman symbols, like the *fasces*, or rods bundled together to symbolize unity, frequently seen carved in stone. His famous march on Rome, the "vampire city", was a classical allusion, to Julius Caesar's army marching on Rome; this was no less true because Mussolini personally arrived by train. As a Fascist pamphlet distributed by the Ministry of Public Education in 1922 proclaimed, Ancient Rome "is our own myth, we dream of a Roman Italy, wise and strong, disciplined and imperial". And in a curious fusion of pagan and Christian, older students at the Scuola di mistica fascista (School of the Fascist Mystique) were informed by visiting lecturer Cardinal Ildefonso Schuster of Milan in 1937 that, "God has chosen to reward the Duce by drawing him closer to the great spirits of Augustus and Constantine".[8]

As part of his campaign called *la Romanità*, the Duce sponsored monthly journals promoting Roman antiquity (one, *Roma*, gradually became blatantly racist). In 1925 he created the Institute of Roman Studies and, in 1927, the Museum of the Roman Empire. He delivered a ghost-written speech on Roman history, and had his speeches translated into Latin, which was promoted as a spoken language.

Mussolini did not invent the use of heritage to promote narrow nationalism. During the Renaissance in Florence the Tuscan dukes had promoted the nobility of their presumed Etruscan origins. Victorian Britain had adopted Roman antiquity as part of its theatrical architecture of empire, even as its neo-Gothic revival had glorified the country's homegrown medieval culture. The Greeks were celebrating Alexander the Great as the unifier of Greece.[9] The Germans were rediscovering their own superior culture in pre-historical Aryan roots, and the French—abandoning their claim to the ancient Roman Empire, which had been renewed at mid-century under Napoleon III—were researching their Celtic superiority.

But as far back as the 1860s Italian Catholic nationalists had claimed that Italy stood above all other nations because for centuries the Church had carried out a "civilizing mission".[10] All European culture, they claimed, from law to philosophy and literature, depended upon ancient Rome, because "Latin is culture".[11] Forget Greece; even in the late Renaissance Italian scholars had preferred Latin authors like Plautus and Tacitus, because they were considered more "vigorous" thinkers than the Greeks.[12]

Moving physically into the imperial past, Mussolini began to be portrayed in profile on commemorative medals, like a Roman emperor. Pictures and mosaics showed him astride a horse, like Caesar Augustus on his bronze mount (now plastic) atop the Capitoline Hill. Roman-style busts of the Duce—DUX, always written in capital letters ancient Roman style—made of coloured plaster, stucco, marble and bronze sprang up like mushrooms in public buildings. With the passage of time, they acquired an increasingly military, abstractly Romanized look.

In a mirror reflection, the flesh and blood Mussolini was transformed into an ancient statue, a Pygmalion in reverse. An awed reporter seeing Mussolini address the Senate in Rome in May 1936 testified to this apotheosis: "He [Mussolini] has the rigidity and the everlasting quality of stone, and the powerful vitality of bronze. His look reveals a firm, immutable, irrevocable spirit. He is Caesar, alive."[13]

He wanted to be Caesar, at least. Mussolini's family tree was traced, and it turned out that his ancestors were Roman soldiers who had settled in the Romagna region in the 2nd century AD. In the same way, Lorenzo the Magnificent had had his family name, Medici, traced, erroneously, to mythical Etruscan ancestors in Florence.

Awkwardly, despite this Fascist classicism running amok, before World War I classical studies had been firmly dominated worldwide by German scholars, with their disciplined scientific methodology. With exceptions, Italian archaeology of the time was more snooty than scientific—an aristocratic pastime in which inspiration counted more than severe logic.

Besides differences of method, German scholars viewed the concept of "classical" in an utterly different way from the Italians. Romans put Rome first, but German classicists relegated Rome to second place behind Greece. The Germans, and the French as well, still taught the theories of the 18th century Prussian art historian, Johann J. Winkelmann, who taught the absolute superiority of ancient Greek culture (see Chapter V). (This Greek-style German classicism, incidentally, would feed into Nazi propaganda, as in the statuesque 1938 Olympic athletes filmed by Leni Riefenstahl.) Winckelmann had had little impact upon Italian classicists, who considered the neo-Winckelmanns of Germany "too Greek".[14] World War I had exacerbated the clash between the two cultures of classicism.

As a gratuitous insult to Italy, the most influential Roman archaeologist of the 19th century had been not Italian, but German. Theodore Mommsen had irritated not a few Italians, first by downplaying the originality of Latin culture and then by winning the 1903 Nobel Prize for Literature for his mammoth *History of Rome*.

Early 19th-century Italian classicists had tended to concentrate on the dignified and severe purism of the Roman Republic, from Cato to Cicero. The more militarized and aggressive imperial Rome and late antiquity came to be considered legitimate fields of study in Italy only after publication in 1911 of a translated textbook by Emanuel Loewy, an influential Austrian scholar who taught the primacy of the Roman Empire.

This convenient shift in emphasis flowed into Mussolini's imperial propaganda. Especially after 1929, some Italian textbooks were changed so as to place greater stress upon the importance of Rome over ancient Greece, that German academic fiefdom.[15] In regime-published books they celebrated Julius Caesar and Caesar Augustus as historical precedents. Pseudo-academic books were rushed into print with race-boosting titles like *Rome from Old Empire to New* and *The History of the Italian Race from Augustus to Mussolini*. Another hymn of praise was entitled *From Virgil to Mussolini*.

Mussolini's classicists were delighted at their new importance, which translated into university appointments, publications and editorships. In a fusion of Futurism and classicism, they promoted Latin literature as vigorously inspirational and filled with moral and civic energy.[16] Latin studies were relaunched as the language of grandeur, and Latin was officially declared an anti-Marxist language because, it was argued authoritatively, no one who knew it could possible become a Marxist.

To the Roman Catholic Church, *la Romanità* fell as manna from heaven—a conservative ideology whose celebrations would automatically embrace early Christian Rome. In 1929, fifty-nine years after Italian unification, the Vatican accepted Mussolini's offer of a peace treaty with Italy, the first. By the terms of the Concordat Roman Catholicism was made the official state religion. Priests would teach religion in all state schools as an obligatory course and become public employees, whose stipends were guaranteed by the state. The Church showed its gratitude. In 1936 Cardinal Pacelli, the papal envoy to Nazi Germany and the future Pope Pius XII, inaugurated an important lecture series entitled "Rome Where Christ is Roman".[17]

For Mussolini, the Concordat accorded greater legitimacy. In his speech at the School of Fascist Mystique, Cardinal Schuster spelled out a fanciful direct link between Imperial Rome, Christian Rome and Fascism, in flowery prose worthy of North Korea: "God has chosen to reward the Duce by drawing his historical figure closer to the great spirits of Constantine and Augustus, through the work of Benito Mussolini reconnecting Rome and its King to a shining new imperial crown of Roman peace".[18]

That very year Mussolini was organizing, as the culmination of his campaign of *la Romanità*, a great exhibition honouring Augustus and, implicitly, himself as the new Caesar Augustus, the first Roman emperor. Constantine the Great was, of course, the emperor who made Christianity the state religion of Rome after his conversion in 312; just so had Mussolini restored Catholicism as the state religion of Italy.

This did not stop Mussolini from, meantime, supplanting the Church by advancing Italy as the missionary of civilization. Already, Fascist author Antonio Bruers had written a book entitled *La missione d'Italia nel mondo* (Italy's mission in the world, 1928).[19]

"Fascism revindicates for Italy the traditional civilizing mission of the Mediterranean race", said author Gianni Poletti in a pamphlet distributed to Italian students by the official Fascist University Groups (GUF) organization in "Year X of the Revolution", 1932. The Mediterraneans, he claimed, and primarily the Italians, had given "glorious civilizations to the world," thus leading "barbarous humanity toward the correct principles of social existence".[20]

Coming to the aid of barbarous humanity, Mussolini invaded Ethiopia in 1935. His airforce bombarded sword-bearing warriors on horseback. Ethiopia was his, and, as a souvenir, a precious ancient monument was shipped to Rome as a war trophy and raised in front of his brand new Ministry for Colonial Affairs. The

marker—which resembles an Egyptian obelisk save for its writings—is a testimonial to early Christianity in Ethiopia, which
successfully obtained its return only in 2005—nearly sixty years
later.

By 1935, the Fascists controlled all the tools of culture: publishing,
education, the arts, the media, the archaeological sites. Such raw
and totalizing political control from the centre had come as a particular novelty; Italy had been cobbled together from diverse duchies
and principalities only half a century before Mussolini. Until Fascism, the country's cultural wealth and diversity had kept
campanilismo defiantly alive, meaning that each town tended to look
to its own town bell tower. To build a totalitarian state, Mussolini
had imposed harsh police measures and military controls. But without his cultural politics, this would not have sufficed in such a
sophisticated country.

The government held a tight fist over the archaeological heritage
in two ways. First, by accumulated laws originating in the Renaissance, every heritage site and archaeological trove on Italian soil
was state property. In his destruction of the forum area and his tearing down of nineteen churches ("parasites") in the centre of
historical Rome during his urban building programme of 1931,
Mussolini violated that existing law. Despite this, in 1939 he rein-
forced state protection of the heritage in legislation which
incorporated the centuries of earlier laws and which still enjoys
broad support as a protection from speculators.

The second way the state controlled the heritage was its selection
of site and museum managers. The practice was ready-made for the
Fascist regime to assume control of the heritage apparatus under
party loyalist Giuseppe Bottai.[21] Neither heritage minister Bottai nor
any other archaeologist unwilling to risk his post objected when the
Duce decided to tear down a medieval and Renaissance quarter in
order to pave over a giant swathe of ancient Roman forum so as to
create a military parade avenue.

The political stamp of approval was necessary for all teachers and
professors of archaeology and related studies in classics, papyrology (the study of ancient written documents, and not only of
papyri), epigraphy (the study of inscriptions), and art history. In
1931 Mussolini ordered all university teachers to swear loyalty oaths
to Fascism. Anyone not signing risked his post. Only one in a hundred refused to sign, or just twelve university professors out of a

total of 1,250.[22] The result was "archaeology cultivated by weak brains," in the words of Antonio Cederna.[23]

Even more than most, the antiquarians turned out in support of the regime, including its racist colonial policy. "Especially the scholars of Latin and Roman ancient history became nationalistic, openly and actively aligned in favour of the regime, in the wake of the promotion of 'Roman' themes connected to the colonial campaign", according to Italian historian Mariella Cagnetta.[24]

The Accademia dei Lincei, the equivalent of the US Academy of Arts and Sciences, was then, as now, Italy's most prestigious cultural institution, whose members were top intellectuals and scholars of Italy, including archaeologists and classicists. All were sent a questionnaire whose answers would reveal their religion. This was an early anti-Jewish, anti-Marxist measure. Only two Accademia members, political philosophers Benedetto Croce and Francesco De Sanctis of Naples University, refused to sign the questionnaire about religion. Both were expelled.[25] When the Fascists' tame philosopher, Giovanni Gentile, called upon all intellectuals to sign Fascist articles of faith in 1931, Croce said, "I could not *not* sign."

The consequences were serious. A young archaeologist, Emilio Magaldi, was accused of anti-Fascist sentiments and exiled to his home village, where he could find no better work than as an elementary school teacher. He never returned. "His life was destroyed", said archaeologist Baldassare Conticello, a former superintendent of Pompeii, in an interview.

In 1938 the Italian parliament introduced racial laws against the Jews, with only ten opposing votes in the Senate. As soon as the law was passed, the prestigious head of the Italian archaeological establishment in Athens, Alesandro Della Seta, was fired because he was a Jew. There was worse to come. Mario Segre, a young Italian Jewish classicist sent from Rome to conduct epigraphical research in Athens, and his wife were arrested there by Nazis and sent to their deaths at Auschwitz.

In the *Romanità* campaign Pompeii loomed large. Its excavations assured a seemingly endless stream of sensational new discoveries and brilliant trophies testifying to the skills of the forebears of the 20th-century Italians. Like those in the Roman forums, its temples and basilica showed that majesty of ancient, Imperial Italy with which Mussolini wished to be identified.

Like other regional sites, Pompeii was managed by a superintendent chosen by minister Bottai in Rome. In 1923, one year after
Mussolini's Black Shirts marched on Rome, archaeologist Vittorio
Spinazzola had been directing Pompeian excavations for nearly thirteen years, keeping conscientious records of the ongoing
excavations. His work was particularly interesting because, proceeding along the great avenue, the Decumanus Inferiore, running
between the gladiatorial amphitheatre and the theatre district, he
was showing the economy of Pompeii at work—not only great
houses, but food stalls and even a workshop for dyeing clothes.

Spinazzola had been appointed prior to the Fascist coup, and was
considered too close to the previous Liberal government. He was
axed, and in the aftermath the government publishing office
declined to print his thirteen years of excavation reports, because
written by a non-Fascist. The decision left scholars worldwide with
a twelve-year gap in knowledge about discoveries at Pompeii until
they were finally published in 1953.[26]

From Rome, minister Bottai chose archaeologist Amedeo Maiuri
to replace the politically incorrect Spinazzola in 1924. Maiuri was
one of those men who, in the Chinese phrase, can ride the crest of
every wave. He entered Pompeii as the fiduciary appointee of a Fascist dictator and a hereditary monarch, and retired in 1962, thirty-
seven years later, when Italy was a republic and a democracy.

Through his authority and such a long tenure, Maiuri left a
greater mark upon Pompeii than any other archaeologist before or
since, with the sole exception of Giuseppe Fiorelli in the Risorgimento era. He acquired almost mythical status, and even his
opponents admire his achievements. "It is fair to say that in his first
eight years Maiuri accomplished more for archaeology at Pompeii
than anyone in the forty previous years", Vittorio Bracco, an expert
on Fascist culture, acknowledges.[27] Speaking at a commemoration
organized in Naples by the Italian Institute for Philosophical Studies
in 1987, Giovanni Pugliese Carratelli praised Maiuri: "He was a
superman, a dynamo".

Today's Italian archaeologists have little use for words like
"superman", but archaeologist Mario Capasso, a specialist in Neapolitan archaeology and epigraphy, praises Maiuri for his efforts to
recover the past in a scientific and systematic manner. "His goal
[was] a total vision of the entire area being investigated, down to its
apparently less interesting aspects of daily life".[28]

Maiuri had graduated from the University of Rome as an expert in Byzantine philology. Shortly afterward he was sent to work on Italian archaeological projects scattered throughout Greece: Athens, Crete, Cos, Halicarnassos and finally to Rhodes. He returned to Italy when war broke out in 1914. Maiuri continued Spinazzola's interrupted excavation of the Decumanus Inferiore. He completed excavation of the 3.12-kilometre ring of city walls and of the huge *palestra*, or gymnasium, adjacent to the amphitheatre, with its elegant porticoed walkway and large swimming pool. In his free time he taught at the University of Naples and wrote prolifically, producing books, 300 scholarly papers, and poetic ramblings on Pompeii for popular magazines.

It was on his watch that Lytton's novel of 1834, *The Last Days of Pompeii*, by then ninety years old, became a great success, the *Gone with the Wind* of the silent film era. Cinema mattered to Mussolini; Fascist party members, including from the party network of workers' and youth clubs like Balilla, received ticket discounts. But some party authorities expressed concern at the less than heroic behaviour of their ancient Roman ancestors in the movies.

The history colossals began to lose their appeal, and by 1925 bankers refused loans to finance them. That year producer/director Amleto Palermi nevertheless persuaded Italian investors to finance production of a brand new, colossal version of *Last Days* under Palermi's own label Grandi Films, on the grounds that it would relaunch the entire Italian film industry. A budget of 3,000,000 lire was approved.

This would be the fourth remake in Italy. Maiuri for one was unimpressed. He already disliked the book because, he said, it was "inconsistent", showing lava arriving at Pompeii when there was none. He acknowledged that the errors were understandable in consideration of the relatively little actually known about the buried cities, the literary fashions of the early 19th century, and the reading public's tastes at that time. But Lytton's vision of Pompeii was "historically and humanly false", lacking in "real and true penetration of the spirit of the city and its inhabitants".

The public saw it differently. Novel, opera and previous movie versions had given *Last Days* the familiarity of an opera plot, with style and performances more important than story line. And style they found: by the time Palermi's exquisite archaeologically accurate sets were made, and the actors and 5,000 extras were dressed as ancient Romans, the costs had soared over budget to 7,000,000 lire—

five times the normal cost of an Italian production during that period.[29]

The film begins like a documentary, with the camera panning slowly—as the script explains—from the "smoking peak of Vesuvius" across a sweep of the ruins of Pompeii, focusing briefly upon the very house Lytton had imagined for Glaucus, the House of the Tragic Poet. The camera settles upon the Stabian baths, which suddenly spring to life with several naked men splashing about in a pool. In its adjacent courtyard the Greek god-looking Glaucus is practising the discus throw, to the admiring eyes of his wealthy girlfriend, Giulia. In front of a *taberna* not far away, blind Nydia plays her flute.

The Palermi remake of Lytton's novel opened all over Italy in January 1926. Within the year audiences in Berlin, Vienna, London,

39. The silent screen version of Bulwer-Lytton's *The Last Days of Pompeii* was a ground-breaking colossal made in Italy in 1926. Frame #744 shows blind flower seller Nydia and Glauco, whom she secretly loves. The setting is a fair copy of Gell's 1824 drawing of the House of the Tragic Poet.

40. In the 1926 Italian version of Bulwer-Lytton's novel, *The Last Days of Pompeii*, ancient nudity was permissible in movies, just as it had been for the Victorians. The background is the forum baths of Pompeii; the message, that Pompeii meant sex.

New York and Paris were thrilling to its scrupulously accurate sets and its costumes, true to the era save perhaps for the long, flapper-style necklaces worn by both men and women—when the women wore clothing, that is. One of the great pluses of the film, permitted because the story was pagan, were the bare-breasted ladies cavorting, Alma-Tadema style, in baths and temples, along with a few shots of nude female and male buttocks.

Nearing the end the stalwart soldier appears, still at his post by the Herculaneum Gate. A caption explains (the capital letters are in the original): "Pompeii is abandoned. Only the legionnaire stands immobile under the fury of the fire and of the cinders, faithful to duty, symbol of the majesty of the EMPIRE OF ROME."

Soldierly self-sacrifice was not far in the future. In 1936 Hitler and Mussolini moved politically closer to each other than previously.

Two years later Italy promulgated racial laws. It was 1938, and Maiuri, now a member of both the Accademia del Lincei and the Accademia d'Italia, gave an address to the latter, in which he spoke favourably of the racist legislation. He explained "the concept of archaeology as militancy"—political militancy, that is. Coincidentally, that very year, 1938, Maiuri discovered inside a cupboard at Herculaneum markings that resembled a Christian cross, if so, it would be the first ever found at any Pompeian site. The finding suited the political mood of conciliation with the Church.

Maiuri's greatest achievement was to conduct an exploration of Herculaneum, open to the skies. Herculaneum had been explored by tunnels in the 1750s and then, after a few failed attempts, abandoned altogether as too deep to bother with. In the early 1900s archaeologist Charles Waldstein attempted to create an international commission, but World War I had blocked his project. Under Maiuri the open excavation began in 1928, and within a decade Maiuri had opened the forum and several important buildings.

In 1940 Mussolini, who had once boasted of having visited "one or two" museums in his life and had admired the Vatican because its buildings were so big, came to Pompeii. Flanked by his uniformed party chieftains from Rome, Maiuri gave the Duce a personal tour of the site. Although Hitler watched the military parade down the new boulevard called the Viale dell'Impero Romano, he never made it to Pompeii. The Prince of Hesse had already visited, and later a delegation of Nazi officials, to enormous embarrassment because no provision had been made for feeding them, and the guards took up a kitty to buy fresh mozzarella.

Mussolini's exploitation of archaeology for the domestic and international promotion of his regime allowed and indeed encouraged Maiuri to operate on the grand scale, cutting great swathes needlessly into the site. Maiuri alone expanded excavated Pompeii by at least twenty-five per cent. The pick—a Mussolini symbol—would crash into a building, and the building would be stripped, then left to weeds and weather. Its best pieces went to the Naples Museum. The rest travelled legally to foreign museums and, mostly illegally, disappeared into private collections.

By the end of Maiuri's tenure, three-fifths of the total walled area of Pompeii were excavated—far more than he or future superintendents could keep safe from vegetation, ice damage, pollution,

41. Mussolini (front row, fifth from left) toured Pompeii in 1940 with archaeologist Amadeo Maiuri (to Mussolini's right). Fascism exploited Pompeii as
testimony to a presumed Italian racial heritage justifying its self-proclaimed
colonial "civilizing mission". The result of this celebratory archaeology was
over-excavation.

theft and the pressure of tourism. Although Maiuri made efforts to
maintain buildings excavated over a century before his time, his
work left a deplorable quantity of problems for future generations to
resolve. What good he did—and anyone knowing Italian bureaucracy has to be impressed by anyone who overcomes the difficulty of
any achievement—too often was excavation for its own sake.

Intellectual loss aggravated the effects of Fascism upon the physical site. Pompeii was one of the obligatory year-long study steps for
archaeology students, and Fascist-tainted scholarship continued by
default for decades after the war. The more bombastic academics
had signed oaths of Fascist loyalty in exchange for salaries, promo-
tions and publications that would not have otherwise appeared; and
after the war these same men and women continued to promote

their protégé graduate students, chosen because cast in the same mould. "The most enthusiastic backers of Fascism had been—perhaps not by coincidence—the least expert and inept students and youth ... in general deriving from narrow groups of the intellectual elite", according to historian Marco Palla."[30]

German archaeology differed from Italian. Hitler became chancellor of the Reich in 1933, eleven years after Mussolini had marched on Rome and at least five years after Mussolini launched *la Romanità* as a propaganda campaign. If Mussolini used the map of the Roman Empire for regime propaganda, Hitler used German pre-history (as well as folklore and mountain peaks). Archaeology held special appeal for Nazi propagandists, for who if not archaeologists could "prove" racial superiority?

The attraction was mutual. Among all university professors in Germany, the proportion of archaeologists identified as Nazi (fifteen per cent) was higher than in any other field (ten per cent). Indeed, early archaeology and prehistory were so thoroughly Nazified that after the war only one German scholar of prehistoric times remained at his post. The rest were either dead or "so politically tainted as to preclude rehabilitation", according to historian Jonathan Petropoulos.[31]

Here the two countries differed. In the bitter reckoning after World War II, Fascist Italy was considered a half-degree less poisonous than the Third Reich. No purge similar to Germany's took place in Italian universities. Professors and textbooks remained unchanged in Italy at the war's end (the latter largely due to lack of funds), with the result that ideas and people remained the same, and the more bombastic, less qualified professors, and the students they chose as their academic successors, stayed in place, making life difficult for the others, like the late, brilliant Ranuccio Bianchi Bandinelli.

No less than greedy king or unscrupulous art dealer, an ideology can plunder a cultural heritage site. Mussolini's overly aggressive excavation of Pompeii and Rome in order to exploit archaeology as a propaganda tool, together with compromising two generations of scholars via career advancement based upon political correctness, wreaked more destruction than all the Austrian captains of fortune, the arrogant Spanish, the drunken custodians of the early Risorgimento and the thieving bandits of Vesuvius. In a bitter postscript, Vesuvius began to erupt in 1943.

During World War II excavations at Pompeii were suspended. In July 1943 Mussolini's supreme council turned on him. The south of Italy joined with the king to switch allegiance, making common cause with the Allies against the Germans. The Duce chose to remain with Nazi Germany. With Germany's support, he retreated to the north, creating a new and fictitious country, the Republic of Salò.

Naples became a theatre of war as the Allies pressed upwards from Sicily. The familiar plume of smoke from Vesuvius participated, helping Allied pilots find their way toward their bombing target—the German army, dug into mountain hideouts. To be rid of them, Allied pilots were ordered to bomb all Nazi barracks in the Naples vicinity. When the pilots asked how they were to recognize these barracks, they were told to look for metal roofing because, as is well known, all Italian houses have red tile roofs.

There was one exception: the metal roofing covering the areas under excavation at Pompeii. Allied bombers saw the roofs glinting in the sunlight and successfully bombed their way down the Decumanus Maximus. Not long afterward more collateral damage occurred when Allied fighter planes destroyed the medieval Abbey of Montecassino, one hundred miles further north.

The good news was that the German troops withdrew northward to Rome. The Allied Military Command (AMC) settled into Naples. The Germans responded by having their bombers attack hapless Naples. Having taken Naples, the Allies liberated the Vesuvius Observatory, a 19th-century creation of King Ferdinando of the Big Nose. Breaking into the observatory, they found its director, Professor Giuseppe Imbò of Naples University, reading the seismograph. His lone helper, an Italian soldier, was at his side.

They ordered Imbò to get packing. He responded politely that, because Vesuvius was showing every sign of awakening, it might prove useful to have someone on hand who knew how to work the seismograph, and only he, Professor Imbò, knew how to use it. The dubious Allies reluctantly agreed, allowing him and his helper to occupy a corner of the building.

During the night soon afterward, German bombs killed 300 Neapolitans. On that day of mourning, 18 March 1944, before bodies could be buried, Vesuvius began to enter an eruptive cycle. "What a lovely sight!" gushed a reporter for *Stars and Stripes*, the US forces' newspaper. Indeed, lovely red-hot lava had begun streaming down the slopes.

Because American and British bombers had been ravaging the entire area for months, they were blamed for the eruption. Italian journalist Vittorio Palliota has explained why: "It sometimes happened that English and American pilots on a mission to Naples fooled around on the way back by dropping leftover bombs into the crater. These episodes were used as proof for propaganda that the Allies intended to provoke an eruption of Vesuvius."[32]

Director Imbò and his steadfast soldier and no less steadfast custodian were anxiously following the eruption. For days the professor would leave the observatory from time to time only to climb to a position from which he could peer into the volcano's fiery crater. Giant boulders burst from it like popcorn in a popper, to soar hundreds of yards into the air.

This modern Pliny carefully recorded what he saw:

> The explosive activity of Vesuvius began with the projecting of cinders and incandescent matter on 22 March, became very intense and continuous until 6 o'clock and then intense and almost continuous from 10 pm throughout the morning of the 23rd. It has become mediocre and discontinuous but still continues, reviving at intervals characterized by the formation of burning clouds and very copious electrical charges.[33]

At intervals the volcano cast up cinders to a height estimated at 1.6 miles, giving rise to the formation of the characteristic Plinian tree-shape cloud. The cinders then drifted on the strong winds from north and north-east to fall slowly in the south-south-west.

Watching in horror, the AMC officer, Lt Col Kincaid, saw a 600-foot-wide river of lava pour down the southern slope of the volcano, then split into three separate lava streams that raced toward the farm villages scattered on the slope "at the rate of three to four metres per minute". To evacuate the inhabitants of the endangered villages, Kincaid summoned ten military trucks. General Charles Poletti, the Italian-American commander of the AMC, rushed to Naples to view the damage, as American military cinematographers filmed the shower of ash in the streets before scampering away as lava rolled toward them down streets, crushing and crumpling buildings in its way. No one was on hand to photograph Vesuvius's last hiccough—a new layer, fifteen feet thick, of pyroclastic material, dumped atop the Villa of the Papyri at Herculaneum, to bury it still deeper than before.

Naples had first been bombed by the Allies, then by the Germans. With the eruption a wave of hysterical fear gripped the populace. A mob of angry women surged into the streets, screaming and praying, before converging upon a notorious brothel which catered to the foreign soldiers. According to writer Curzio Malaparte, author of *La Pelle* (in English, *The Skin*), the prostitutes were dragged from the brothel, naked, as the good women yelled at them to repent so as to save Naples from Vesuvius.

CHAPTER XIV

The Library at the End of the Tunnel

42. Harbour scene

Picking up the threads of his explorations after World War II, an undaunted Amedeo Maiuri, for two decades Mussolini's foremost archaeologist, plunged back into work throughout the Vesuvian territory. The new research showed that one detail from the past had to be corrected. The supposedly Christian cross which Maiuri had discovered just in time for the Fascist regime's reconciliation with the Roman Catholic Church was merely a marking left inside a nook from a small shelf propped up by a wooden upright.

Despite such minor setbacks and his limited resources, it was a triumph when Maiuri's excavators bared a stretch of Herculaneum's ancient ring wall to the north-west. Tantalizingly, just beyond this section of wall lay the magnificent Villa of the Papyri, still sealed in silence after two centuries. A few faltering probes had been made, but they failed, and the villa had remained just as it was in the 1750s, when military engineer Karl Weber had partially excavated it through an elaborate network of tunnels. Its 750-foot length makes this among the larger Roman villas, and from it dozens of fine Hellenistic statues in bronze and marble had been triumphantly hauled off to Neapolitan palaces.

But the villa's signal importance came from another treasure: its books. Other Vesuvian towns, other great villas, have been and will be excavated, and their art treasures fought over by museums. But to our own day the intellectual library which Weber found inside the Villa of the Papyri has never been equalled. This is still the only library from antiquity extant. The ideas its books contained fuelled the Senate orations of Cicero, the ambitions of Julius Caesar, and the poetry of Virgil, Lucretius and Horace.

Weber's slave labourers had hauled up to the surface somewhere between 1,100 and 1,800 precious carbonized papyrus scrolls, some whole, some in fragments. An exact tally would depend on who was counting, and in what condition a charred scrap becomes a scroll. In addition, in the dim light and underground chaos no catalogue or even a count of the scrolls was ever made. At one point Weber and his senior officer, Alcubierre, reckoned the same batch diversely: Weber, seventeen; Alcubierre, twenty-six. Countless other *volumen*, as the scrolls were called, were lost, burned or otherwise destroyed, as we have seen.

It is a certainty, however, that one of the several rooms in which Weber had found caches of papyri was a library, furnished with reading table and two book cabinets. Scrolls were in one cabinet; others lay in a tumble on the floor. Significantly, in a row atop the cupboards were small bronze busts of Greek philosophers. One was of Epicurus. This then was not only a library; it was a Greek library.

But most great villas from that period had two separate libraries, one for books in Greek, the other, in Latin. Presumably the villa had a second library. Had Weber overlooked the Roman library, still somewhere inside the sprawling villa? The pressure on Maiuri to proceed the few hundred yards beyond the wall and into the villa in search of its lost Latin library was immense. But in 1958, as other sites claimed his attention and funds, the Herculaneum exploration was abandoned.

After Maiuri retired four years later, scholars and archaeologists resumed their appeals for a new excavation of the villa utilizing modern archaeological criteria and modern technology—for instance, as one archaeologist proposed, reasonably enough, by installing an elevator so as to continue the exploration by tunnel. Exactly like their 18th-century peers, the post-World War II scholars longed to find new scrolls, particularly in Latin. They yearned for new information about the history, literature, science and thought of Rome at that very particular moment in the Empire's early history.

But even as the elevator project and other proposals were bandied about, farm work and construction of new buildings atop the buried villa continued, and city hall moved into a Renaissance palazzo directly overhead, making future open excavation difficult.

In the meantime, some 400 scrolls had been opened and read, or roughly half of those which seem remotely readable, and about one in ten turned out to be in Latin. Opponents of excavating the villa (mostly because of the high costs) said this proved that no separate Latin library existed. Those in favour pointed to the fact that scroll troves had been found in five separate places, one of them seemingly a store room. Besides, the various batches had all been lumped together, meaning that no provenance could be shown. The books in Latin might have come from either the store room or from the crates in the garden.

The arguments in favour of launching a new exploration gained momentum in the early 1980s after scientists established that the first eruptive action at Herculaneum had been a savagely violent

43. The Herculaneum library of scrolls discovered in the 1750s remains unique in history. Under the International Philodemus Project, papyrologists, like this American scholar, are painstakingly transcribing fragments of charred papyri from Herculaneum in the Biblioteca Nazionale at Naples.

blast of poisonous, searing air. This contradicted previous theories of how the volcano's successive surges had buried Herculaneum. Its implication was that such a horrific blast could have blown papyrus scrolls forcibly all over the villa, including down corridors or stairwells. In the last analysis, if scrolls had been found in five locations, why not in a sixth or seventh?

Even as the debate raged, more of the fragile scrolls had been successfully unrolled, and the true shape of the library had become clear. The first to have been unrolled and read in the late 18th century was by one Philodemus, a Greek émigré intellectual active in Rome during the mid-1st century BC. Eager for new works by Herodotus or other familiar names from antiquity, the 18th-century intellectuals were sorely disappointed: who had ever heard of Philodemus?

But later scholars, more sophisticated, had heard of him. Probably Jewish, this brilliant intellectual was born at Gadara in Syria around 110 BC and studied in Athens. After twelve years as a wandering scholar on the eastern frontier of Asia, he reached Rome, where he became the centre of a coterie of admirers and students, and influenced the finest minds of his time.

Philodemus had trained at the School of Epicurus, and, as the slow unrolling of the Herculaneum scrolls continued, they were found to contain not only Philodemus' poems and commentaries, but thirty-seven books from a masterpiece by Epicurus, *On Nature*. Of the 300 scrolls known to have been written by Epicurus, most are lost, and those that exist are medieval copies presumed to contain errors from the recopying process. These were the closest Epicurean texts to the original ever found, although even they had been transcribed by ancient Greek stenographers in different hands at different times.

The Herculaneum library contained works by rival philosophers as well, including prominent Stoics, and such scientific texts as *On Geometry* and *On the Size of the Sun*. One, newly translated, is a comic play in Latin about a miser, from a scroll recomposed from diabolically tiny fragments and read by the Norwegian classicist, Knut Kleve, in 2001. But the core of the villa library has remained the writings of Epicurus and of his disciples like Philodemus himself, his teacher in Athens, Zeno, and Zeno's younger contemporary, Demetrius of Laconia. The library of the Villa of the Papyri was thus above all Epicurean.

To speak of an Epicurean today suggests mostly an excessive fondness for foie gras, white truffles and vintage Brunello di Montalcino. But this is wide of the mark, for when Epicurean ideas began to circulate in Rome, and then to the rest of the Roman world, they were revolutionary. This was an early version of humanism, and bound up in the history of the Villa of the Papyri and its library. It is also an intimate component of our own ideas of happiness, for as a direct result of a revival of interest in Epicurean thought in the 18th century, the "Preamble" to the US Constitution declares the "pursuit of happiness" to be an inalienable right. Philodemus introduced these heady notions to a relatively backward Rome, military in organization and spirit. Its intellectual culture reflected not the rhythm of Sappho's poetry, but the tramp of soldiers' feet, the Etruscans' teachings of geometry and engineering.

To the extent that it was influenced by Greek philosophy, Rome was then under the sway of the Stoics. Stoicism, popular among the aristocrats and governing class in the late republican period before the empire, promoted traditional values, like manly virtue and stalwart action (shut up and die for the greater good).[1] The Epicureans won few points among old-fashioned Roman Stoics by their promotion of individualism and the right to happiness.

In early Christianity, Epicureanism was also disliked as a philosophy which averred that man is mortal, death is final, and the search for happiness during lifetime, legitimate. Epicureanism was presented as synonymous with self-indulgence. It is true that Epicurus in his famous *Letter on Happiness* preached the individual's right to happiness, but this was also connected to ethical behaviour; true happiness, he said, presumes virtuous behaviour in order to attain a perfect, rational, and Zen-like calm. Partying and sex ("the delights from youths and women") are part of life's joys but have their limitations: "Banquets, parties, the delights from youths and women, a good fish and all that makes a rich table, do not of themselves bring the sweetness of life; that [derives] from the lucid analysis of the reasons for selecting this and rejecting that". To this day this letter contains such grace that when an Italian publisher reprinted it as a pamphlet in 1996, he reported selling a million copies.

Born in 341 BC, Epicurus founded a school in Athens known as The Garden (*Kepos*). In the seclusion behind the high walls of The Garden, fellowship was nourished through scroll study, mellow talk, and discussion of life's choices. The Garden was therefore a kind of Paradise, not unlike the perfect walled garden envisioned by

medieval monks for their secluded but, in that case, solitary meditations. From Epicurus' *Letter to Menoeceus*: "We consider it a great gift
even to be happy with little. Not because we have to content ourselves with little, but because if we do not have a lot, we can content
ourselves with little … the more one enjoys abundance, the less one
needs it". True happiness also requires overcoming the fear of death
and accepting the fact that death is nothingness. Meantime, take
delight in the wonders of life, for it is not the length of time on earth
that matters, but the depths of one's appreciation of life as a miracle.

Roman thought was further influenced by a corollary of this: that
in order to make rational ethical choices, one should observe and
analyse nature carefully before taking action. This prompting of natural studies is one reason why these became important in the
Roman world, including to Pliny the Elder. Before Philodemus'
time, no system of higher education had existed in Rome, and little
Latin literature was available. When Caesar and Cicero were children, it was unusual for a well-born young Roman to read
philosophy, by which was meant Greek philosophy. Even the language, Latin, especially as spoken in the interior, was a handicap,
for it was still being developed and was crude in comparison with
Greek. Its lack of compound words did not yet permit the subtlety
of thought of Greek.

Rome having no institute of higher learning, Caesar studied in
Rhodes while his contemporary, the orator Cicero, spent three years
studying in different Greek cities. In Athens Cicero heard lectures at
all three schools: the Epicureans, the Stoics and the Aristotelians.
Aristotle's writings, Cicero recorded, were "a river of gold".

By the time Caesar and Cicero were adults, scholarly travel had
begun to flow in the opposite direction. Intellectuals fleeing uncertainty, war and poverty at home flocked to wealthier Rome; just so
had royal patronage drawn scholars, philosophers, doctors and
poets to Alexandria two centuries before, and the Nazi-Fascist wars
of Europe brought enriching intellectuals to the USA in the 1940s.

Emigré intellectuals required patrons. For years Cicero had given
a room in his home in Rome to Diodotus, a blind Stoic. Cato the
Younger had given hospitality to Athenodorus, head librarian at
Pergamum (in today's Turkey). These émigré scholars were "half
mentor and half servant" to the upper-class youth of Rome, to whom
they would read aloud, explain texts, and teach educated Greek.[2]

The Greek educators encouraged questioning about everything,
from the workings of a volcano to the nature of the human soul and

the innards of the octopus. In this way the Greek thinkers had calculated that the world is round, and Democritus and Epicurus had
advanced the notion that the world is composed of "atoms".

For Rome this cultural revolution, effervescent and Hellenizing,
brought new ways of behaving and thinking. Values changed. The
novel ideas had to be recorded; to make this easier, Latin shorthand
was invented. Roman physicians, who had previously been satisfied
by studying under Etruscan soothsayers who examined entrails for
inspiration, took up an interest in Greek medicine. Intellectual spar-
ring was part of the education, and this pleased some and offended
others, for Greek professors taught diversity and insisted upon
debate. To do so they brought with them their books—Greek books.

The first Greek library had reached Rome only in 167 BC, as plunder from Macedonia. A century later, there were still no public
libraries in Rome, although some prominent men owned private
libraries—usually in country estates—in which works in Greek pre-
dominated. Cicero, who wrote philosophy himself in his spare time,
reread the "golden river" of Aristotle in the library of a villa at Tus-
culum outside Rome owned by his friend Lucullus. The scholar
Varro also had a library, plus what he called his "museum".

Philodemus was the most successful of all the émigré scholars in
Rome at the time. His native Gadara was a sophisticated city in
Syria, and his father either a slave or freed slave who, like many
others, had been swept up by war.. Eventually the family settled in
Athens, where Philodemus studied under Zeno in The Garden—the
school of Epicurus—and then taught there before setting out as a
wandering scholar for eleven years.

Arriving in Rome in his mid-thirties, Philodemus began giving
public readings of his poems and essays. In the same way, the travelling intellectuals on the Alexandrian Library lecture circuit had
lectured for money. He also acquired a patron: an aristocrat from
one of Rome's most influential families, named Lucius Piso. Like a
Hollywood star converting to Buddhism, Piso took up Philodemus'
Epicureanism and became an enthusiast. It was a two-way street; for
Piso, Philodemus wrote a history of Greek philosophy—and a series
of erotic epigrams.

Piso's patronage sent Philodemus' popularity soaring to the stars.
To the dismay of the Stoics, an elite Epicurean circle rather like
Bloomsbury or the Algonquin began to meet regularly with
Philodemus at a villa on the Aventine Hill of Rome, for good talk,
scroll chatter and fellowship. No trace of that villa exists, though in

the theatre of my imagination I place it arbitrarily where the orange garden overlooks the Tiber from a bluff on the hill by the ancient church of Santa Sabina.

In the Epicurean tradition their dinner meetings took place on the twentieth of each month, the master's birthday. To the students and friends gathered within the stone walls of the Roman transplant of the Garden, the world was well lost. Under fragrant laurels and pomegranate trees, with the heady scent of jasmine and lemon blossom, Philodemus explained the Greek way and the Epicurean way, while in a room set aside as a library the students read the writings of the master himself and of his disciples, like Zeno.

As for politics, Epicurus wrote: "You must free yourself from the prison of politics and the daily round".[3] But on the other hand one of Philodemus' key works is *On the Good King*, whom he advises to exercise justice with great care. Significantly, it is dedicated to Piso:

> Let us again exhort the king to be virtuous: to hate extreme or rude or bitter conduct, and to exercise, to the greatest possible extent, gentleness, fairness and mildness in his carriage, and harmony in his behavior, these virtues being conducive to a stable monarchy; and not to rule through fear.[4]

One of the habitués of the transplanted Garden was the first important lyrical poet to write in Latin, Lucretius, who espoused Epicureanism and celebrated it, almost aggressively. In his six-book-long poem *De rerum natura*, written two centuries after Epicurus died, Lucretius argued in pure Epicurean fashion against the existence of the gods as conceived in the Greco-Roman tradition. Similarly, Horace has passages of poetry that echo the writings by Philodemus, as do Robert Lowell's *Imitations*.

All of this was little to the taste of the 1st-century BC ruling caste of Rome, on the cusp of cobbling together, and ruling, the greatest empire the world would see until Queen Victoria. A kinder, gentler ruler did not pave roads down which six soldiers could march abreast, drive tunnels through mountains in Africa to outwit enemies, or fling bridges for troops to storm over rivers.

Gossips whispered that things in the Garden on the Aventine were not as they should be. Among them was Cicero, who complained at the signs of decadence and warned that "feminizing" men participated in the Epicurean soirées. Worse yet, sipping the wine, harking to the siren song of individual happiness, mellowing out in fellowship with other seekers and students, were the lower orders. Unlike at Oxford or Harvard in the 1950s, women were allowed into the fellowship of the Garden, along with the elderly and slaves, the latter also encouraged to learn to read. (In this, according to Diogenes Laertius in his 2nd-century AD *Lives of the Philosophers*, Epicurus had been unique, moreover advising his own slave Mys to take up the study of philosophy.)

The sensual atmosphere is made clear in a touching epitaph written by Philodemus to honour a youth named Trygonian, who had fallen ill and died. In older translations the dead Trygonian—his name in Greek means "Little Dove"—is evoked by Philodemus as one of "the effeminates", an "orgy-lover", yet delicate and worthy of a headstone on which will grow white violets, and no cruel brambles. A newer translation by poet George Economou draws us closer to Philodemus and his world: "Here the delicate form of one tender as a dove lies,/Trygonion, special among a crazy bunch of eunuchs …".[5]

Enter Julius Caesar. Caesar was married, but it had all gone sour. His wife was the daughter of General Pompey, and these once political allies had become bitter enemies. Caesar's two-year term as co-consul was ending in 58 BC, when he was forty-two, and he was about to leave Rome for Gaul (France) at the head of an army. In his absence he needed someone in Rome powerful enough to guarantee that for the next two years Pompey would not usurp power.

It was a complication that Caesar's wife was Pompey's daughter. This Caesar resolved with expedience, by divorcing her on an obviously trumped-up excuse; during a woman's religious rite a man had stolen into the ladies' quarter of the household, and though he was forced to acknowledge that his wife bore no blame, he said icily, "Caesar's wife must be above reproach".

In an equally cold political calculation, he now married Calpurnia, the daughter of that enthusiast of things Greek, Lucius Piso, patron of Philodemus. Piso was the scion of a famously old and aristocratic Roman family and had been a consul in the Campania region around Naples. To marry Piso's daughter was, for Julius Caesar, the equivalent of marrying the daughter of John Adams or of the Duke of Marlborough.

As if by magic, Piso was appointed to succeed Caesar as co-consul, even though, before this, Piso had never evinced interest in politics, and on the contrary, in 57 BC, after eighteen years in exile, had publicly declared that "no sane man should engage in public affairs," an Epicurean statement if ever there was one, and offensive to old-school Roman Stoics. When Piso's two-year appointment

came to an end, as if by magic he became governor of the giant territory of Macedonia (so vast that it included Athens)—where, as it
happened, Caesar's enemy, Pompey, was head of the Roman military command. Accompanying the new proconsul in Macedonia
was Philodemus, Piso's ad hoc aide and consultant.

In either case, Caesar had manipulated events so that, first in
Rome and then abroad, his newest father-in-law, Piso, had become
his proxy in the war of ambition against his former father-in-law,
Pompey; and Piso, newly powerful, introduced Philodemus to
Rome, and Philodemus introduced Epicurean thought. Initially,
Caesar had also tried to cajole political support from the elegant ora-
tor Cicero, four years older than himself, but had been rebuffed.
Relations remained occasionally friendly between the two, but that
was not an offence Caesar would forget; besides, Cicero was known
to be an admirer of Pompey.

In 55 BC Piso, with Philodemus in tow, had just returned from
Macedonia when Cicero launched two broadsides against him.[6] In a
famous speech of insults spoken in the Senate, Cicero called Caesar's father-in-law "repulsive" and "coarsely dressed". Piso's hair is
all in a tangle, he has "dirty habits" (*sordium*), and he wastes his time
in "idleness and inactivity".

In a second speech of insults Cicero reminded the senators that
sumptuary laws prohibited overseas consuls from owning ships
beyond a certain size, so as to limit, physically, the possibility for a
Roman governor to carry home more than a fair share of foreign
plunder. Yet while Piso was in Macedonia as governor, Cicero
charged, he had grabbed all the prized Greek statuary and bronzes
he could lay his dirty hands on in shrines there and shipped it all
back to Italy: fine Hellenistic marble statuary, busts of philosophers,
and one great marble statue of a winged Athena.

Piso survived these insults and more. When Caesar, fifty-five years
old, was murdered in 44 BC (by twenty-three dagger thrusts, according to Suetonius), Piso and the weeping Calpurnia received his body
and made arrangements for cremation on a pyre in the Campus Martius near the tomb of Caesar's daughter, Julia. Roman women tore off
their jewellery and the gold *bulla* (pendants) boys wore on their
tunics and tossed them onto the pyre. The funeral over, the rabble
tried to burn down the houses of the chief conspirators, Brutus and
Cassius. Six months later Piso received Caesar's will from the Vestal
Virgins, who had been holding it for safekeeping. The bequests, incidentally, included the gardens on the Tiber banks where Cleopatra

had lived, left by Caesar to the Roman public for a park; the Botanical Gardens are still there, still a public park in Trastevere.

As an old man Piso remained important enough to be reappointed consul in 23 BC. During the previous decade the Emperor Augustus had been writing a memoir about his reign, *Res gestae divi Augusti*. Together with his last will and testament, the dying emperor placed this memoir in the hands of Piso.[7]

What happened to Philodemus and his books? What happened to Piso's statuary, the busts of philosophers? A strong case can be made that they had all belonged to the Villa of the Papyri, where Weber found them. But there are differences of opinion. In fact, questions about the villa—who owned it, how its library came to be there, and what role the library played in it—have beguiled and bedeviled generations of scholars.

The internationally known dean of Italian papyrologists, the late Marcello Gigante of Naples University, was among the majority who believe that the villa had belonged to Piso, and that its library was assembled and brought there by Piso's protégé, Philodemus.[8] Gigante's first witness for the defence was the Herculaneum library itself. The library of writings primarily by Philodemus and his master, Epicurus (three busts of Epicurus were found in the villa) was found near Naples, already known as a centre for Epicurean teaching; it is generally believed that Philodemus had retired and died somewhere near Herculaneum. In Gigante's view, all this suggests that the villa had belonged to Piso, who had served as consul to the Campania region around Naples before he became consul to Rome (and Caesar's father-in-law). Wealthy and powerful men like Piso, Philodemus' enthusiastic patron in Rome, would have had several such villas; Cicero, who was never actually rich, had eight. The library then presumably belonged to Philodemus, who brought it to the villa for the long summers.

A later date of construction could have ruled this out, but it was already known that, around 50 BC, the twenty-year-old Virgil had travelled to Naples to study Greek under a teacher named Siron, a follower of Epicurus. In a crowning achievement, Professor Gigante had tracked down and successfully transcribed a hitherto lost Herculaneum scroll which recorded Virgil's attending a lecture in the villa at Herculaneum.

This important link between the Epicurean school of Naples, Virgil and the villa proved that the villa had certainly existed from at least the mid-1st century BC; that it had a teaching function, and that some of the greatest minds of their times had convened in the villa, with its rich Epicurean library.

But this does not prove that Piso owned the villa, nor that Philodemus taught there. Archaeologist Andrew Wallace-Hadrill, author of two authoritative books on Pompeii and director of the British School at Rome, has argued that no hard evidence of the existence of a separate Latin library has been found in the villa. Neither an epigraph giving Piso's name, nor a portrait bust showing Piso, has ever been found.

Another sceptic is American scholar David Blank of the University of Southern California at Los Angeles, a director of the international Philodemus research project. He argues that other wealthy individuals lived at Herculaneum. There is no reason why Piso and only Piso could have owned the villa, nor that only Philodemus could have brought the Epicurean library there. On the contrary, the entire library may have been purchased and only recently brought to Herculaneum from somewhere else. The crate of books found in the Great Peristyle of the villa may have been coming rather than going, a new delivery from some book dealer rather than an old legacy. This, at least, can be disputed: more probably the crates had been placed in the garden because post-earthquake restoration was still underway in the villa, as in countless other buildings. Elsewhere at Pompeii similar crated objects had been found stored among signs of belated restoration, as at Murecine, as we shall see.

A further complication is that around 130 years passed between the lecture attended by Virgil in the villa and the eruption of Vesuvius which buried it. That time lapse in the life of the villa has never been reconstructed.

However, some of the rediscovered scrolls proved to be multiple copies of the same book. This demonstrates that, on the eve of the eruption of AD 79, a century after Philodemus was in his prime, the library still played a crucial role in the life of the villa. Student followers of Epicurean theories of fellowship and good talk gathered in what perhaps saw use as a sort of academy or Aspen Institute, where the teachings of the master were discussed. If this is so, then what has been rediscovered is a Greek school of philosophy, The Garden, perhaps heir to that of the pre-Christian-era Gulf of Naples, transferred to the villa overlooking the sea from a high cliff.

Two tantalizing hints continue to evoke the figures of Piso and his protégé Philodemus within the context of the Herculaneum Library. One is the great white marble Athena that is now a pride of the

Naples Museum. Its description matches that of the Greek statue of Athena which Cicero had denounced Piso for acquiring in Macedonia and bringing to Rome, like Lord Elgin bringing pieces of the Parthenon to London.

Secondly, in a bitter-sweet epigram of mourning addressed to his friend Sosylus, Philodemus describes memories of their strolling together in a summer garden on a cliff overlooking the sea. Spring has come, he says,

> Already here, Sosylus, is the rose, here the ripe chickpea, the small early cabbages, the glistening sardine, the salty curds of fresh cheese, the frothy leaves of curly lettuce. But we shall not go upon the headland, nor as we always did in times past, Sosylus, find ourselves in the belvedere. Yesterday we were still at play. Today we bury him.

In 1752 Karl Weber had stumbled by candle-light into the belvedere of the deeply buried Villa of the Papyri—that belvedere from which Weber removed a geometric inlaid marble trompe l'oeil floor, now in the Naples Museum. Can there be real doubt that the the belvedere, mentioned in this sorrowing epigram of springtime and loss, is not a reference to the very belvedere of the villa, high on its headland overlooking the sea at Herculaneum? In the lee of that headland the treasure of Epicurean scrolls had been unloaded at the same dock where the statues from Macedonia had arrived. There they had been placed on wooden carts to be hauled up the steep cliff, four stories above the level of the boat dock. And there they had remained until Vesuvius claimed the villa and the scrolls.

Or so all but the most severely sceptical may believe.

The late Baldassare Conticello was a dapper, Sicilian-born archaeologist with a prodigious memory backed by sturdy scholarship. In 1980, not long before he was appointed superintendent of Pompeii, the entire territory south of Naples was devastated by an earthquake. His first task was therefore to attempt to shore up some of the newly damaged ancient buildings and walls at Pompeii, which—already exposed for two centuries—risked collapse.

The problems of ordinary administration then had to be addressed. Weeds had to be brought under control, for their roots chewed up stone. Metal roofs were rusting down onto rapidly fading frescoed walls. The budgetary strains were enormous; at the time, only half the the huge ticket revenues Pompeii earned ever reached the administration, having been lost mysteriously before it reached officialdom. What did arrive was automatically sent to the heritage ministry in Rome for redistribution back to all the Vesuvian sites, but also as subsidies to less popular archaeological sites.

Conticello also saw that what money returned to Pompeii tended to go toward restoration of the same buildings again and again—those houses most favoured by tourists. Little remained either to launch new projects or to maintain the vast number of buildings the public found uninteresting, however important they might be to science and history. If the building were, moreover, at Herculaneum, as opposed to Pompeii, it ranked farther down the list of priority projects. If it was an academic project, as opposed to a restoration of a popular building, such as the House of the Vettii or the brothel of Pompeii, it had less priority. And if it concerned the reading of papyrus, it had no priority at all.

Conticello desired to go beyond the ordinary. Approached by that Cinderella of academia, the minuscule papyrus lobby, Conticello listened. Their proposals captivated him. Heeding the arguments of Italian and international scholars, he was instrumental in arranging government funding for a new exploration of the Villa of the Papyri.

This would be the most ambitious adventure in the history of Pompeian archaeology for three decades. To carry it out, the best minds of modern Italian scholarship and engineering would do their utmost. Working with Conticello were archaeologist Antonio De Simone of the University of Naples and geologist Umberto Cioffi of Infrasud Progetti, SpA, which belonged to the Italian state financial holding company, IRI-Italstat, and had already built most of the highway tunnels in and around Naples.

To find the hypothetical lost Latin library was not a goal at the outset. This was to make an accurate map, with a mind to eventual expropriations; from above ground it was impossible to know the precise layout of the villa so far below. Speed mattered: there was always the risk that new shopping malls or other buildings would pop up to add to the complications atop the villa.

For months, aided by technicians, Conticello and his colleagues had again and again analysed photocopied enlargements of army mining engineer Weber's map hanging in the Archaeological Museum of Naples. And they had studied Weber's old excavation reports, no easy task. Born near Schwyz, Weber had spoken Schwyzerdeutsch in his childhood and Italian to his northern Italian wife. Most of the reports written in his neat, rounded hand were in the 18th-century official Spanish of the south Italian throne.

The Veneruso shaft which Weber had excavated to reach down to his horizontal spider web of tunnels was now a well inside a greenhouse redolent with the sweet scent of carnations, which were sold throughout Europe. The farmer owning the land watered his carnations with water from this very well, and had agreed to their probing down through it only on condition that any drilling to remove old debris would cause no vibrations that put his property at risk.

At sixty feet underground the technicians had reached a layer of rock-hard lava. Vibrations began, and the machines could no longer be employed. Work had proceeded by hand. But the carnation farmer had grown tired of the intrusion. He withdrew authorization. The preliminary exploration came to a halt.

The frustrated excavators had to find an alternative entry into the villa. They knew that Weber had dug two more shafts, but the locations had long since been forgotten. Then the one called Ciceri I was rediscovered by engineer Antonio Jorio and archaeology writer Carlo Knight.

From above the Ciceri I shaft the shoreline was visibly altered, for it had been shoved forward half a mile by the AD 79 eruption. But otherwise the view was almost the same as that which the community of the Villa of the Papyri would have seen from the belvedere: the islands of Capri and Ischia floating in the distance and the slopes of Mount Vesuvius. There were differences: the 1944 eruption had obliterated the plume of smoke which had been the hallmark of the volcano, beloved of artists and of pilots, and the once densely forested slopes of the volcano were now home to 600,000 people—all of whom remain at risk from an eventual new eruption.

Finally, on 16 December 1986, the first archaeological descent into the villa in some 230 years could begin. The adventurous climb would be down the well shaft on some newly attached aluminium ladders, but mostly on the 18th-century iron ladders still in place. It was an emotional moment for the trio preparing to enter the villa. The first to enter were Conticello, geologist Cioffi, and archaeologist De Simone. The workmen would follow with geoseismic testing equipment. "In truth we were terrified. I had to press my foot down on each of the antique iron rungs and hope it would not collapse", Conticello recalled in an interview. "We had cords tied around us like Alpinists so that if the tunnel began to collapse, we could be pulled out."

Theirs was a voyage down through the geology of eruptive time. First they descended through fifteen feet of pyroclastic matter left by the 1944 eruption, and then past a thirteen-foot layer of solid lava

from the eruption of 1631. Below this were ten more feet of pyroclastic material. Finally they reached the thirty-six-foot shelf of
consolidated mud which had engulfed Herculaneum in a violent,
boiling surge in AD 79, and had buried the city while shoving its
roofs forward. At the bottom of the well shaft they stood more than
seventy feet underground. The reassuring sight of twin columns,
marked on Weber's map, showed them their exact position.

Carrying flashlights, they advanced slowly as a tube sent down
air. Coming to a low ceiling, they had to creep forward briefly on
hands and knees before they could stand upright again, or almost.
At intervals of from nine to eighteen feet they saw the small niches
which had once held the candles whose feeble light had shown the
forced labourers where to dig. And on a wall a date had been scribbled: 1753. "We were so thrilled, we hugged each other like school
boys", Conticello recalled.

Then they realized they were standing exactly where Karl Weber
had made his first discovery of the villa: on the floor of the round
belvedere where the trompe l'oeil floor in opus sectile marble had
been found. As it had for Weber, this led them down the long walkway into the Great Peristyle, and then into the villa proper, where
Conticello began to test Weber's old measurements. "And they were
precise", a delighted Conticello reported. Even the Great Peristyle
with its long pool was exactly where Weber had shown it. Although
the early excavators had removed its showier mosaics, many
brightly coloured mosaics were still visible at the pool bottom.

However, in the tunnels at the bottom the problems the modern
excavators faced were also the same as they had been for Weber and
the slave labourers of the 18th century. If anything, they were worse,
Cioffi realized.[9] The tunnels had to be cleared of rubble. No tunnel
was more than thirty-five inches wide and rarely more than five feet
high, and in some stretches much lower. "Today's workmen are
taller than Weber's forced labourers. And besides, ours wore hard
hats", Cioffi recalled. "No one could stand upright without banging
his head". This was so even though he specifically hired short workmen. Systems of forced air and lighting impervious to the dripping
of water had to be introduced, and especially small-sized picks and
shovels manufactured. Such was the discomfort that workmen,
awed at the suffering which their predecessors must have endured,
could tolerate no more than two-hour shifts.

Poisonous gas remained a risk. In the 1750s, terrifying sparks and
even "una llama de fuego" (a flame) had been seen more than once,
and a pick-axe striking against rock in a gas-filled tunnel had actu-

ally started a fire. The villa excavation had halted, but briefly reopened in 1761, only to be quickly shut down again when deadly volcanic gases seeped into the tunnels. Today's technicians addressed this by installing a modern testing system.

Their exploration had advanced the knowledge of the villa in several ways. Weber's map had given an erroneous orientation of the villa. The new map corrected this, showing the precise location of the underground situation of the villa in relation to the land above it, a prerequisite for future excavations of any kind. They also discovered that, although Weber showed the villa all on one level, like a ranch house, in fact it had raised portions connected by steps. Outside, roots of grape vines were found beside the belvedere—the Epicurean Garden itself, a delighted Professor Gigante theorized when he heard that news.

The exploration had also demonstrated that further tunnelling underground would be very, very difficult indeed, if not impossible for the time being, given the difficulties of water seepage, lack of air and the continued risk of poisonous gas. If the villa were to be explored, another solution would have to be found.

In January, 1999, I stood before a giant canyon. From a ramp leading down into it I could see a pool of water at the bottom and, to one side, four storeys of terraced building. On one of the terraces student archaeologists, looking as if they were making a picture puzzle, were piecing together a shattered wall fresco; nearby was an ancient rowing boat, upside-down. The noise of the earth-moving equipment was deafening.

The underground exploration of the Villa of the Papyri had been discarded in favour of this one, open to the skies. To accomplish this, Conticello had managed to persuade the government to expropriate a limited number of the farm properties above ground. One building overhead could not be expropriated, however. It was the 17th-century villa, later refurbished in the neo-classical style and now used as city hall. In other cases the desired expropriation was complicated by the fact that some land owners expected exorbitant payments.

The ambitious new excavation, which had cleared away thousands of tons of earth, had taken place under the direction of archaeologist De Simone. It had already shown that before AD 79, the sprawling villa, shown on Weber's map as having only one storey, in fact had three. Weber had found only the uppermost level. Clearing away the seafront facade, De Simone had uncovered two more storeys, terraced like stepping-stones down the side of a cliff to the sea level and a probable boat dock—hence the finding of a boat. A shallow probe made into a few of the villa's seafront rooms had revealed handsome mosaic floors. A baths complex had also been discovered lying between the villa and the city wall.

Archaeologist De Simone had established that, though the villa was enlarged later, its nucleus dated from the mid-1st century BC. This reconfirmed papyrologist Gigante's dating of the villa to Piso's era. There was a downside, or rather several. It was known that a stream passed between the wall and the villa. This small river had been deviated by the lava mud surge of AD 79. Water was streaming into the newly excavated area, requiring a pump at work twenty-four hours a day, every day. In addition, discovery of the baths and of the additional storeys of the building—whose existence no one had imagined—had brought a significant cost overrun. The grumbling of the bean-counters at the cultural ministry was drowned out only by the ferocious racket of the bulldozers. As yet, no new papyri had been found. Nor was there new evidence firmly linking the villa to Piso or Philodemus.

A few days after my visit the bulldozers fell silent. The exploration beyond the newly opened facade had been stopped due to lack of further funding from the Italian government. The new administrators of Pompeii under Professor Pier Giovanni Guzzo were sceptical about the value of further exploration of the villa. His opposition was seriously logical: why excavate the new site, adding more maintenance obligations, when that already open to visitors, scholars, thieves and pollution was not yet properly maintained, and funds were finite? Another objection—this at least debatable—was that expropriations patchwork style were pointless. And wasn't the hunt for papyrus just another version of the old treasure hunt?

Even private foreign contributions to excavating the villa were later discouraged as a result, and when Packard Foundation officials stepped in with an offer, they were rerouted toward the refurbishing of town houses and other buildings inside the walls of Herculaneum. All was rigorously logical. But it ignored two things. First, papyri are not treasure, save to the most serious of scholars, whose interest is history, not conventional loot.

Secondly, the Villa of the Papyri is unfinished business. In consideration of the immense income from Vesuvian sites, excavators have considerable margin of choice. Their priorities could extend to completion of the excavation of the Villa of the Papyri, halted largely due to piranha-like demands for payment for expropriated lands. Sad but true, the excavated sites of Vesuvius lie in crime territory, but this should be faced boldly, not passively accepted.

Three years later I again stood on the ramp and gazed across the gaping mud canyon at the newly visible cliff-side facade of the Villa of the Papyri. It was the year 2002, and I was in the company of a British scholar of classical Greek who had worked for many years on deciphering and translating the writings of Philodemus. At the time, Professor Richard Janko, author of a translation of Philodemus' writings on poetry just awarded the Goodwin Award of Merit of the American Philological Association, was at University College, London; today he is chairman of the classics department of the University of Michigan at Ann Arbor.

We knew that as much as half of the interior of the upper level of the villa was still sealed, along with most of the lower level. The possibility of finding the Latin library or other new scrolls, if they exist, had been left dangling. Janko spoke for many when he described his frustration at sight of the abandoned excavation.

"I feel as if I were within a meter of knowing what lies inside the rooms of the villa. It is right there. And we just do not know." So it has remained—an enigma waiting for resolution.

Conticello, meantime, was kicked upstairs in the ministry of cultural heritage, becoming its central inspector in Rome. De Simone returned to academic life before being called to begin an important new exploration, as we shall see. Papyrologist Gigante was dead. He had died without learning the end of the story to which he had contributed so generously. However, for those eager to see inside it, the villa already existed and could be seen elsewhere—in a replica built in California.

It was ridiculous ... Here was this strange old man, sitting in rural Surrey [England], saying he wanted to recreate, in Malibu, on the borders of Hollywood, a Roman villa that no one had ever seen and was lying sixty feet under the ground in Italy. I wrote a long report advising him against it because I thought there was a serious risk both he and the building would be ridiculed.[10]

The sceptic was Stephen Garret, London architect and consultant working in Los Angeles. It was a typically soggy English day in November 1968, and the world's richest man, John Paul Getty, had summoned Garret, who had already designed building projects for

44. American petroleum tycoon John Paul Getty, who travelled in Italy as a student and again in the 1930s, wrote a novella set in ancient Pompeii. This photograph by Milton Gendel shows the connoisseur and collector Getty in his home near Rome.

Getty in Italy and in California. Now the "strange old man" wanted Garret to design a brand new museum in California as a showcase for Getty's personal collection of works of art, then housed somewhat casually on the sixty-four-acre Getty citrus ranch in California.

What sort of building would be appropriate? Getty had a passionate dislike of modern architecture, as was well known. With equal passion Getty admired the architecture of antiquity. As he wrote in his autobiography, "The beginnings of my interest can be traced back to my earliest visits to Italy and Greece, where I saw the crumbled and fragmentary remnants of the architectural marvels that these long-dead civilizations had produced."

But when Getty proposed that the model for the building be the ancient Roman Villa of the Papyri, Garret was taken aback, especially when he learned that the building had never been seen because it lay entirely underground. The replica of the Villa of the Papyri was to be reconstructed on the basis of Karl Weber's map from the 1750s, which Getty had seen when he toured Herculaneum the first time back in 1913.

Getty ultimately became a true connoisseur and talented amateur antiquarian, almost as knowledgeable of Greco-Roman antiquities as of Big Oil. As a student in England, Getty had moved in aristocratic circles where collections of classical antiquities on show were part of the stately home way of life. Even so, imagining Pompeii preceded his collecting. As a youth Getty wrote a novella about Pompeii called *A Journey from Corinth*, in which the boy tycoon indulges in a flight of almost Arcadian fantasy into antiquity. Some of the story's details curiously dovetail the beginning of Lytton's 1834 novel, *The Last Days of Pompeii*. As in *Last Days*, Getty's young hero was born in Greece, is named Glaucus, and moves to Neapolis (Naples) from Corinth.

Getty in writer's mode was still Getty, and the first pages of the novel are a long disquisition on the dangers, especially financial, of the sea voyage to Naples. Money mattered to him: just as Getty had been financially astute in oil, he bought fine examples of genres of antiquities just before they became popular. Preparing himself subsequently to become a collector on the grand scale, Getty began by being professionally tutored in New York City in the late 1930s. "He only wanted to buy regal works of art", as a New York dealer recalled.[11]

In November of 1940, he was in Rome at the Excelsior Hotel on Via Veneto, where he sat reading Gibbon's *Decline and Fall of the Roman Empire.* He began making his purchases there, having decided to concentrate on acquiring busts of Greek and Roman heroes and the decorative arts of the 18th century. At that time neither was keenly sought by other collectors. Getty was both prescient in taste and a bargain hunter. At the time he built the museum, his collection was the third most important collection of classical antiquities in the US and worth $200 million, by his own evaluation, far more than he had paid for it.

The museum replica of the Villa of the Papyri was designed with the help of archaeologist Norman Neuerburg of California State University, at a cost of $17 million. In addition, Getty provided a $2 billion endowment to ensure its perennial maintenance, and this allowed creation of a separate scholarly library.[12] The museum was to be free of charge to visitors, and Getty calculated that the net personal cost to him was $3 per visitor or, with 300,000 annual visitors, $900,000 per year.

According to Getty's biographer, Russell Miller, the choice of the Villa of the Papyri as a model was linked to his acquiring a large-scale statue of Herakles (Hercules) which Getty believed had once stood in the Villa of the Papyri at Herculaneum. The statue had been found in 1790 outside Rome, near the Emperor Hadrian's Villa at Tivoli, and purchased by the English Marquess of Lansdowne, but Getty believed that it was among the statues that Piso, the former consul in Macedonia, had installed in the Villa of the Papyri, but which had been purchased not long before the eruption and eventually installed in Hadrian's Villa outside Rome.

Construction of the J. Paul Getty Museum began in 1970. Weber's one-storey floor plan of the villa, was adapted for a two-storey museum. The famous elongated reflecting pool ran down the centre of Getty's porticoed peristyle, and outside was a handsome replica of the geometric marble inlay (*opus sectile*) floor of the belvedere.

The museum opened its doors in January 1974, to scathing criticism on aesthetic grounds. The *New York Times* called the building "pretentious and somewhat sterile". Architectural critics scorned it variously as Disney-like and too attuned to "popular taste". The building was even put down as unethical for its use of the "architectural imagery" of the past (hey, we're in the 1970s), because its design was based on a rich man's whim, and because the technology employed in the repro ancient Roman villa differed from that used to build the original. In short, the new building did not rise to the demands of a high aesthetic.[13]

The people voted with their feet. During its first year the new museum attracted some 350,000 visitors—so many that Getty asked local authorities permission to add more parking space. The permit was rejected on grounds that the neighbours were already in a state over the hundreds of thousands of visitors flocking to his museum and did not want more.[14] When the Malibu museum was set to be refurbished in the year 2000, the same objections delayed work for over a year.

Views of the reconstructed Villa of the Papyri—newly restored as the Getty Museum Villa to distinguish it from the Getty Center designed by Richard Meier, which opened in 1997—have changed radically since those days. Even the architects like it these days. "Postmodernism has played itself out", Peter J. Holliday of California State University explained at a conference on the heritage of

45. When opened in 1974 at Malibu, California, the repro Villa of the Papyri, built by John Paul Getty as a museum of classical antiquities, was deplored by architectural modernists but loved by the public. Exploration of the real villa at Herculaneum was partly financed by Getty.

Pompeii and Herculaneum which took place in Philadelphia in 2002.[15] Getty's repro Greek-influenced villa played a role in the search for a new aesthetic by its "introduction and legitimization of a new form of classical vocabulary".

It is argued that the Villa of the Papyri contributed to changing the face of contemporary American architecture by its re-introduction in the mid-1970s of some of the forms of neo-classical architecture. For Getty, hunched over his easy chair in England, the knowledge that his personal taste exhibited at Malibu had given dozens of buildings across America a different and more pleasant look would have brought a wry smile.

As Getty said in 1957, "You can criticize a man's wife, his children, in fact almost anything about him. But if you criticize his taste in art, you offend him mortally."

The crowds at both Malibu and, now, flocking to the two Getty museums in California, plus the architecture establishment's acceptance of a new kind of neo-classicism, have long since vindicated Getty's taste. Like Getty's collection of statues and paintings from antiquity, the reproduced villa at Malibu turned out to be one smart bargain.

EPILOGUE

Lost Again

46. Cupids fishing, engraving

In the spring of the year 2000, once more I stared down into a gaping hole. Vesuvius was, as usual, the backdrop, though not, this time, for the Villa of the Papyri. This excavation was called Murecine, which meant "Little Walls," because that was what the farmers had been able to see. From where I stood I could see the ruined buildings of ancient Pompeii, rising from its lava shelf a half-mile distant.

What I saw in the mud thirty feet or so below my feet resembled a vast, flooded basement several hundred yards long. A half-dozen pumps struggled mightily to keep seeping water at bay as workers with wheelbarrows carted away more mud. Junior archaeologists wearing rubber boots splashed and slid through the water and mud as they worked.

Above ankle level, however, the rooms which had been revealed for the first time since that August day of AD 79 were of extraordinary and unexpected elegance. Far beneath the rustic "walls", visible to local farmers for centuries, lay a succession of buried rooms, whose walls were lusciously painted with muses in fluttering gowns who held musical instruments and perfume bowls. On one wall a river god reclined, on another a goddess—a *nike*—raised a wreath of victory high overhead. I saw in the centre of one of these rooms a cleverly designed fountain; this would have been a dining room, a *triclinium*, for stone benches provided seating, or reclining, on three sides. Another room with a long work counter had plainly served as a kitchen. Archaeologist Antonio De Simone, who had overseen the excavation of the Villa of the Papyri, was enthusiastically shouting his explanation of this stunning new site and its complexities.

The deafening noise came only in part from the massive pumps, and herein lay the story. Just as water poured in underfoot, an endless stream of cars and motorcycles and gigantic trucks whizzed along almost overhead. Towering over us upon high earthen embankments was a huge highway. This divided toll highway, whose ceaseless traffic is clearly visible to visitors as they exit ancient Pompeii, is the main connection between Naples and Salerno, and brings tourists to Pompeii through one of its exits. Indeed, it is one of the busiest highways in Italy, and notoriously accident-ridden.

The archaeologist who had once shown Mussolini around Pompeii, Amedeo Maiuri, had survived the fall of Fascism to continue as superintendent of Pompeii for more than a decade after the end of World War II. In the poverty of the early postwar period excavations at Pompeii were relaunched with a vengeance as part of a campaign of public works.

Highway building was even more important. At Murecine, therefore, the good intentions of those desiring to improve the archaeology of Pompeii met the good intentions of those desiring to improve the economy of the south of Italy. Put another way, the national desire to promote high culture, a non-Fascist, specifically Italian heritage, and mass tourism appeared to coincide with the need to find jobs for the unemployed and to foster industrial development by building roads. It seemed a perfect match.

Until the 1950s the excavations at Pompeii had been scattered, patchwork fashion. No one could walk through Pompeii from beginning to end. But Maiuri had a vision: to make a clean sweep that would open up and unify all the excavated areas of Pompeii. Pompeii's walls form an ellipse. To make his dream into reality, he would have to connect the dots. All that lay in a direct line from the gladiatorial amphitheatre at one end of the ellipse all the way to the basilica and forum at the opposite would have to be cleared. The result would be an unfettered vision of the entire city.

The problem was dirt. To cart away all the thousands of tons of earth and rubble removed from a site had always been a gigantic problem at Pompeii. In this case the problem would be sorely aggravated by the sheer quantity of material that would have to be hauled elsewhere. Meanwhile, construction of the new highway had already begun at either end, meaning that one construction crew had begun at Naples, the other at Sorrento. Pompeii lay midway between the two. As the construction crews converged in the broad valley just south of Pompeii, Maiuri realized that the builders would need slag and rubble in order to raise a solid support for the double highway that would cross that valley originally shaped by the waters of the Sarno River. The earth bed for the new *autostrada*, therefore, could be made of the volcanic rubble and pebbles that would otherwise form a giant hill when his planned new excavation of Pompeii began on the grand scale. In exchange, the construction company building the Naples–Salerno highway could provide workmen and equipment to excavate at Pompeii. In other words, the workmen's salaries were paid in the coin of volcanic slag. The swap was nothing less than genial.

The pressure to complete the highway rapidly was enormous, and Maiuri sometimes found himself with a hundred men digging their hearts out—far more in numbers than the coerced prison labourers who had been utilized by Spanish overseers in the 18th century.

Indeed, work proceeded so rapidly that only the sloppiest and most cursory of records were kept, when kept at all. But, most fortunately, by the same token the crews focused on gardens and courtyards, because they were easiest to excavate, as Pompeian officials acknowledge gratefully today. This meant that many buildings and rooms were spared for future generations to rediscover because they yielded less lapillae.

Then the rot set in. Approaching from their two directions, the road builders ran slap into a previously unsuspected complex of ancient Roman buildings lying directly in the path of the new highway, in the little area the farmers called Murecine (also known as Moregine—The Walls). In accordance with Italian law, all work, no matter how urgent, had to be stopped while a team of archaeologists explored the site, as they did between April and December of 1959.

Their findings did not immediately arouse interest. True, there were a few painted walls, but the decorations were relatively uninspired. What seemed far more important was the finding on a bench of 125 wooden tablets, still inside their a basket-like container that had served as a wicker briefcase. The tablets, which bore traces of a waxed coating and scratchings in Latin, could be, and were, removed, along with the basket. Before locking them in a warehouse, Maiuri somewhat dismissively declared that the tablets represented "domestic accounts".[1]

Meanwhile, the better portions of the painted wall panels were being detached from their walls for safe-keeping. No one knew exactly what the buildings were, apart from the three identifiable, by the presence of *triclinium* benches, as dining rooms. Then the excavators ran into tremendous problems. Water was streaming right through the excavation. Obviously the AD 79 earthquake had channelled a part of the Sarno River near the site right into the buildings.

The water and the waiting construction crews made a decision imperative. The purposes of archaeology being satisfied, Maiuri could in good conscience allow his road-building partners to resume their work. With scarcely less efficiency than an erupting volcano, the newly discovered buildings were entirely, deeply reburied. The necessities of roadway engineering meant that a portion of the presumably domestic complex now lay directly beneath the earth support and concrete skin of the new autostrada, the A3.

The uninspired wall paintings were tucked away in a storage room, out of public view. The wicker briefcase needed no storage. No one having experience in conservation of wicker, it simply disintegrated. As for the wooden tablets, the dry air of Naples slowly but surely shrivelled them to one-half their original size.

In the years that followed, scholars discovered that the tablets were documents of financial registrations, bank business and commercial accounts. The tablets, still under intense study, tell the story of Pompeii's crucial maritime trade and how banking worked in the port city. Since they were written on both sides, they provide well over 200 pages of documents. Tablet Number 60, which records a woman taking out a loan on 20 March of AD 43, offers an example of the flavour and content:

> Accounts of Titinia Anthracis: payment made to Euplia of Milo, Theodorus's daughter, of 1,600 sesterces upon the authority of her tutor Epichares of Athens, who is the son of Aphrodisius. Euplia received the money in cash from the lockbox in the home of her creditor. Questioned by Titinia Anthracis, Aphrodisius's son Epichares of Athens declared that on behalf of Theodorus's daughter Euplia of Milo he would guarantee repayment of the 1,600 aforementioned sesterces.[2]

47. The artefacts of daily life in antiquity found in the Vesuvian sites fascinated the public worldwide. This engraving from August Mau's *Pompeii. Its
Life and Art*, published by Macmillan in New York in 1899, shows a four-folio
waxed tablet notebook next to a legal document with witnesses' signatures
visible (right).

For all his gifts, Maiuri had made a second tragic error. In the rush
to improve Pompeii by making a pact with the *autostrada* builders,
he had failed to realize the extent of the newly discovered neighbourhood at Murecine. Nor did he realize what buildings he had
found. As a result, he did not have the highway route shifted, as has
since been done elsewhere; the Via Cassia Veientana at the Valle dei
Baccanti north of Rome is a successful example of a highway shifted
to salvage a similar habitat. His misjudgement compromised an
entire and uniquely fascinating neighbourhood and conditioned
future archaeology.

In 1999 the A3 *autostrada* linking Naples and Sorrento had such
heavy use that it was being called Death Alley. To save lives, two
more lanes were being added to the four existing. Because the state
still owned all antiquities, the ministry for cultural heritage required
the same clearance from the superintendent of Pompeii, at that time
the meticulous Pier Giovanni Guzzo, as it had in Maiuri's day. Work
on the Villa of the Papyri having been stopped, Professor Antonio

De Simone of Naples University was summoned to conduct the new assessment for the government, working along with a fellow university archaeologist, the distinguished Salvatore Ciro Nappo.

In the year 2000 this second excavation of Murecine began. Once again financing came from the road-building company, Autostrade Meridionali. First the archaeologists penetrated alongside the highway itself. Then they explored underneath it. The results of this second investigation were literally astounding.

Continuing to pursue the various wall structures, the archaeologists realized that the indifferent paintings were merely the upper panels of a far more ambitious and fascinating ancient decorating scheme for a sprawling construction that lay more deeply buried underneath. In addition to the AD 79 eruption, during the Renaissance a new eruption had buried the building further still, giving the impression of a floor level many feet above the original floor.

Gradually a dozen rooms emerged: the big kitchen with its oven and long counter, a total of eight separate dining rooms (one with an elaborately engineered fountain system), and an adjacent spa with rooms for hot and cold water pools. Its elegant windowed frontage gave onto one of the fjord-like lagoons at the mouth of the Sarno River; this lagoon would have been shallow, for a boat with a flat

48. Ankle deep in water, an Italian archaeologist works at the luxury complex of river-front buildings at Murecine, near Pompeii and buried in the eruption of AD 79. A diverted channel of the Sarno River cut through the building cluster, recently reburied beneath a speedway overhead.

keel was also found. Steps leading to an upper floor showed that more rooms topped the dining area and kitchen.

Also, in the corridor between the baths and the hotel a new basket of treasures was discovered inside a latrine tucked beneath a staircase. Taking no risks, the archaeologists had the basket removed, mud encasement and all, for study. Inside, as X-rays revealed, were no less than forty pieces from a table service of silver weighing four kilos. The pieces ranged from a big serving platter with decorated edges down to a serving spoon; one cup, intended to amuse, depicts a country woman improbably feeding grapes from her apron to her chicken, which is standing upon an altar. This was only the third table service from antiquity at Pompeii; the previous two were the Boscoreale service found in 1895; the other was found by Maiuri himself in 1930 in the House of the Menander at Pompeii (in the National Archaeological Museum at Naples). After five years of painstaking work this third precious trove of silver was safely removed from the basket for conservation. This time,

49. A rare find at the Murecine complex (also known as Moregine) on the Sarno River was a wicker basket, still intact. When opened carefully, it was found to contain a hoard of forty serving items of sterling silver, including these platters and cups.

thanks to new conservation techniques, the basket too has been preserved.

Grand as it was, this was only the beginning. Next-door was a second group of buildings, including a tavern with rooms above it, presumably for the coachmen, slaves and boatmen in the service of the expense account crowd convivially cutting their deals in the hotel–spa complex. Skeletons too were found, including of children. One was of a woman in her thirties, still wearing a thick gold upper arm bracelet in the form of a snake. Engraved inside it was a dedication that read, in Latin, "Master to his slave girl". "My hand was shaking as I took it off her arm," said De Simone. The bracelet is particularly important as the first material evidence ever found intimating the existence of a sentimental relationship between an owner and his female slave.

The new complex of buildings has been hailed as the most fascinating found since the systematic excavation of the villa at the Pompeian suburb of Oplontis had begun back in 1964. The Murecine paintings too are exceptional, considered the finest found since discovery of the Villa of the Mysteries in the 1930s.

Returning again and again to Murecine, I watched as the buildings came into view. At the time of the eruption these buildings were freshly refurbished; indeed, in some rooms the post-earthquake renovation was still underway. Ownership of the complex, which I privately called the Five-Star Riverside Hotel and Wellness Spa, was proven not only by the waxed tablets. In the big kitchen which served the eight private dining rooms, some sixty marble panels for the new floor of the baths were stacked against the counter. Each slab was marked with "SULP," for Sulpicii—those very bankers whose business archives Maiuri had found in the (disintegrated) wicker briefcase. The city further up the Gulf of Naples had not been damaged by the earthquake preceding the AD 79 eruption. These rich bankers from Puteoli first snapped up the hotel portion, largely undamaged by the quake of AD 68, and then the spa, which they decided to renovate.[3]

For the archaeologists, the rule was that the show must go on. No matter how important this miniature village was, the highway had precedence. The walls and every removable element of three of the dining rooms, down to a fountain table and collapsible lattice wooden door with its bronze lock still in place, were taken away with meticulous care for restoration and future museum display.

As for the rest—the long kitchen counter, the almost-complete new baths, the five other dining rooms—I watched them disappear. One wheelbarrow load after another, the earth which had been removed was dumped back into the huge hole. Today the entire complex is lost from sight, invisible and buried beneath the now widened highway visible in the distance from Pompeii and linking Naples to Sorrento.

Just so, four centuries before this, the great architect Domenico Fontana, the first to rediscover Pompeii, had sorrowfully submitted to reburying it when a duke ordered him to continue digging a ditch for pipes (still visible today at Pompeii) that would carry water to grind the ducal wheat.

Today's devastation grinds on in other forms. Vandalism is one.

Not far away at Nola, the town whose citizens got into such a pitched battle with the Pompeians that gladiatorial events were cancelled for seven years, builders of a shopping center recently dug straight into a Bronze Age village which had been buried by Vesuvius in 1,800 BC, as carbon dating proved. Exactly like Pompeii, this village had simply disappeared under a blanket of ashes so thick that no one knew of its existence until excavation for the shopping centre began.

"The villagers had to leave so quickly, they left their dirty dishes," the archaeologist heading that excavation five miles or so from ancient Pompeii told me. Their village of thirty horseshoe-shaped houses, each with a sleeping loft, were cunningly built, with an air-space between otherwise fragile walls to keep the homes cool in summer and warm in winter.

In their flight from the volcano's wrath the villagers left behind a fine jug—it looks exactly like today's milk pitcher—in their ceramics kiln, waiting to be fired. The jug was taken to authorities in Naples for conservation. The kiln remained on the site, obviously.

A few weeks afterward vandals destroyed the kiln, for fun.

Fortunately, not all of today's stories have sad endings.

The newest important excavation in the territories around Pompeii is of a mystery-shrouded building—more probably, a complex of buildings—buried some forty feet underground near Somma Vesuviana, the small town that lies due north of Mount Vesuvius, just below the hump called Mount Somma. Visiting the site in October 2005, I once again found veteran Italian archaeologist Antonio

De Simone hard at work. "Many Roman villas along the coastline between Naples and Pozzuoli (ancient Puteoli) have been excavated, but this is unique and uniquely important", said De Simone, who serves as Italian scientific advisor of the project. "We think it may be the villa in which both the Emperor Augustus and his father died". Relatively few archaeological research projects have been conducted on the inland villas surrounding Mount Vesuvius, De Simone added. The costly excavation, utilizing high-tech excavation equipment, is financed by the University of Tokyo, with on-site direction by Professor Masanori Aoyagi flanked by a binational team of archaeologists as field directors, Satoshi Matsuyama and Claudia Angelelli.

That an important building lay underground has been known since 1929, when a local doctor and archaeology enthusiast learned that a farmer trying to dig a well had found a wall blocking his way. Try as he might, the farmer had been unable to destroy the wall. Intrigued, the doctor launched a tiny exploratory excavation. Almost immediately his workmen found the wall. Its strikingly large size showed that it was part of an important building—so important that archaeologists from the Fascist state's cultural establishment took over.

The finding of mammoth square columns, typical of imperial architecture, combined with the sheer size of the mystery wall, suggested to the archaeologists that this may have been a great lost villa described by both Suetonius and Tacitus. If so, it had belonged to the family of Caesar Augustus. Here Augustus' father had died, and here, sixty years before the eruption of AD 79, Augustus himself had died. Famous in its time, the exploration attracted a parade of illustrious visitors and scholars. Both came to a halt with World War II.

Sixty years later, the excavation was revived by the University of Tokyo, supported by the University of Naples. First the 1930s site had to be rediscovered. Old maps led the archaeologists straight to the cottage of a farmer, who had built his small stone house directly atop the old dig, incorporating the monumental wall into its foundations.

A fund-raising campaign in Japan allowed the purchase of the cottage and surrounding field. When the excavation was finally launched, the scientific team—it now included a vulcanologist from Naples University—learned that their mystery building had not been destroyed in the AD 79 eruption at all, but in the late 5th century AD. Later, three or more subsequent eruptions entombed it more deeply still. "But the point is that from the time of its construction until that medieval eruption, the building was occupied", said Professor De Simone in an interview on the site. "This means that it reflects five hundreds years of use".

At the time of writing, a great porticoed hall and another large room are visible. To enter them is to experience the same sensation Karl Weber or Maiuri must have felt: our footsteps are the first for centuries. The back entrance of the hall leads to a narrow road important enough to be paved with traditional Roman flat stones of basalt. The imposing doorway, whose colours still glow from its stucco decoration, may have led to a formal garden.

Inside that door, the portico roof has collapsed, but once it was held up by a dozen massive square columns in a double row. Unless they supported a five-storey building (and there is no sign of this), their exaggerated size, one by 0.5 metres, is a nice demonstration of imperial Roman grandiosity for its own sake, which is to say architectural propaganda.

Niches for statues appear in the curved walls of this hall, which in my own mind—not the cautious archaeologists'—is a grand carriage hall where the emperor's fine covered wagon, decorated with ivory and gilt, would have been kept. Two fine statues have been found so far, both in marble worked in the Roman Hellenistic-style. Surprisingly, the statue of a woman—the subject is yet to be identified—was found intact and still standing proudly in her niche. Workmen, using a miniature digger, were cautiously scraping away at a wall of lavic mud and rubble when, with uncanny dramatic force, her face emerged from the mud—a white marble ghost of Vesuvius. The statue would have been visible in its niche for centuries, yet had remained in place and untouched. In an adjacent room a humble oven, built centuries after the statue was placed into her niche, was also found, testimony to the subsequent decline in the social status of the inhabitants.

This showcase cooperative project is expected to continue at least until 2008. In practice, the duration and extent appear open-ended. The building was surely part of a sprawling estate, and other buildings almost certainly lie buried nearby beneath vineyards and orchards. "We buy from a farmer one field at a time", as Satoshi Matsuyama put it. "And each purchase means that new funding must be found."

The century-old Italian law states that all archaeological remains on its territory belong to the Italian government. The compromise is that the excavation at present is entirely financed by the University of Tokyo, which has legally purchased the land. At some point when the project is considered complete, the University of Tokyo has agreed to donate the land to the Italian government.

Rigorously multi-disciplinary, the excavating team includes, in addition to a vulcanologist, experts in conservation, architecture, geography and informatics. Another specialist is Akira Matsuda of the Institute of Archaeology, University College London, an expert in community relations at heritage sites. This too is a novelty. Most of the farmers living in Somma Vesuviana, with over 35,000 inhabitants, or on scattered farms had never seen a Japanese citizen apart from in movies. As the Prussian Winckelmann had been for the Neapolitan royals in the late 18th century, the Japanese archaeologists were aliens. Some—so the Japanese feared—might resent presumed interlopers digging in local backyards. "We had to try to interest the local cultural figures, and explain ourselves to them", said Matsuda.

To do so, Matsuda made speeches in the town and called at the villages to explain the project. "I try to get to know the key person of each area. And I invite as many local people as possible to our excavation site when I speak to them at schools, public halls, holiday events, in cafés and on the street."

The results were gratifying. On learning that the excavators had found an important statue of Dionysus that lacked whole bits, even an arm, a local resident came forward shyly. Long ago, the resident confided to De Simone, the family had come into possession of various pieces of carved marble. One of the pieces was an arm.

Recounts Matusda proudly: "We were able to reconstruct the entire splendid statue of Dionysus, thanks to involving the community". In an area as crime-ridden as the Neapolitan hinterland, the return of valuable archaeological elements is literally astounding.

Somma Vesuviana lies directly beneath Mount Vesuvius, and even closer to it than Pompeii. And therein lies the next threat, for infrared studies show that the cauldron of the volcano is sealed by what amounts to a gigantic Champagne bottle cork. Beneath this cork a sea of magma stretching some forty square miles—that is, from the centre of the Gulf of Naples to the rim of mountains behind Vesuvius—is bubbling away

Experts consider a new eruption overdue. In recent centuries eruptions have occurred every fifty years or so; the last was in 1943.

An international committee of scientists warned in 1999 that Vesuvius, which harbours a destructive force greater than that of a nuclear bomb, is among the world's fifteen volcanoes most likely to erupt.

Should it erupt, a thirty-metre-tall wall of volcanic material, heated to 500°C., will hurtle outward from the cone at the speed of 100 kilometres per hour. As has happened for at least four millennia, all in its path will be entombed—people, first of all.

Since World War II ended, some 600,000 people have come to live in houses directly on the slopes of the volcano—those slopes once so densely-forested that they could hide Spartacus and his entire army of escaped rebel slaves. An evacuation will not be easy: when an earthquake measuring 4 on the Richter Scale struck five kilometres directly below Vesuvius in October 1999, the Italian civil protection authorities pretended not to hear the subsequent appeals to stage a trial evacuation. A trial, they decided, would cause intolerable chaos.

The potential damage to the cities painstakingly reclaimed after AD 79 is also terrifying to contemplate. Pompeii, Herculaneum, Oplontis, Nola and Somma Vesuviana can be protected only to limited extent. A recent attempt was made to defuse the volcano by bombing it, even though the Allied bombs dropped into Vesuvius in December 1943 as unwanted cargo did not stop that eruption.

The risks of a new eruption remain sufficiently real that the government actually offered financial compensation to those Vesuvius-dwellers willing to move to a safer distance. Such awareness is an advance, for, as Baldissare Conticello, former superintendent of Pompeii told me, "In the 1980s, when I warned about this at press conferences, no one would publish it".

On the brighter side, advances in vulcanology should allow advance warning. Despite chaos, many will escape, as they have in the past.

And after all, the lost cities of Vesuvius have been buried, not once, but many times over, layer upon layer, and rediscovered. For three centuries the ghost towns of Vesuvius have also captured the imagination of some of the world's most gifted artists and writers, photographers and scientists. In poetry, stone, movies and, now, the annals of cyberspace, the ghosts of Vesuvius continue to haunt the imagination.

50. Quantities of skeletons recently discovered on the original shoreline at Herculaneum contradict archaeologists' assertions that relatively few died in that resort town. Typical of today's scientific archaeology, the skeletons are under study for DNA content.

Notes

PREFACE

1 Pliny the Younger, *Letters*, Book VI, Letters XVI and XX.

CHAPTER I

1 Willem Jongman, *The Economy and Society of Pompeii*, Grieben, Amsterdam, 1988, on the shards at Ostia. In Pompeii, street signs were not written, but were small rectangular picture plaques of baked earthenware. Off the main Forum is one showing two men carrying on their shoulders a pole from which an amphora hangs; this was Amphorae Street.
2 Ray Laurence, *Roman Pompeii, Space and Society*, Routledge, London, 1994, p. 51.
3 Lucius Annaeus Seneca, *Naturales Quaestiones*, Book VI, 1, 3–4, AD 62, in Patrizia Antignani (ed.), *Pompei e Ercolano: Monumenti e miti della Campania Felix*, Pierro, Naples, 1996, p. 11.
4 L. Richardson, Jr., *Pompeii: An Architectural History*, Johns Hopkins University Press, Baltimore, 1988, p. 7.
5 Pliny the Younger, *The Letters of Caius Plinius Caecilius Secundus*, trans. Melmoth, Revd F.C.T. Bosanquet, George Bell and Son, London, 1895, Book VI, Letters XVI and XX, pp. 193–8, 200–4, slightly adapted for readability. Subsequent quotations are from the same letters.
6 University of Naples researchers Giuseppe Mastrolorenzo and Piero Paolo Petrone, "Studi scientifici sull'eruzione e i suoi effetti", in Mario Pagano (ed.), *Gli antichi ercolanesi*, catalogue, Electa, Naples, 2000.
7 See Epilogue, on Murecine
8 Antonio Ghirelli, *Storia di Napoli*, Einaudi, Turin, 1973, pp. 25–7.
9 Domenico Fontana, diary entry 1592, in Carlo Bonucci, *Pompei descritta da Carlo Bonucci architetto*, 3rd edn, Naples, 1827; also in Antignani, *Pompei e Ercolano*, pp. 44–5.

CHAPTER II

1 D.A. Parrino, *Nuova guida de forastieri per l'antichitá curiossime di Pozzuoli*, Naples, 1709, cited in Patrizia Antignani (ed.), *Il miglio d'oro*, Pierro, Naples, 1996, p. 16.
2 Francesca Longo Auricchio traces his career in "Le prime scoperte a Ercolano", *Cronache Ercolanese*, no. 27, 1997, p. 2.

3 Pagano, *Gli antichi ercolanesi*, p. 75.

4 The building was a Greek-style theatre built in the age of Augustus. For an idea of its interior finishing, visitors to Rome can see similar coloured marble panelling *in situ* in the restored interior of the Pantheon, which was built by the son-in-law of Augustus.

5 Pagano, *Gli antichi ercolanesi*, p. 79. A Greek theatre is open to the skies (though make sure that the sun will not disturb the viewers, Vitruvius had advised). In it the performers stand in the floor space called the orchestra, between stage and the rising tiers for seating. In the otherwise similar Roman theatre, the orchestra served for seating for politicians and important guests.

6 Some of the marble panelling recovered at that time are in the Church of Saint-Etienne at D'Elboeuf sur Seine.

7 Cited in Auricchio, "Le prime scoperte", p. 3.

8 The statues are known as La Grande and the two Piccole Ercolanesi.

9 Joseph Addison, *Remarks upon Several Parts of Italy*, 1705, in Roger Hudson (ed.), *The Grand Tour*, Folio Society, London, 1993, pp. 189–90.

10 Maria Forcellino, "La formazione e il metodo di Camillo Paderni", *Eutopia*, vol. 11, no. 2, 1993, pp. 49–64.

11 Nicoletta Zanni, "Lettere di Camillo Paderni ad Allan Ramsay 1739–1740", *Eutopia*, vol. 11, no. 2, 1993, pp. 65–77.

12 Ibid., p. 76.

13 Letter to Allan Ramsay, 20 November 1739, in the British Museum and published in Forcellino, "La formazione e il metodo di Camillo Paderni".

14 Charles de Brosses, *Lettres sur Herculaneum*, Paris, 1750, p. 276.

15 In Giuseppe Fiorelli, *Giornale degli scavi di Pompei*, Naples, 1861. Fiorelli, who directed the excavations at Pompeii after Italian unification, quotes from interviews circa 1765 made on site by the then excavations director Franscesco La Vega. Two of the original statues found by Alcubierre still stand in niches in the North Wing courtyard in the former Palazzo Caramanico, now a university institute. *Giornale degli scavi di Pompei* was the official site daily journal of excavations.

16 Zanni, "Lettere di Camillo Paderni ad Allan Ramsay", p. 76.

17 Quoted in Christopher Charles Parslow, *Rediscovering Antiquity: Karl Weber and the Excavation of Herculaneum, Pompeii and Stabiae*, Cambridge University Press, Cambridge, 1995. p. 33. Unless otherwise specified, other details of these early excavations are from the official royal *Cronache Ercolanensi*; from archaeologist Amedeo Maiuri, *Pompei*, Libreria dello Stato, Rome, 1931, or "Anno X Era Fascista". Especially regarding Karl Weber, Parslow's excellent book was the result of five years of research in the Naples archives and is fascinating reading for all serious students of the 18th-century excavations of the Vesuvian area.

18 Michele Ruggiero, *Storia degli scavi di Ercolano ricomposta su' documenti superstiti*, Naples, 1885, p. xiii.

19 De Brosses, *Lettres sur Herculaneum*, Letter to President Bouhier, 28 November 1739.

20 Parslow, *Rediscovering Antiquity*, p. 80.

21 Camillo Paderni, *Monumenti antichi rinvenuti ne reali scavi di Ercolano e Pompej & delineati e spiegati da D. Camillo Paderni romano*, undated. A facsimile reprint of this hand-written MS with no date has been published, with the authorization of the Biblioteca dell'Ecole de Rome, by Arte tipografica, Naples, 2000. The MS was an 1879 gift to the Ecole Française by a descendant of Napoleon.

CHAPTER III

1 Quoted in Benito Iezzi, "Viaggiatori Stranieri nell'Officina dei Papiri Ecolanesi", in Marcello Gigante (ed.), *Contributi all Storia dell Officina dei Papiri Ercolanesi, I Quaderni della Biblioteca nazionale di Napoli*, series VI/I, vol. 2, *I Papiri Erconanesi IV*, Istituto Poligrafico e Zecca dello Stato, Rome, 1986, p. 163.

2 The sculpture has been on view to the public at the Naples Archaeological Museum since early 2000.

3 Padre Antonio Piaggio, in his *Memorie* diary (1769–1971), cited in Francesca Longo Auricchio and Mario Capasso, "I rotoli della villa ercolanese: Dislocazione e ritrovamento", in *Cronache Ercolanesi*, vol. 17, Gaetano Macchiaroli, Naples, 1987, p. 38.

4 Iezzi, "Viaggiatori stranieri nell'officina dei papiri ercolanesi", p. 165.

5 Ibid., Letter from Bishop Juan Andres, who toured Herculaneum in 1785.

6 William Gell, *Pompeiana, The Topography, Edifices, and Ornaments of Pompeii*, London, 1817, p. vii. Gell quotes a letter of 1755 from Carlo Paderni in Naples to Thomas Hollis in London and published that year in *Philosophical Transactions of the Royal Society of London*. See also Auricchio and Capasso, "I rotoli della villa ercolanese", p. 37.

7 Ammianus Marcellinus, XIV, 6, 18, quoted in Luciano Canfora, *The Vanished Library, A Wonder of the Ancient World*, trans. Martin Ryle, University of California Press, Los Angeles, 1990, p. 196.

8 Iezzi, "Viaggiatori stranieri nell'officina dei papiri ercolanesi", p. 163.

9 Ibid. p. 169.

10 Auricchio and Capasso, "I rotoli della villa ercolanese", p. 38. The authors cite Martorelli, a Neapolitan scholar and contemporary of Paderni.

11 Agnese Travaglione, "I papiri ercolanesi", *BNN/Quaderni*, series IX, no. 1, La Biblioteca Nazionale di Napoli, Naples, 1977, p. 89.

12 Mario Capasso, University of Lecce, speaking at the International Conference of Papyrology, Florence, 26 August 1998.

13 Auricchio and Capasso, "I rotoli della villa ercolanese", p. 38.

14 Paolo Moreno (ed.), "Winckelmann 2000", *Archeo*, December 2000, p. 68; Parslow, *Rediscovering Antiquity*, pp. 216–17.

15 Charles Burney, in Hudson, *The Grand Tour*, p. 249.

16 J.J. Winckelmann, *Gedanken über die Nachahmung der Greischiechen Werke in der malerey und Bilderkunst*, Saxon State Library, Friedrichstadt (Dresden), 1755; translated into English by Henrich Füsseli, as *Thoughts on the Imitation of Greek Works*, A. Millar, London, 1765. For a synthesis see David Irwin (ed.), *Writings on Art*, Phaidon, London, 1972.

17 Ibid., pp. 104–6 and 113–22.

18 Winckelmann, *Gedanken über die Nachahmung der Greischiechen Werke*.

19 J.J. Winckelmann, in Eric Fermé (ed.), *Art History and its Methods*. Phaidon, London, 1995. p. 72

20 E. Caird, *Hegel*, Blackwood Philosophical Classics, London, 1883, pp. 5–8, in Will Durant, *The Story of Philosophy, the Lives and Opinions of the Great Philosophers*, Simon & Schuster, New York, 1926, 1961, p. 221.

21 Auricchio and Capasso. "I rotoli della villa ercolanese", p. 26, Letters to Berends and to Muzl Stosch.

CHAPTER IV

1 Gina Carla Ascioni, *Ercolano nella cultura artistica del Settecento e dell'Ottocento*, exhibition catalogue, Electa, Naples, 2000, p. 36.

2 Letter from Antonio Grimaldi, prince of Monaco, to the French foreign minister, 1714, cited in the fascinating biography by the Italian scholar Mirella Mafrici, *Fascino e potere di una regina, Elisabetta Farnese sulla scena europea*, Avagliano Editori, Cava de' Tirreni, 1999, p. 33.

3 Visible today in the Naples Archaeological Museum, it is newly restored.

4 A. Arata, "La politica dei Farnese e il Cardinale Alberoni", in *Archivio storico per le province parmensi*, vol. VII, 1929, pp. 120–1. Cited in Mafrici, *Fascino e potere di una regina*, p. 23.

5 Cited in Mafrici, *Fascino e potere di una regina*, p. 163.

6 M.R. de Courcy, "La renonciation des Bourbons d'Espagne au trone de France", *Revue de Deux Mondes*, Paris, 1888. Cited in Mafrici, *Fascino e potere di una regina*, pp. 21–2.

7 Giuseppe Coniglio, *I Borboni di Spagna*, Dall'Oglio, Milan, 1970, pp. 196–232.

8 Mafrici, *Fascino e potere di una regina*, p. 165.

9 From a letter of 16 July 1732, by Count Rottembourg, the French ambassador to Madrid. The count said that the king's only pleasures had become attending Mass and reading his breviary. Cited in Mafrici, *Fascino e potere di una regina*, p. 165.

10 From Paolo Maria Doria, "Il politico moderno", Biblioteca Nazionale di Napoli, Brancacciano, V D III, 8 cit., f. 50 v, cited in Mafrici, *Fascino*

e potere di una regina, p. 51. Doria was a jurist and philosopher from Naples.

11 Antonio Ghirelli, *Storia di Napoli*, Einaudi, Turin, 1973, p. 109.

12 From Sir Sacheverell Sitwell's *Southern Baroque Art*, cited in Desmond Seward (ed.), *Naples, A Traveller's Companion*, Constable, London, 1984, p. 225.

13 The decorators were Francesco Solimena and Francesco de Mura.

14 De Brosses, *Lettres sur Herculaneum*.

15 Ibid.

16 The painting, believed to have been commissioned by Charles himself, can be seen at the Capodimonte Museum. In it the pope appears to hide.

17 Thomas Gray, in Hudson, *The Grand Tour*, p. 187.

18 J.J. Winckelmann, "Lettera sulla Scoperta di Ercolano al Signor Conte de Bruhl", in J.J. Winckelmann, *Opere*, Prato, 1831, p. 61. Winckelmann's two famous open letters on Herculaneum addressed to Count von Bruehl were first published as: J.J. Winckelmann, *Sendschreiben von den herculanischen Entdeckungen: an den hochgebohrnen Herrn Heinrich Reichsgrafen von Brühl*, Verlegts George Conrad Walther, Dresden, 1762; in English as J.J. Winckelmann, *Critical Account of the Situation and Destruction by the First Eruptions of Mount Vesuvius, of Herculaneum, Pompeii, and Stabia; the Late Discovery of their Remains; the Subterraneous Works Carried on in Them; and the Books, Domestick Utensils, and Other Remarkable Greek and Roman Antiquities thereby Happily Recovered; the Form and Connection of the Ancient Characters being Faithfully Preserved, in a Letter, (originally in German) to Count Bruhl, of Saxony*, T. Carnan, F. Newbery, London, 1771.

19 A painting of Charles's departure for Spain, by the Neapolitan landscape artist Antonio Joli, can be seen in the National Museum of Capodimonte.

20 Ghirelli, *Storia di Napoli*, p. 126.

21 Cited in Frances Haskell, "Mecenatismo e collezionismo nella Napoli dei Borbone durante il XVIII secolo", in Marina Causa Piconi (ed.), *Civiltá del Settecento a Napoli 1734–1799*, exhibition catalogue, Electa, Naples, 1979, p. 12.

22 Giannone, *Istoria civile del regno di Napoli*, 1723 pamphlet cited by Fernand Braudel, in Seward, *Naples, A Traveller's Companion*, p. 275. Two-ninths of the land were owned by the nobles and just one-ninth by farmers.

23 Giuseppe Galasso, "Tradizione, metamorfosi e identità di un'antica capitale", in Giuseppe Galasso (ed.), *Napoli*, Laterza, Bari, 1987, pp. xii–xvii.

24 Ibid., pp. xvi–xxi.

25 Braudel, in Seward, *Naples, A Traveller's Companion*, p. 276.

26 Ferdinando Bologna, "The Rediscovery of Herculaneum and Pom-
    peii", in Ferdinando Bologna (ed.), *Rediscovering Pompeii*, l'Erma di
    Bretschneider, Rome, 1990, p. 91.
27 Parslow, *Rediscovering Antiquity,* p. 270.

                        CHAPTER V

 1 A. Wilton and I. Bignamini (eds), *Grand Tour, Il fascino dell'Italia nel
    XVIII secolo*, catalogue, Skira, Milan, 1997, p. 29 (published in Eng-
    land as John Ingamells (ed.), *Grand Tour. The Lure of Italy in the 18th
    Century,* Tate Gallery, London, 1996).
 2 Bologna, "The Rediscovery of Herculaneum and Pompeii", p. 86.
 3 Carlo Barbieri, "Direzione pe' viaggiatori in Italia. Colla notizia di
    tutte le poste e lor prezzi", Battista Sassi, Bologna, 1772; in English as
    "The Roads of Italy, … wherein are found all the Cities, Towns, Vil-
    lage, Rivers, Remarkable Views etc.", London, 1774. In Ingamells,
    Grand Tour, p. 113.
 4 Bologna, "The Rediscovery of Herculaneum and Pompeii", p. 70.
 5 From Pompeii, House of Julia Felix, inv. 27874, National Archaeolog-
    ical Museum, Naples.
 6 Besides Fragonard and Robert, they included Louis-Jean Desprez,
    Claude-Louis Chatelet, and Jean-Augustin Renard.
 7 Ingamells, *Grand Tour*, p. 164.
 8 Ibid.
 9 Jean Patrice Manandel, "Pittori stranieri a Napoli", in Piconi, *Civiltá
    del Settecento a Napoli*. One of the fifteen, Piranesi's *Casa di Pompeii*,
    belongs to the Ashmolean Museum (inventory 1044), Oxford.
10 Ibid., in the catalogue introduction by French minister of culture,
    Jean-Philippe Lecat.
11 In Hamburg, Ernst George Harzen and the architect Ludwig Her-
    mann Philippi.
12 Jean-Jacque Levecque, *Piranesi*, Alfieri e Lacroix, Milan, 1989, p. 50.
13 Ingamells, *Grand Tour*, p. 116.
14 Levecque, *Piranesi*, p. 31.
15 Pagano, *Gli antichi ercolanesi*, p. 75. Italian archaeologist Pagano
    hypothesizes that they may have passed from the then young Pom-
    peian archaeologist Francesco La Vega to Galliani and then to G.B.
    Piranesi.
16 That original can be seen in Gabinetto Segreto of the National
    Archaeological Museum of Pompeii.
17 Frank Salmon, "The Impact of the Archaeology of Rome", in Claire
    Hornsby (ed.), *The Impact of Italy, The Grand Tour and Beyond*, British
    School at Rome, London, 2000, p. 60.
18 Hudson, *The Grand Tour*, p. 207.
19 Marie-Noelle Pinot de Villechenon, "Napoleone, Mazzolani, Ercol-

ano e Pompei", in Marie-Noelle Pinot de Villechenon, *Gli affreschi nelle illustrazioni neoclassiche dell'album delle "peintures d'Herculanum" conservato al Louvre*, Franco Maria Ricci, Milan, 2000.

20 Nicola Spinosa, "I Vedustisti stranieri a Napoli e nel sud dell'Italia", in *Viaggio in Italia. Un corteo magico dal Cinquecento al Novecento*, exhibition catalogue, Electa, Milan, 2001, pp. 381–5. This synthesis of Neapolitan landscape painting is from his excellent essay.

21 See the *Gulf of Naples as seen from the villa of Sir W. Hamilton at Portici*, by John Robert Cozens, a watercolour on paper in the Victoria and Albert Museum (inventory 121-1894), from the W. Beckford Collection. It shows a patch of stormy sea and a big cliff with a solitary, wind-whipped tree.

22 See Eugenio Lo Sardo (ed.), *Athanasius Kircher S.J., Il Museo del Mondo*, catalogue, De Luca, Rome, 2001. In the Rome exhibition at Palazzo Venezia in 2001 a facsimile of Kircher's "volcano" was on view.

23 Cited in Spinosa, "I Vedustisti stranieri a Napoli", p. 382.

24 Madame Vigée-Lebrun, cited in Seward, *Naples, A Traveller's Companion*, p. 204.

25 See catalogue, *Viaggio in Italia*, p. 196.

CHAPTER VI

1 The links between Hamilton and Winckelmann are detailed in the fascinating biography by David Constantine, *Fields of Fire, A Life of Sir William Hamilton*, Weidenfeld & Nicolson, London, 2001.The painting by Fabris showing the concert at the Fortrose establishment, in which the young musician wears the famous light-blue outfit, is on view in the Scottish National Portrait Gallery, Edinburgh. In a letter cited by Constantine, Leopold Mozart mentions Catherine's embarrassment at being asked to play for the Mozarts, father and son, at the Hamiltons' home, the Villa Sessa.

2 Maurice Krafft, *Volcanoes, Fire from the Earth*, Thames and Hudson, London, 1993 (originally published by Gallimard, Paris, 1991), p. 41.

3 William Gell and John P. Gandy, *Pompeiana, The Topography, Edifices, and Ornaments of Pompeii*, 3rd edn, London, 1852. p. 37.

4 William Hamilton, Pietro Fabris, *Campi Phlegraei, Osservazioni sui vulcani delle Due Sicilie*, London, 1776. Quoted in Seward, *Naples, A Traveller's Companion*, p. 131.

5 Krafft, *Volcanoes*, pp. 81–2.

6 Brian A. Sparkes, *The Red and the Black, Studies in Greek Pottery*, Routledge, London, 1996, p. 47. Sparkes points out that Thomas Dempster's *De Etruria Regali*, Florence, 1723, fostered the tendency to attribute Greek vases to Etruscan potters.

7 Johann Wolfgang von Goethe, *Italienische Reise*, 1818. *Goethe's Travels in Italy*, trans. A.J.W. Morris and Charles Nisbet, Bohn's Standard Library, George Bell, London, 1892, p. 330.

8 Sparkes, *The Red and the Black*, p. 50. The sale catalogue was entitled *Collection of Etruscan, Greek and Roman Antiquities from the Cabinet of the Honourable William Hamilton*. See also Chapter VII.

9 Constantine, *Fields of Fire*, p. 37.

10 Ibid., p. 38.

11 Ibid., p. 41.

12 Sparkes, *The Red and the Black*, p. 52: "d'Hancarville misinterpreted the ancient literary evidence to enhance the (supposed) value that clay vases had in antiquity" .

13 Constantine, *Fields of Fire*, pp. 38–9.

14 Sparkes, *The Red and the Black*, p. 50.

15 Anon., Private collection, Rome, 1798; illustrated in I. Jenkins and K. Sloan (eds), *Vases and Volcanoes: Sir William Hamilton and his Collection*, exhibition catalogue, British Museum, London, 1996, fig. 22, p. 53.

16 Cited in Christopher Hibbert, *Nelson, A Personal History*, Viking, London, 1994, p. 89.

17 Constantine, *Fields of Fire*, p. 179.

18 Horace Walpole, *Correspondence*, Yale Edition, London 1937–83, 40 vols, vol. XI, p. 249, cited in Chloe Chard, "Emma Hamilton and Corinne", in Hornsby, *The Impact of Italy*, p. 168.

19 Chard, "Emma Hamilton and Corinne", p. 131. Chard cites B. Connell, *Portrait of a Whig Peer (2nd Viscount Palmerston)*, London, 1957, p. 276, and Patricia Jaffé, *Lady Hamilton in Relation to the Art of her Time*, exhibition catalogue, Arts Council of Great Britain, London, 1972. p. 50.

20 Lori-Ann Touchette, "Emma Hamilton and her Attitudes", in Hornsby, *The Impact of Italy*, p. 135. Touchette cites Earl of Ilchester (ed.), *Journal of Elizabeth, Lady Holland*, London, 1908.

21 Anne Miller, *Letters from Italy*, E. and C. Dilly, London, 1776, pp. 272–3.

22 Jacob Jonas Björnsthäl, *Letters from his Foreign Travels*, first printed Stockholm, 1774 (my translation from an Italian edition).

23 Letter to Pasquale Carcani, undated, cited in Francesca Longo Auricchio and Mario Capasso, "Nuove accessioni al dossier Piaggio", in Gigante, *Contributi alla storia della officina dei papiri ercolanesi*, p. 46.

24 Aurichio and Capasso, "Nuove accessioni al dossier Piaggio", p. 5, note. Autograph memoir of Padre Piaggio the authors found in the archives of the Società napoletana di Storia Patria.

25 Ibid., p. 28, based on British Museum autograph documents by Padre Piaggio.

26 Charles Burney, *The Present State of Music in France and Italy: or the Journal of a Tour Through those Countries*, London, 1771. Letter of 1770

quoted in Gigante, *Contributi alla storia della officina dei papiri ercolanesi*, p. 171.

27 Agnese Travaglione, "I papiri ercolanesi", *BNN/Quaderni*, vol. 9, no. 1, 1997, pp. 85–98.

28 Jean-Jacques Barthelemy, in Iezzi, "Viaggiatori stranieri nell'officina dei papiri ercolanesi", p. 167.

29 Gigante, *Contributi alla storia della officina dei papiri ercolanesi*, p. 28.

30 Ibid., p. 55.

31 Cited in Giuseppe Coniglio, *I Borboni di Spagna*, Dall'Oglio, Milan, 1970, p. 74.

CHAPTER VII

1 Simon Schama, *Landscape and Memory*, Fontana Press, Bath, 1996, p. 541.

2 Maria Antonella Fusco, "Il luogo comune paesaggistico nelle immagini di massa", in Antonio Ghirelli, *Storia d'Italia*, Einaudi, Turin, 1982, vol. 3, p. 777.

3 Raphael Samuel, *Theatres of Memory*, Verso, London and New York, 1994, vol. 1, p. 111.

4 Ibid., p. 111.

5 Constantine, *Fields of Fire*, p. 40.

6 Cited in ibid., p. 41.

7 Ibid., p. 24.

8 In other versions Daphnis invented song to console himself from being blinded.

9 Stefano De Caro, *Guida alla visita del "Gabinetto Segreto" nel Museo Archeologico Nazionale di Napoli*, catalogue to the collection of the National Archaeological Museum of Naples, Electa, Naples, 2000, note. p. 93.

10 William Hamilton, "An Account of the Worship of Priapus", in Richard Payne Knight, *A Discourse on the Worship of Priapus*, Spilsbury, Snowhill, London, 1786.

11 *Oxford Classical Dictionary*, Oxford University Press, 1996, p. 1245.

12 James Davidson, *Courtesans and Fishcakes, the Consuming Passions of Classical Athens*, Fontana, London, 1998, p. 169.

13 Juvenal, "The Ways of Women", trans. G.G. Ramsay, Loeb Classical Library, Harvard University Press, Boston, 1918, penultimate paragraph, ll. 1–5.

14 Lionel Cust and Sidney Colfin (eds), *History of the Society of Dilettanti*, Macmillan, London, 1898, pp. 140–50.

15 Nicholas Penny, "A Brief Life", in Michael Clarke and Nicholas Penny (eds), *The Elegant Connoisseur: Richard Payne Knight 1751–1824*, catalogue, Manchester University Press, Manchester, 1981, p. 3.

16 For the entire text of Knight's "A Discourse of the Worship of Priapus," see http://www.sacredspiral.com.

17 Sparkes, *The Red and the Black*, p. 52: "d'Hancarville misinterpreted the ancient literary evidence to enhance the (supposed) value that clay vases had in antiquity."
18 Constantine, *Fields of Fire*, pp. 36–7.
19 De Caro, *Guida alla visita del "Gabinetto Segreto"*, p. 25.
20 See Antonio Varone's interesting report on a newly excavated house with a pleasure alcove, "Un nuovo programma decorativo a soggetto erotico", in Pietro Giovanni Guzzo and Vincenzo Scarano Ussani, *Veneris figurae, immagini di prostituzione e sfruttamento a Pompei*, Electa, Naples, 2000, pp. 61–5
21 A second presumed brothel has been found at Puteoli (today's Pozzuoli), but without wall paintings which would definitively establish its purpose.
22 Guzzo and Scarano Ussani, *Veneris figurae*.

CHAPTER VIII

1 Cited in Hibbert, *Nelson*, p. 79.
2 Hester Lynch Piozzi (Mrs Thrale), *Observations and Thoughts Made in the Course of a Journey through France, Italy and Germany*, London, 1789, in Hornsby, *The Impact of Italy*, p. 150. For Mrs Thrale's collected letters see E. A. Bloom and L. D. Bloom (eds), *The Piozzi Letters: Correspondence of Hester Lynch Piozzi (formerly Mrs. Thrale)*, 3 vols, Newark, 1989–93.
3 Giuliana Toso Rodinis, *La commedia degli intrighi e degli amori, le più belle lettere da Napoli di Dominique-Vivant Denon (1782–85)*, Olschki, Florence, 1977, p. 182.
4 In 1791 Dominique-Vivant Denon drew a double image of her as two of the three graces, published that year in the Paris *Gazette des Beaux-Arts*.
5 Hagen Schulze, "Cerchiamo gli antichi per capire noi stessi", *Il Sole-24 Ore*, 25 January 1998, p. 24. Professor Schulze teaches Modern and Contemporary History at the Freie Universitat, Berlin.
6 Ibid.,p. 24.
7 Roland Schaer, *L'invention des musées*, Gallimard, Paris, 1993, p. 69.
8 Under the terms of the Treaty of Tolentino.
9 In the print cabinet of the Bibliotheque National, Paris.
10 Constantine, *Fields of Fire*, p. 185. Hamilton's most recent biographer says there is no proof such a letter existed but that it is likely.
11 Hibbert, *Nelson*, p. 71.
12 Ibid., p. 165.
13 Sparkes, *The Red and the Black*, p. 55.
14 Schaer, *L'invention des musées*, p. 71.
15 In the Musée du Louvre.
16 P.C. Sadgrove, *The Egyptian Theatre in the Nineteenth Century 1799–1882*, Ithaca Press, Reading, 1997.

17 Gilles Neret (ed.), *Description de l'Egypt, publiée par les ordres de Napoleon Bonaparte*, complete edn, Taschen, Cologne, 1997, p. 130.
18 Jean Châtelain, *Dominique-Vivant Denon et le Louvre de Napoleon*, Librairie Academiques, Perrin, Paris, 1973.

CHAPTER IX

1   Cited in Antonietta Drago, *I Borboni di Spagna e Napoli*, Mondadori, Milan, 1972, p. 89.
2   Cited in Constantine, *Fields of Fire*, p, 243. From a dispatch to Charles Grenville.
3   Ibid., p. 243.
4   In the judgement of Giovanni Indelli, writing in Gigante, *Contributi alla storia della officina dei papiri ercolanesi*, p. 46.
5   John Hayter, *A Report Upon the Herculaneum Manuscripts in a Second Letter Addressed by Permission to his Royal Highness the Prince Regent*, London, 1811. Professor Francesca Longo Auricchio of Naples University has published an Italian language version as "John Hayter nella Officina dei Papiri Ercolanesi", in Gigante, *Contributi alla storia della officina dei papiri ercolanesi*, 163–4.
6   La Vega was otherwise one of the positive notes in a bleak period, for he tried to take careful stock of the excavations, leaving written records, and he preserved two of Weber's precious maps of underground Herculaneum for posterity.
7   Alfonso Scirocco, *Gioachino Murat*, Istituto Italiano per gli studi filosofici e Soprintendenza per i Beni artistici e storici, Elio de Rosa, Naples, 1994, p. 14.
8   Auricchio, "John Hayter nella officina dei papiri ercolanesi", p. 179. The letter by Drummond, which Professor Auricchio located in the Bodleian Library, is dated 13 December 1808, Ms. Gr. Class. C 10, ff. 113–16v.
9   Quoted in Joan Bear, *Caroline Murat*, Collins, London, 1972.
10 Drago, *I Borboni di Spagna e Napoli*, p. 6.
11 Chard, "Emma Hamilton and Corinne", p. 157.
12 That painting is now in the Museum of San Martino in Naples.
13 The painting, like the full-length portrait of Murat described above, is in the Capodimonte Museum of Naples.
14 Salmon, "The Impact of the Archaeology of Rome", pp. 221, 232. On the topic see also Alistair Rowan *Bob the Roman: Heroic Antiquity and the Architecture of Robert Adam, Sir John Soane's Museum*, Soane Gallery, London, 2003.
15 Andrea Milanese, "Michele Arditi e la 'catena delle arti': l'acquisizione delle raccolte borgiane e la loro sistemazione nel Real Museo di Napoli", in A. Germano and M. Nocca (eds), *La collezione Borgia, curiositá e tesori da ogni parte del mondo*, exhibition catalogue, Electa, Naples, 2001, p. 55.

16 Cited in Bear, *Caroline Murat*, pp. 89, 107.

17 Gell and Gandy, *Pompeiana*, Introduction.

18 From Auguste François Creuze de Lesser, *Voyage en Italie e en Sicile, fait en MDCCCI et MDCCCII*, Paris, 1806, pp. 176–7, cited in Gigante, *Contributi alla Storia della Officina dei Papiri Ercolanesi*, p. 128.

19 Marcello Gigante, "I papiri ercolanesi e la Francia", in Gigante, *Contributi alla storia della officina dei papiri ercolanesi*, p. 33.

20 Milanese, "Michele Arditi e la 'catena delle arti'", p. 55.

21 De Caro, *Guida alla visita del "Gabinetto Segreto"*.

22 In ibid., pp. 83, 89. The drawings were originally published as *Priapées et sujets divers, gravés par D.-V. Denon*.

23 Quoted in Edith Clay (ed.), *Lady Blessington at Naples*, Hamish Hamilton, London, 1979; translated into Italian as *Lady Blessington a Napoli, 1813–26*, Beta, Salerno, 1974.

CHAPTER X

1 David Brown, "'Terra Pictura' della Terra dei Poeti, J.M.W. Turner e l'Italia", in G. Marcenaro and P. Boragina (eds), *Corteo magico dal Cinquecento al Novecento*, exhibition catalogue, Electa, Milan, 2003, p. 389.

2 Gell and Gandy, *Pompeiana*, p. viii.

3 Seward, *Naples, A Traveller's Companion*, pp. 256–8.

4 P.B. Shelley, *The Letters of Percy Bysshe Shelley*, F.L. Jones (ed.), Clarendon Press, Oxford, 1964. Cited in Seward, *Naples, A Traveller's Companion*, pp. 253–4.

5 Barbara Cinelli, "Il ritratto dell'artista", in Barbara Cinelli, *La Maiestà di Roma*, Electa, Naples, 2003, p. 298.

6 Noted by John Bowen, "Pictures from Italy", in Hornsby, *The Impact of Italy*, p. 208.

7 Ingamells, *Grand Tour*, pp. 302–3.

8 Gell and Gandy, *Pompeiana*, p. 139.

9 Edith Clay (ed.), *Sir William Gell in Italy, Letters to the Society of Dilettanti, 1831–1835*, Hamish Hamilton, London, 1976.

10 The so-called Elgin Marbles arrived by sea from Greece between 1802 and 1812. They were purchased by Lord Elgin, who feared that the Turkish rulers of Greece would allow them to be destroyed.

11 George Gordon, Lord Byron, *English Bards and Scotch Reviewers: A Satire*, 1809, XXIII. In this 9,000-word verse satire Gell appears in the penultimate stanza, to wit:

> Let Aberdeen and Elgin still pursue
> The shade of fame through regions of virtù;
> Waste useless thousands on their Phidian freaks,
> Misshapen monuments and maim'd antiques;
> And make their grand saloons a general mart
> For all the mutilated blocks of art;
> Of Dardan tours let dilettanti tell,

> I leave topography to rapid Gell;
> And, quite content, no more shall interpose
> To stun the public ear—at least with prose.

12 Clay, *Sir William Gell in Italy.*
13 Gell and Gandy, *Pompeiana*, p. v.
14 Donald Saff and Deli Sacilotto, *Printmaking, History and Process*, Holt, Rhinehart, New York, 1978, pp. 89–136.
15 Saff, and Sacilotto, *Printmaking*. Intaglio means "engrave," or cut into. Steel-plate intaglio, popular for scenic travel book illustrations in the 19th century, is today used almost exclusively for postage stamps and currency.
16 A broom-closet-sized darkroom with a hole through which an image could pass, upside down, for copying onto paper. This served to provide correct proportions of buildings such as temples.
17 From the fascinating essay by Kathryn Sutherland, "'Events … Have Made Us a World of Readers:' Reader Relations 1780–1830", in David B. Pirie, *The Romantic Period*, Penguin, London, 1994, pp. 1–48.
18 Salmon, "The Impact of the Archaeology of Rome", p. 221.
19 Riccardo Redi, "La tragedia di Pompei, in teatro", in Riccardo Redi and P.L. Raffaelli (eds), *Gli ultimi giorni di Pompei*, exhibition catalogue, Electa, Naples, 1994, p. 63.
20 Fernando Mazzocca, "Da Oriente a Occidente: Nuovi protagonisti sulla scena romana", in Cinelli, *La maestà di Roma*, p. 360.
21 All biographical notes unless otherwise stated are from Sibylla Jane Flower, *Bulwer-Lytton, An Illustrated Life, Lifelines 9*, Shire, Aylebury, 1973. I am also indebted to the curator of Knebworth, Clare Fleck, who introduced us to Lord Lytton's private world and collected information on translations of *Last Days*.
22 Cited in ibid., p. 15
23 Ibid., p. 16.
24 Victor Alexander George Robert Bulwer-Lytton, 2nd Earl Lytton, *The Life of Edward Bulwer, First Lord Lytton*, Macmillan, London, 1913, vol. 1, pp 443–4.
25 Clay, *Lady Blessington at Naples.*
26 John Auldjo, letter from Naples, 26 July 1836, in Earl of Lytton, *The Life of Edward Bulwer, First Lord Lytton, by his Grandson*, Macmillan, London, 1913, vol. 1, p. 444.
27 Laurence Goldstein, "The Impact of Pompeii on the Literary Imagination", *Centennial Review*, vol. 23, no. 3, 1979, p. 229.

CHAPTER XI

1 Marcello Barbanera, *L'Archeologia degli italiani*, Editori Riuniti, Rome, 1998, note p. 194.
2 Umberto Eco, "Viaggio a Napoli", *Il Maratra*, no. 14–15, 1964.

3 Maiuri, *Pompei*, p. 170. The letter appeared in *Il Tempo*, 10 March 1848. Also see Giuseppe Fiorelli, *Appunti autobiografici*, Stefano De Caro (ed.), Di Mauro, Naples, 1994.
4 The original phrase was *patria carità*—the cherishing of nation.
5 Fiorelli, *Appunti autobiografici*, p. 16.
6 A. Giardina and A. Vauchez, *Il mito di Roma da Carlo Magno a Mussolini*, Laterza, Rome-Bari, 2000, p. 189.
7 Vittorio Vidotto, cited in ibid., p. 189.
8 Fiorelli, *Appunti autobiografici*. From a previously unpublished report by Fiorelli's successor as director-general of antiquities, Felice Barnabei.
9 Ibid., p. 24.
10 Ralph Trevelyan, *The Shadow of Vesuvius*, Folio Society, London, 1976, p. 84.
11 Maria Antonella Fusco, "L'Arte", in Galasso, *Napoli*, pp. 431–6.
12 Available for consultation in the Library of the Sovrintendenza di Pompeii.
13 Nunzia Meluccio, "Le collezioni del Palazzo Reale di Portici: da Museo d'Antichità a sede della Facoltá di Agraria", in *La reggia di Portici nelle collezioni d'arte tra Sette e Ottocento*, catalogue, Elio de Rosa, Naples, 1998, p. 40.
14 The description is by Ghirelli, *Storia di Napoli*, see pp. 228–33.
15 As portrayed in a painting of the occasion by Calabrian artist Eugenio Tanò.
16 Fiorelli, *Appunti autobiografici*, p. 27.
17 Ernesto De Carolis, "A City and its Rediscovery", in A. Ciarallo and E. De Carolis (eds), *Pompeii, Life in a Roman Town*, catalogue, Electa, Milan, 1999. De Carolis traces a useful synthesis of the succession of directors of Pompeii from the late 18th century through the 1960s.
18 Fiorelli, *Appunti autobiografici*, p. 14.
19 *La Repubblica*, 24 June 1999, Napoli Cronaca.
20 Barbanera, *L'Archeologia degli italiani*, pp. 3, 39–48.
21 For a complete review and details on these various laws, see Andrea Emiliani, "Musei e museologia", *Storia d'Italia, i documenti*, vol. 5, 1973, pp. 1615–60.
22 Baldassare Conticello, "Scienza, cultura e cronaca a Pompei nella prima metá del nostro secolo", in Redi and Rafaelli, *Gli ultimi giorni di Pompei*, p. 15. The late distinguished Professor Conticello was a former superintendent of Pompeii.

CHAPTER XII

1 Lytton Strachey, *Eminent Victorians*, Putnam, New York, 1918. "By Pompeii, Dr. Arnold was not particularly impressed. 'There is the same sort of interest with which one would see the ruins of Sodom and Gomorrah but indeed there is less'."

2 Walter Kendrick, *The Secret Museum: Pornography in Modern Culture*, University of California Press, Los Angeles, 1997.

3 Edward Bulwer-Lytton, *The Last Days of Pompeii*, London, 1834, Chapter Ten.

4 R. Jenkyns, *The Victorians and Ancient Greece*, Blackwell, Oxford, 1980, pp. 84–5.

5 Redi, "La tragedia di Pompei", p. 63.

6 *Maestá di Roma da Napoleone all'unitá d'Italia*, catalogue, Electa, Naples, 2003, p. 372.

7 Goldstein, "The Impact of Pompeii on the Literary Imagination", p. 240.

8 Amadeo Maiuri, *Pompeii ed Ercolano fra case e abitanti*, Giunti, Florence, 1956, 1998, p. 190.

9 To borrow the words of Lee Behlman of Kansas State University, in his address, "Victorian Stoicism and Pompeii, in Edward Poynter's 'Faithful unto Death'", at a symposium on "Antiquity Recovered: Pompeii and Herculaneum in the Philadelphia Collections", Philadelphia, October 8, 2002.

10 Sir Arthur Conan Doyle, *The Sign of Four*, London, 1892. His second novel, it is still in print under Penguin Classics. The weather is so foul, the passage begins, that, "Hence the cocaine. I cannot live without brain-work. What else is there to live for? Stand at the window here ...".

11 Vern G. Swanson, *Sir Lawrence Alma-Tadema, The Painter of the Victorian Vision of the Ancient World*, Ash & Grant, London, 1990, p. 50. Cited in R.J. Barrow, *Lawrence Alma-Tadema*, Phaidon, London, 2000, p. 85

12 Swanson, *Sir Lawrence Alma-Tadema*, p. 22

13 Maxwell L. Anderson, "Pompeii and America", in Bologna, *Rediscovering Pompeii*, pp. 95–6.

14 Art critic Harry Quilter, *Preferences in Arts, Life and Literature*, London, 1892, cited in Swanson, *Sir Lawrence Alma-Tadema*, p. 22.

15 A. Clutton Brock cited in Swanson, *Sir Lawrence Alma-Tadema*, p. 48.

16 Chard, "Emma Hamilton and Corinne", p. 161. Chard cited Joan Kerr (ed.), *Heritage: The National Women's Art Book*, Craftsman House, Sydney, 1995, p. 219.

17 Redi, "La tragedia di Pompei", p. 63.

18 Mario Verdone, "Preistoria del film storico", *Bianco e Nero*, vol. 24, no. 1–2, January–February 1963, pp. 20–5.

19 Cited in Swanson, *Sir Lawrence Alma-Tadema*.

20 Chard, "Emma Hamilton and Corinne", p. 161. According to Chard, Freud "emphasizes the strong basis in popular belief for the conviction that scholarship and erotic life are utterly distinct ... 'Mathematics enjoys the greatest reputation as a diversion from sexuality'".

21 John David Rhodes, Interview, Rome, December 5, 2000. Prof. Rhodes is the author of *Stupendous Miserable City: Pasolini's Rome*, University of Minneapolis Press, Minneapolis andLondon, 2007.

22 Vittorio Martinelli, "Sotto il volcano", in Redi and Raffaelli, *Gli ultimi giorni di Pompei*, p. 35.

23 Davide Turconi, "I film storici italiani e la critica americana dal 1910 alla fine del muto", *Bianco e Nero*, vol 24, no. 1–2, January–February 1963, pp. 41–56.

24 Martinelli, "Sotto il volcano", p. 34.

25 Redi and Raffaelli, *Gli ultimi giorni di Pompei*, pp. 41–2. Pasquali's version, too, thrilled the Roman audiences. The daily *Il Messaggero* reported, "The enthusiasm is indescribable … The historical reconstruction of the celebrated novel by Bulwer Lytton is excellent."

26 Cited in John David Rhodes, "'Our Beautiful and Glorious Art Lives': The Rhetoric of Nationalism in Early Italian Film Periodicals", *Film History*, vol 5, no. 12, 2000, pp. 308–21. This brilliant essay synthesizes the complex interaction of early Italian cinema and nationalism.

27 Ibid., p. 317.

28 *Film*, 23 April 1914, Naples. Cited in ibid., p. 319.

29 Siegfried Kracauer, *From Caligari to Hitler*, Princeton, 1947, p. 47. "An article published in January 1920 by Rudolf Pabst testifies to the thoroughness with which the Germans prepared for the reconquest of a prominent economic and cultural position. Pabst severely criticized the current advertising shorts for subordinating entertainment to propaganda … To serve as a means to an end this screen entertainment would have to seem an end itself." The model, Kracauer concludes, was the Italian historical superspectacle, particularly *Quo Vadis?* and *Cabiria*.

CHAPTER XIII

1 Mariella Cagnetta, *Antichisti e impero fascista*, Dedalo, Bari, 1979, pp. 125–9.

2 Stefania Parigi, "La Rievocazione dell'antico", in Redi and Raffaelli, *Gli ultimi giorni di Pompeii*. This fascinating volume offers a series of detailed essays on Italian cinema productions of Lytton's *The Last Days of Pompeii*, with photographs.

3 Marinetti became a Fascist and remained loyal to Mussolini. He joined the Republic of Saló after it was formed in north Italy in November 1943.

4 In the text, "*apparato di genitali in pietra e in affresco*".

5 Giardina and Vauchez, *Il mito di Roma*, p. 213, citing Antonio Cederna, *Mussolini Urbanista*, Laterza, Rome-Bari, 1990.

6 Marco Palla, *Mussolini e il Fascismo*. Giunti, Florence, 1993, p. 69.

7 Carlo Bordoni, *Cultura e Propaganda nell'Italia Fascista*, D'Anna, Messina, 1974, p. 192.

8   Giardina and Vauchez, *Il mito di Roma*, p. 257–8.
9   Antonio La Penna, "La Tradizione classica nella cultura italiana", *Storia d'Italia*, vol. 5, 1973, pp. 1319–72.
10 Giardina and Vauchez, *Il mito di Roma*, p. 190. This was the theory of Vincenzo Gioberti, leader of the Liberal Catholics known as neo-Guelfs.
11 La Penna, "La Tradizione classica", p. 1323, citing Lorenzo Valla, *Proemio to Elegantarum linguae latinae*.
12 La Penna, "La Tradizione classica", p. 1332.
13 Giardina and Vauchez, *Il mito di Roma*, p. 242.
14 Vittorio Bracco, "La dimensione imperiale", *Archeologia del Regime*, Volpe, Rome, 1983, p. 36.
15 Luciano Perelli, "Sul culto fascista della romanità", *Quaderni di Storia*, vol. 3, no. 5, January–June 1977, p. 197.
16 Ibid.
17 Luciano Canfora, *Ideologia del Classicismo*, Einaudi, Turin, 1980, p. 78.
18 Cited in ibid., p. 80.
19 Antonio Bruers, *La missione d'Italia nel mondo*, Campitelli, Foligno, 1928, p. 207.
20 Gianni Poletti, *Fascism is the Fourth Heroic Renaissance in Mediterranean Civilization*, GUF, Milan, 1934. Poletti presents the Italians as the heirs of all Mediterranean peoples, including the Greeks: "Archaeological studies and an examination of the physical characteristics of the people who gave birth to the Mycenian, Greek and Roman civilizations have thoroughly demonstrated how the founders of these civilizations all belonged to the same ethnic brand ... which occupied the Eastern Mediterranean ... these were the true Italics from whom we derive our origin."
21 In a formal restoration, the Rome city council named a street for Bottai in 1999.
22 Giorgio Bottai, *Preferirei di no*, Einaudi, Turin, 2001.
23 Antonio Cederna, *Mussolini urbanista, Lo sventramento di Roma negli anni di consenso*, Laterza, Bari, 1980, p. 68
24 Cagnetta, *Antichisti e impero fascista*, p. 10.
25 See Michele Sarfatti, *Gli ebrei nell'Italia fascista, Vicende, identitá, persecuzioni*. Einaudi, Turin, 2000.
26 Printed as *Pompei alla luce degli scavi nuovi di Via dell'Abbondanza*, in 1953.
27 Bracco, "La dimensione imperiale", p. 29.
28 Mario Capasso, "Maiuri e i papiri ercolanesi", in *Atti del seminario di studi sulla figura e l'opera di Amedeo Maiuri svoltosi il 20 giugno 1987*, Bibliopolis, Napoli, 1990, p. 45.
29 Redi and Raffaelli, *Gli ultimi giorni di Pompei*, pp. 27–34.
30 Palla, *Mussolini e il Fascismo*, p. 68.
31 Jonathan Petropoulos, *The Faustian Bargain, The Art World in Nazi Germany*, Oxford Press, Oxford, 2000, p. 15.

32 Vittorio Paliotti, *Vesuvius, A Fiery History*, Azienda Autonomo di Soggiorno, Naples, 1973, p. 172.

33 Giuseppe Imbò, "L'eruzione del Vesuvio", 1944. Cited in *Il Vesuvio* anthology, Pierro, Naples, 1996, p. 96.

CHAPTER XIV

1 Ronald Syme, *The Roman Revolution*, Oxford University Press, Oxford, 1939, pp. 247, 57.

2 Elizabeth Rawson, *Intellectual Life in the Late Roman Republic*, Duckworth, London, 1985, pp. 40ff.

3 Cited in Jonathan Barnes, "Hellenistic Philosophy and Science", in *Oxford History of the Classical World*, J. Boardman, J. Griffin and O. Murray (eds), Oxford University Press, Oxford, 1986, p. 372.

4 Marcello Gigante, *Philodemus in Italy*, trans. Dirk Obbink, University of Michigan Press, Ann Arbor, 1995, p. 72. Material in this chapter is also from my interviews with the late Professor Gigante at Naples in 2000 and at Pompeii in 2002.

5 Philodemus, 26.3 GP. George Economou, *Harmonies and Fits*, Point Riders Press, Norman, Oklahoma, 1987; see also Philodemus, *Acts of Love, Ancient Greek Poetry from Aphrodite's Garden*, George Economou and Wendy Doniger (eds), Modern Library, New York, 2006. The traditional translation into English is by A.S.F. Gow and D.L. Page, *The Greek Anthology: The Garland of Phillip and Some Contemporary Epigrams*, Cambridge University Press, Cambridge, 1968.

6 The speech was delivered in late 57 BC after 18 months of exile. The two speeches attacking Piso are *Pro Sestio* and *In Pisonem* (55 BC).

7 *Res gestae divi Augusti* would be edited and published by Tiberius. Several copies from cities outside Rome have survived.

8 Gigante, *Philodemus in Italy*, p. 2.

9 L. Franchi dell'Orto (ed.), *Ercolano 1738–1988: 250 anni di ricerca archeologica*, Atti del Convegno Internazionale Ravello-Ercolano-Napoli-Pompei (30 ottobre–5 novembre 1988), L'Erma di Bretschneider, Rome, 1991, pp. 237–41; B. Conticello, and U. Cioffi, "Il rientro nella Villa dei Papiri di Ercolano", in Luisa Franchi dell'Orto (ed.), *Restaurare Pompei*, SugarCo, Rome, 1991.

10 Cited in Russell Miller, *The House of Getty*, Henry Holt, New York, 1995. p. 291. This incident and other details here are, unless otherwise noted, from Miller's chapter, "A Lecher, a Miser, a Womaniser".

11 Martin Zimet, of Frency & Co., New York, cited in Robert Lenzner, *The Great Getty*, Crown, New York, 1985, p. 178.

12 J. Paul Getty, *As I See It, An Autobiography*, Prentice-Hall, New Jersey, 1976, p. 281.

13 Peter J. Holliday, "From Herculaneum to Malibu: The Reception of the Getty Museum Villa", paper delivered at a symposium in connection with the exhibition "Antiquity Recovered: Pompeii and

Herculaneum in Philadelphia Collections", October 2001. Professor Holliday is from California State University, Long Beach.

14 Getty, *As I See It*, p. 291.
15 Holliday, "From Herculaneum to Malibu".

EPILOGUE

1 Maiuri, *Pompeii ed Ercolano fra case e abitanti*, p. 270.
2 Jean Andreau, "Banking and Borrowing in a Roman Port", *Archaeology*, May/June 2001. My slightly adapted translation.
3 Judith Harris, "Five-Star Inn with Great Art", *Archaeology*, July/August 2000, and, in the same magazine, "The Lap of Luxury", May/June 2001.

Select Bibliography

Ascioni, Gina Carla, *Ercolano nella cultura artistica del Settecento e dell'Otto-cento*, catalogue, Electa, Naples, 2000

Ash, Russell, *Sir Lawrence Alma-Tadema*, Pavillion, London, 1995

Auricchio, Francesca Longo, "John Hayter nella officina dei papiri ercol-anesi," *Contributi alla Storia della Officina dei Papiri Ercolanesi*, no. 2, 1986

——, "Le prime scoperte a Ercolano", *Cronache Ercolanesi*, no. 27, 1997

—— and Capasso, M., "I rotoli della villa ercolanese: Dislocazione e ritrova-mento", *Cronache Ercolanesi*, no. 17, 1987

——, ——, "Nuove accessioni al dossier Piaggio", *Contributi alla Storia della Officina dei Papiri Ercolanesi*

Barbanera, Marcello, *L'Archeologia degli italiani*, Editori Riuniti, Rome, 1998

Bear, Joan, *Caroline Murat*, Collins, London, 1972

Bonfait, O. and Pinto, S. (eds), *Maestà di Roma, da Napoleone all'unità d'Italia*, catalogue, Electa, Rome, 2003

de Brosses, Charles, *Lettres familières sur l'Italie en 1739 et 1740*, Laterza, Bari, 1973

Byatt, A.S., *Unruly Times*, Hogarth Press, London, 1989

Chatelain, Jean, *Dominique-Vivant Denon et le Louvre de Napoleon*, Librairie Academiques, Perrin, Paris, 1973

Ciarallo, A. and De Carolis, E. (eds), *Pompeii, Life in a Roman Town*, catalogue, Electa, Milan, 1999

Clay, Edith (ed.), *Sir William Gell in Italy, Letters to the Society of Dilettanti, 1831–1835*, Hamish Hamilton, London, 1976

—— (ed.), *Lady Blessington at Naples*, Hamish Hamilton, London, 1979; in Italian as *Lady Blessington a Napoli, 1813–26*, Beta, Salerno, 1974

Coniglio, Giuseppe, *I Borboni di Spagna*, Dall'Oglio, Milan, 1970

Constantine, David, *Fields of Fire, A Life of Sir William Hamilton*, Weidenfeld & Nicolson, London, 2001

Conticello, Baldassare (ed.), *Rediscovering Pompeii*, catalogue, L'Erma di Bret-schneider, Rome, 1990

Cust, L. and Colvin, S. (eds), *History of the Society of Dilettanti*, Macmillan, London, 1898

Davidson, James, *Courtesans and Fishcakes, the Consuming Passions of Classical Athens*, Fontana, London, 1998

De Caro, Stefano (ed.), *Giuseppe Fiorelli, appunti autobiografici*, Di Mauro, Naples, 1994

——, *Guida alla visita del "Gabinetto Segreto" nel Museo Archeologico Nazionale di Napoli*, presentation of museum collection, Electa, Naples, 2000

Deiss, Joseph Jay, *Herculaneum*, Harper & Row, New York, 1966, 1985

De Simone, A. and Ciro Nappo, S. (eds), … *Mitis Sarni Opes*, Denaro Libri, Naples, 2000

Drago, Antonietta, *I Borboni di Spagna e Napoli*, Mondadori, Milan, 1972

Fermé, Eric (ed.), *Art History and its Methods: A Critical Anthology*, Phaidon, London, 1995

Fisher, Todd, *The Napoleonic Wars, The Rise of the Emperor 1805–1807*, Osprey, Oxford, 2001

Fothergill, Brian, *William Hamilton: Envoy Extraordinary*, Harcourt, Brace, London, 1969

Galasso, Giuseppe, *Napoli*, Laterza, Bari, 1987

Gell, William and Gandy, John P., *Pompeiana, The Topography, Edifices, and Ornaments of Pompeii*, 3rd edn, London, 1852

Germano, A. and Nocca, M. (eds), *La collezione Borgia, curiosità e tesori da ogni parte del mondo*, catalogue, Electa, Naples, 2001

Ghirelli, Antonio, *Storia di Napoli*, Einaudi, Turin, 1973

Giardina, A. and Vauchez, A., *Il mito di Roma Da Carlo Magno a Mussolini*, Laterza, Bari, 2000

Gigante, Marcello (ed.), *Contributi alla Storia della Officina dei Papiri Ercolanesi*, no. 2, 1986

——, *Philodemus in Italy*, trans. Dirk Obbink, University of Michigan, Ann Arbor, 1995

——, De Simone, A. et al., *Cronache Ercolanesi*, no. 27, 1997

Goethe, *Italian Journey*, Penguin, London, 1970

Goldstein, Laurence, "The Impact of Pompeii on the Literary Imagination", *Centennial Review*, vol. 23, no. 3, 1979.

Guzzo, G., Pagano, Capasso et al., *Gli antichi ercolanesi*, catalogue, Electa, Naples, 2000

Haskell, Francis, "Mecenatismo e collezionismo nella Napoli dei Borbone durante il XVIII secolo", in *Civiltà del Settecento a Napoli 1734–1799*, exhibition catalogue, Naples, December 1979–October 1980, 2 vols, Florence, 1974

Hibbert, Christopher, *Nelson, A Personal History*, Viking, London, 1994

Hornsby, Clare (ed.), *The Impact of Italy, The Grand Tour and Beyond*, The British School, London, 2000

Hudson, Roger (ed.), *The Grand Tour*, Folio Society, London, 1993

Iezzi, Benito, "Viaggiatori stranieri nell'officina dei papiri ercolanesi", *Contributi alla Storia della Officina dei Papiri Ercolanesi*, no. 2, 1986

Irwin, David (ed.), *Writings on Art*, Phaidon, London, 1972

Istituto Italiano per gli studi filosofici e Soprintendenza per I Beni artistici e storici, *Gioachino Murat*, Elio de Rosa, Naples, 1994

Jenkins, I. and K. Sloan (eds), *Vases and Volcanoes: Sir William Hamilton and his Collection*, exhibition catalogue, British Museum, London, 1996

Jenkyns, Richard, *The Victorians and Ancient Greece*, Blackwell, Oxford, 1980

Johnson, Edgar, "Introduction", in Edward Bulwer Lytton, *The Last Days of Pompeii*, Sidgwick & Jackson, London, 1979

Jongman, Willem, *The Economy and Society of Pompeii*, Gieben, Amsterdam, 1988

Kendric, Walter, *The Secret Museum: Pornography in Modern Culture*, University of California Press, Los Angeles, 1997

Kluckert, Ehrenfried, "Il Giardino Paesistico", in *Neo-Classicismo e Romantico*, Konemann, Cologne, 2000

Kracauer, Siegfried, *From Caligari to Hitler, A Psychological History of the German Film*, Princeton University Press, Princeton, 1947.

Krafft, Maurice, *Volcanoes, Fire from the Earth*, Thames and Hudson, London, 1993

Kunze, Max (ed.), *Römische Antikensammlungen im 18. Jahrhundert*, Von Zabern, Mainz, 1998

Laurence, Ray, *Roman Pompeii, Space and Society*, Routledge, London, 1994

Levecque, Jean-Jacques, *Piranesi*, Alfieri e Lacroix, Milan, 1989

Lejeune, A. and Lewis, M., *The Gentlemen's Clubs of London*, Bracken Books, London, 1974

Lowenthal, David, *The Heritage Crusade and the Spoils of History*, Viking, London, 1996

Lukacs, Georg, *The Historical Novel*, Moscow, 1937, Marlin Press, London, 1962

Mafrici, Mirella, *Fascino e potere di una regina, Elisabetta Farnese sulla scena europea*, Avagliano Editori, Cava dé Tirreni, 1999

MacKendrick, Paul, *The Roman Mind at Work*, Van Nostrand, Princeton, 1958

Marcenaro, G. and Boragina, P. (eds), *Viaggio in Italia, un corteo magico dal Cinquecento al Novecento*, catalogue, Electa, Milan, 2001

Maiuri, Amadeo, *Pompei*, Libreria dello Stato, Rome, Year X Era Fascista (1932)

——, *Description des fouilles de Pompeii*, Rende, Naples, 1953

——, *Pompei ed Ercolano fra case ed abitanti*, Giunti, Florence, 1958, 1998

Martorelli, Luisa (ed.), *La Reggia di Portici nelle collezioni d'arte tra Sette e Ottocento*, Elio de Rosa, Naples, 1998

Meyer, Karl E., *The Plundered Past*, Hamish Hamilton, London, 1974

Moreno, Paolo (ed.), "Winckelmann 2000", *Archeo*, vol. 178, 16, no. 1, December 2000

Mumly, Frank Arthur, *Publishing and Bookselling, A History from the Earliest Times to the Present Day*, Jonathan Cape, London, 1956

Napo, Salvatore, *Pompeii, A Guide to the Ancient City*, Barnes & Noble, New York, 1998

Neret, Gilles (ed.), *Description de l'Egypt, publiée par les ordres de Napoleon Bonaparte*, Taschen, Cologne, 1997

Pagano, Mario, *Ercolano, itinerario archeologico ragionato*, T&M Edizioni, Naples, 1997

Paliotti, Vittorio, *Vesuvius, A Fiery History*, trans. Zinnia M. Steinhauer, Azienda Autonoma di Soggiorno Cura e Turismo, Naples, (circa 1975)

Parslow, Christopher Charles, *Rediscovering Antiquity: Karl Weber and the Excavation of Herculaneum, Pompeii and Stabiae*, Cambridge University Press, Cambridge, 1995

Piggott, J.R., *Palace of the People, The Crystal Palace at Sydenham 1854–1936*, Hurst, London, 2004

Pirie, David B. (ed.), *The Romantic Period*, Penguin, London, 1994

Pompeii e gli architetti francesi dell'Ottocento, catalogue of exhibition Paris–Naples 1981, Ecole Nationale Superieure des Beaux-Arts et l'Ecole Française de Rome, Rome, 1981

Redi, Riccardo and Raffaelli, P.L. (eds), *Gli ultimi giorni di Pompei*, Electa, Naples, 1994

Ricci, Corrado, *Visioni e figure*, Rome, 1919

Richardson, Jr., J., *Pompeii, An Architectural History*, Johns Hopkins University Press, Baltimore, 1988

Rodinis, Giuliana Toso, *La Commedia degli Intrighi e degli Amori, le più belle lettere da Napoli di Dominique-Vivant Denon (1782–85)*, Olschki, Florence, 1977

Ruggiero, Michele, *Storia degli scavi di Ercolano ricomposta su' documenti superstiti*, Naples, 1885

Saff, Donald and Sacilotto, D., *Printmaking, History and Process*, Holt, Rhinehart, New York, 1978

Salles, Catherine, *Les bas-fonds de l'antiquité*, Laffont, Paris, 1982

Salmon, Frank, "The Impact of the Archaeology of Rome on British Architects and their Work, c. 1750–1840", in Hornsby, *The Impact of Italy*

Samuel, Raphael, *Theatres of Memory*, Verso, London and NY, 1994, vol. 1

Schaer, Roland, *L'invention des musées*, Gallimard, Paris, 1993

Seward, Desmond (ed.), *Naples, A Traveller's Companion*, Constable, London, 1984

Sollers, Philippe, *Le cavalier du Louvre – Vivant Denon*, Plon, Paris, 1995

Swanson, Vern G., *Sir Lawrence Alma-Tadema, The Painter of the Victorian Vision of the Ancient World*, Ash & Grant, London, 1977

Travaglione, Agnese, "I papiri ercolanesi", *BNN/Quaderni*, vol. 9, no. 1, 1997

Van Kessel, Peter (ed.), *The Power of Imagery, Essays on Rome, Italy, & Imagination*, Nederlands Instituut te Rome, Apeiron Editori, Rome, 1992

Verdone, Mario, "Preistoria del film storico", *Bianco e Nero*, vol. 24, no. 1–2, January–February 1963

Wilson, A.N., *The Victorians*, Hutchinson, London, 2002

Wilton, A. and Bignamini, I. (eds), *Grand Tour, The Lure of Italy in the 18th Century*, Tate Gallery, London, 1996; in Italian as *Grand Tour*, Skira, Milan, 1996

Winckelmann, J.J., *Sendschreiben von den Herculanischen Entdeckungen: an den Hochgebohrnen Herrn Heinrich Reichsgrafen von Brühl*. G. C. Walther, Dresden, 1762; in English as *Critical Account of the Situation and Destruction by the First Eruptions of Mount Vesuvius, of Herculaneum, Pompeii, and Stabia … to Count Bruehl*, T. Carnan, Newbery, London, 1771

——, *Geschichte der Kunst des Alterthums*, Dresden, 1764; in English as *The History of Ancient Art)*, 4 vols, Waltherischen Hof-Buchhandlung, Dresden, 1764–7; in English as *The History of Ancient Art*, trans. Henry Lodge, 4 vols, J.R. Osgood, Boston, 1849–73

——, *Gedanken über die Nachahmung der Greischiechen Werke in der Malerei und Bilderkunst*, Saxon State Library, Friedrichstadt (Dresden), 1755; in English as *Thoughts on the Imitation of Greek Works*, trans. Henrich Füsseli, A. Millar, London, 1765

Picture Credits

For their courtesy and generosity I would like to thank the archivists of the Pompeii Soprintendenza, Alfredo Bardi of the Centro Sperimentale Cinematograhico of Rome, Milton Gendel, the J. Paul Getty Trust and Valerio Maioli.

Every effort has been made to contact copyright holders. Any errors or omissions brought to the attntion of the publishers will be made good in future editions.

1, 4 and 15: From William Gell and John P. Gandy, *Pompeiana, The Topography, Edifices and Ornaments of Pompeii*, 3rd edn, London 1852.

2, 3 and 24: From François Mazois, *Ruines de Pompei*, privately published facsimile copy, Ravenna, 2003, courtesy Valerio Maioli.

5, 8, 14, 20, 25, 26, 32, 37 and 42: From V. Mollame, *Les Monuments du Musée National de Naples*, 1890.

6: Private Collection.

7: Palazzo Reale, Caserta.

9: Lazaro Galdiano Museum, Madrid.

10: From *Le Antichitá de ercolano esposte*, 1755.

11, 13, 28, 30, 35, 41, 46 and 49: Courtesy Pompeii Archives.

12 and 48: Photograph courtesy Marcus Whitney.

16 and 18: L'Elefante, Rome.

17: Vatican Library.

19: National Archaeological Museum of Naples.

21: Madrid, Museo Nacional del Prado.

22 and 23: Museo Napoleonico, Rome

27: Knebworth House.

29: From J. Jacoltet, *L'Italie à vol d'oiseau*, Paris, 1859.

31: Courtesy Francesco Nicotra.

33: The Royal Collection © HM Queen Elizabeth II.

34: Courtesy the Spurgeon Archive.

36: Alinari Archives.

38: Private Collection.

39 and 40: Centro Sperimentale di Cinematografia-Cineteca Nazionale, Rome.

43 and 50: Photograph courtesy David Willey.

44: Photograph courtesy Milton Gendel.

45: Getty Museum, Malibu, California.

47: August Mau: *Pompeii. Its Life and Art*, Macmillan, New York, 1899.

Index